Immediate

ENVIRONMENT | POPULATION | POWER | WEALTH | TENSIONS AND CONFLICTS

Sébastien Brodeur-Girard | Claudie Vanasse
Marc Carrier | Marie-Noëlle Corriveau-Tendland | Maxime Pelchat

Éditions Grand Duc
Groupe Éducalivres inc.
955, rue Bergar, Laval (Québec) H7L 4Z6
Telephone: 514 334-8466 ■ Fax: 514 334-8387
InfoService: 1 800 567-3671

ACKNOWLEDGMENTS

The Publisher would like to thank the following individuals for the scientific verification of the content:
René Blais, Professor, Université de Moncton
Martin Larochelle, Professor, Cégep Marie-Victorin
Jean-François Lévesque, Teacher
Daniel Massicotte (Ph.D. in history), Teacher, Cégep Saint-Jean-sur-Richelieu

The Publisher would also like to thank the following individuals for their helpful advice, comments
and suggestions at the various stages of the development of this project:
Patrice Bastien, École Frenette, Commission scolaire de la Rivière-du-Nord
Jean-François Beaudoin, École des Trois-Saisons, Commission scolaire des Affluents
Carl Beaulieu, École de la Courvilloise, Commission scolaire des Premières-Seigneuries
Céline Benoît, École secondaire Mont-de-Lasalle, Commission scolaire de Laval
Michel Bouchard, Juvénat Notre-Dame
Luc Boucher, École secondaire Les Etchemins, Commission scolaire des Navigateurs
Denise Bouffard, École La Frontalière, Commission scolaire des Hauts-Cantons
Marc-André Caron, École secondaire Polybel, Commission scolaire des Patriotes
Annie Fontaine, École secondaire Soulanges, Commission scolaire des Trois-Lacs
Fabien Gabillet, Collège St-Charles-Garnier
Kathy Lang, Académie de Roberval, Commission scolaire de Montréal
Sylvie Lessard, École La Frontalière, Commission scolaire des Hauts-Cantons
Claude Miville, École Pointe-Lévy, Commission scolaire des Navigateurs
Éric Ouimet, École Leblanc, Commission scolaire de Laval
Marcel Poirier, École secondaire Jean-Raimbault, Commission scolaire des Chênes
Geneviève Renaud, École secondaire du Chêne-Bleu, Commission scolaire des Trois-Lacs
Denis Robitaille, Académie Ste-Thérèse
Michel Roy, École de la Courvilloise, Commission scolaire des Premières-Seigneuries
Annie Sarrazin, École secondaire Mirabel, Commission scolaire de la Rivière-du-Nord
Marwan Tomeh, Polyvalente de La Baie, Commission scolaire des Rives du Saguenay
André Viens, École Le Triolet, Commission scolaire du Lac-Témiscamingue

ENGLISH VERSION

Translation: Linda Arui, Natasha De Cruz, Gwendolyn Schulman
Consultant: Christopher J. Bedic, Lester B. Pearson School Board

Immediate

© 2010, Éditions Grand Duc, a division of Groupe Éducalivres inc.
955, rue Bergar, Laval (Québec) H7L 4Z6
Telephone: 514 334-8466 ▪ Fax: 514 334-8387
www.grandduc.com
All rights reserved

Translation of *Immédiat, Manuel de l'élève,*
2e cycle du secondaire, 3e année (ISBN 978-2-7655-0315-6)
© 2010, Éditions Grand Duc, a division of Groupe Éducalivres inc.

GRAPHIC DESIGN: Pige communication
ILLUSTRATIONS: Serge Rousseau, Bertrand Lachance
MAPS: KOREM

These programs are funded by Québec's Ministère de l'Éducation, du Loisir et du Sport
and through contributions from the Canada-Québec Agreement on Minority-Language Education
and Second-Language Instruction.

We acknowledge the financial support of the Government of Canada through the Canada Book Fund (CBF)
for our publishing activities.

Gouvernement du Québec – Refundable tax credit for book publishing – Administered by SODEC

PRODUCT CODE 3900
ISBN 978-2-7655-0380-4

Legal Deposit
Bibliothèque et Archives nationales du Québec, 2010
Library and Archives Canada, 2010

Printed in Canada
2 3 4 5 6 7 8 9 0 F 14 13 12 11

TABLE OF CONTENTS

INTRODUCTION

ENVIRONMENT

POPULATION

POWER

APPENDIXES

LIST OF MAPS

The Student Book covers the five themes that make up the Contemporary World program: Environment, Population, Power, Wealth, and Tensions and Conflicts. Each chapter presents content to help students understand the theme. This content is set out in an encyclopedic style.

The *Immediate* collection is organized in such a way that you will easily find the information you're looking for. The Student Book provides information about the topic to be interpreted (contemporary world problem) and the position to be taken (contemporary world issue). In this way, the content provides guidelines for developing your comprehension and does not necessarily require constant updating.

Introductory Chapter

The *Immediate* Student Book begins with an introductory chapter that provides the rationale for the four areas of the Contemporary World program: geography, politics, economics and history.

The introductory chapter includes a section addressing each area, as well as a section on the media. The latter will help you learn how to exercise critical judgment with respect to the information conveyed by the media.

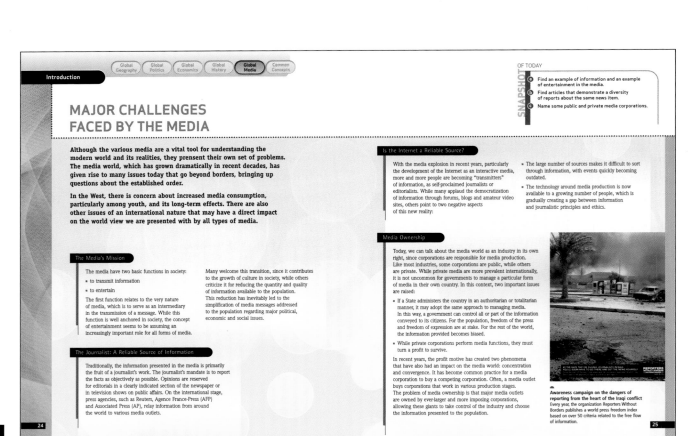

Introduction | Global Geography | Global Politics | Global Economics | Global History | Global Media | Common Concepts

OF TODAY

SNAPSHOT
- Find an example of information and an example of entertainment in the media.
- Find articles that demonstrate a diversity of reports about the same news item.
- Name some public and private media corporations.

MAJOR CHALLENGES FACED BY THE MEDIA

Although the various media are a vital tool for understanding the modern world and its realities, they prensent their own set of problems. The media world, which has grown dramatically in recent decades, has given rise to many issues today that go beyond borders, bringing up questions about the established order.

In the West, there is concern about increased media consumption, particularly among youth, and its long-term effects. There are also other issues of an international nature that may have a direct impact on the world view we are presented with by all types of media.

The Media's Mission

The media have two basic functions in society:
- to transmit information
- to entertain

The first function relates to the very nature of media, which is to serve as an intermediary in the transmission of a message. While this function is well anchored in society, the concept of entertainment seems to be assuming an increasingly important role for all forms of media.

Many welcome this transition, since it contributes to the growth of culture in society, while others criticize it for reducing the quantity and quality of information available to the population. This reduction has inevitably led to the simplification of media messages addressed to the population regarding major political, economic and social issues.

The Journalist: A Reliable Source of Information

Traditionally, the information presented in the media is primarily the fruit of a journalist's work. The journalist's mandate is to report the facts as objectively as possible. Opinions are reserved for editorials in a clearly indicated section of the newspaper or in television shows on public affairs. On the international stage, press agencies, such as Reuters, Agence France-Press (AFP) and Associated Press (AP), relay information from around the world to various media outlets.

Is the Internet a Reliable Source?

With the media explosion in recent years, particularly the development of the Internet as an interactive media, more and more people are becoming "transmitters" of information, as self-proclaimed journalists or editorialists. While many applaud the democratization of information through forums, blogs and amateur video sites, others point to two negative aspects of this new reality:

- The large number of sources makes it difficult to sort through information, with events quickly becoming outdated.
- The technology around media production is now available to a growing number of people, which is gradually creating a gap between information and journalistic principles and ethics.

Media Ownership

Today, we can talk about the media world as an industry in its own right, since corporations are responsible for media production. Like most industries, some corporations are public, while others are private. While private media are more prevalent internationally, it is not uncommon for governments to manage a particular form of media in their own country. In this context, two important issues are raised:

- If a State administers the country in an authoritarian or totalitarian manner, it may adopt the same approach to managing media. In this way, a government can control all or part of the information conveyed to its citizens. For the population, freedom of the press and freedom of expression are at stake. For the rest of the world, the information provided becomes biased.
- While private corporations perform media functions, they must turn a profit to survive.

In recent years, the profit motive has created two phenomena that have also had an impact on the media world: concentration and convergence. It has become common practice for a media corporation to buy a competing corporation. Often, a media outlet buys corporations that work in various production stages. The problem of media ownership is that major media outlets are owned by ever-larger and more imposing corporations, allowing these giants to take control of the industry and choose the information presented to the population.

Awareness campaign on the dangers of reporting from the heart of the Iraqi conflict Every year, the organization Reporters Without Borders publishes a world press freedom index based on over 50 criteria related to the free flow of information.

The introductory chapter includes activities that will help you acquire knowledge that is essential in developing an understanding of today's world, regardless of the theme in question.

In this final year of secondary school, you will learn independance and develop note-taking techniques. This feature, which you will find in the learning and evaluation situations (LES), includes tips to help you do so.

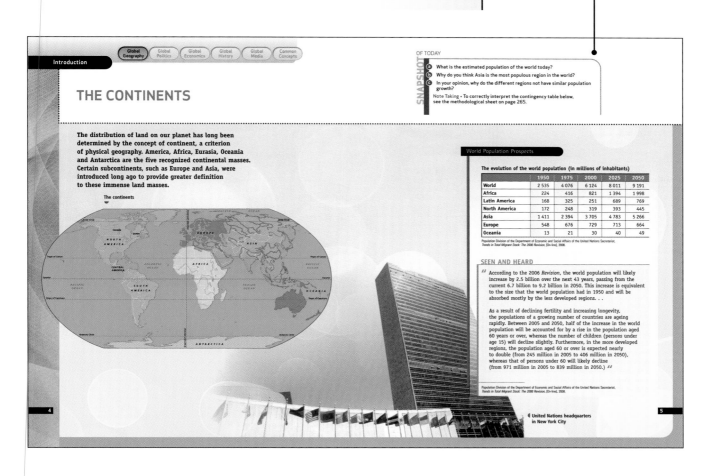

THE CONTINENTS

SNAPSHOT OF TODAY

a. What is the estimated population of the world today?
b. Why do you think Asia is the most populous region in the world?
c. In your opinion, why do the different regions not have similar population growth?

Note Taking • To correctly interpret the contingency table below, see the methodological sheet on page 265.

The distribution of land on our planet has long been determined by the concept of continent, a criterion of physical geography. America, Africa, Eurasia, Oceania and Antarctica are the five recognized continental masses. Certain subcontinents, such as Europe and Asia, were introduced long ago to provide greater definition to these immense land masses.

The continents

World Population Prospects

The evolution of the world population (in millions of inhabitants)

	1950	1975	2000	2025	2050
World	2 535	4 076	6 124	8 011	9 191
Africa	224	416	821	1 394	1 998
Latin America	168	325	251	689	769
North America	172	248	319	393	445
Asia	1 411	2 394	3 705	4 783	5 266
Europe	548	676	729	713	664
Oceania	13	21	30	40	49

Population Division of the Department of Economic and Social Affairs of the United Nations Secretariat, Trends in Total Migrant Stock: The 2006 Revision, [On-line], 2008.

SEEN AND HEARD

" According to the 2006 *Revision*, the world population will likely increase by 2.5 billion over the next 43 years, passing from the current 6.7 billion to 9.2 billion in 2050. This increase is equivalent to the size that the world population had in 1950 and will be absorbed mostly by the less developed regions. . .

As a result of declining fertility and increasing longevity, the populations of a growing number of countries are ageing rapidly. Between 2005 and 2050, half of the increase in the world population will be accounted for by a rise in the population aged 60 years or over, whereas the number of children (persons under age 15) will decline slightly. Furthermore, in the more developed regions, the population aged 60 or over is expected nearly to double (from 245 million in 2005 to 406 million in 2050), whereas that of persons under 60 will likely decline (from 971 million in 2005 to 839 million in 2050.) "

Population Division of the Department of Economic and Social Affairs of the United Nations Secretariat, Trends in Total Migrant Stock: The 2006 Revision, [On-line], 2008.

◀ United Nations headquarters in New York City

Chapters Covering the Themes in the Program

The program elements are presented at the beginning of each chapter to help you make a connection between these elements and the chapter.

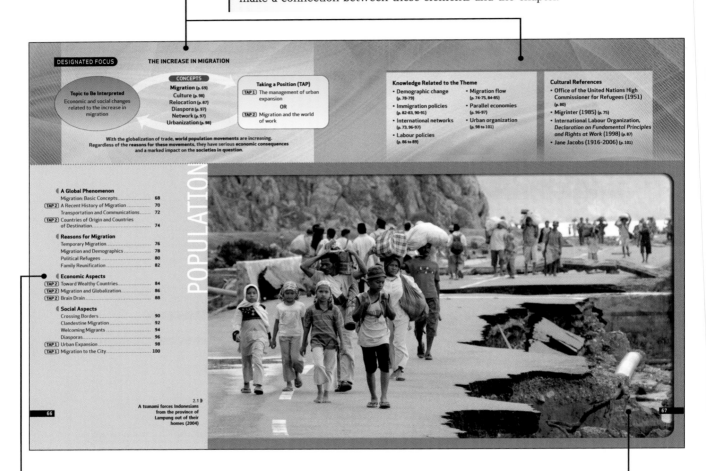

DESIGNATED FOCUS   **THE INCREASE IN MIGRATION**

CONCEPTS

Topic to Be Interpreted
Economic and social changes related to the increase in migration

Migration (p. 69)
Culture (p. 98)
Relocation (p. 87)
Diaspora (p. 97)
Network (p. 97)
Urbanization (p. 98)

Taking a Position (TAP)
TAP 1 The management of urban expansion
OR
TAP 2 Migration and the world of work

With the globalization of trade, world population movements are increasing. Regardless of the reasons for these movements, they have serious economic consequences and a marked impact on the societies in question.

Knowledge Related to the Theme
- Demographic change (p. 78-79)
- Immigration policies (p. 82-83, 90-91)
- International networks (p. 73, 96-97)
- Labour policies (p. 86 to 89)
- Migration flow (p. 74-75, 84-85)
- Parallel economies (p. 96-97)
- Urban organization (p. 98 to 101)

Cultural References
- Office of the United Nations High Commissioner for Refugees (1951) (p. 80)
- Migrinter (1985) (p. 75)
- International Labour Organization, *Declaration on Fundamental Principles and Rights at Work* (1998) (p. 87)
- Jane Jacobs (1916-2006) (p. 101)

POPULATION

2.1 ▶
A tsunami forces Indonesians from the province of Lampung out of their homes (2004)

66

67

A detailed table of contents shows how the chapter is organized. The section titles appear on tabs at the top of each double page spread. This makes it easier to find the content you are looking for, since, unlike most social sciences materials, the information in this book is not presented in chronological order.

Each chapter opens with a striking image that will spark your interest and elicit questions.

For quick reference, the titles of the main sections in the table of contents appear on tabs.

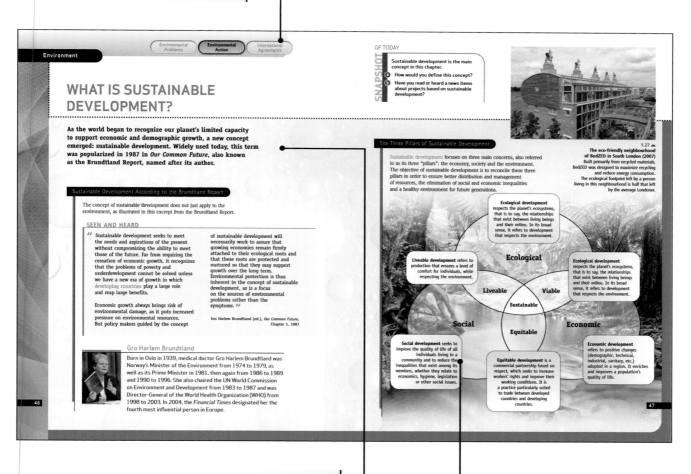

Like the lead sentence in a newspaper article, an introductory text briefly presents the information in each double page spread of this book.

In most cases, the information is presented using a graphic organizer to make it both easier to understand and more appealing.

History Headlines

This reference section presents events that have occurred between the end of the 19th century and today, in chronological order. You can refer to it as needed.

Each article is situated in space and time: the name of the country, the continent and the year are given for each event.

A time line presents a number of historical events. Those that are the subject of an article appear in bold type.

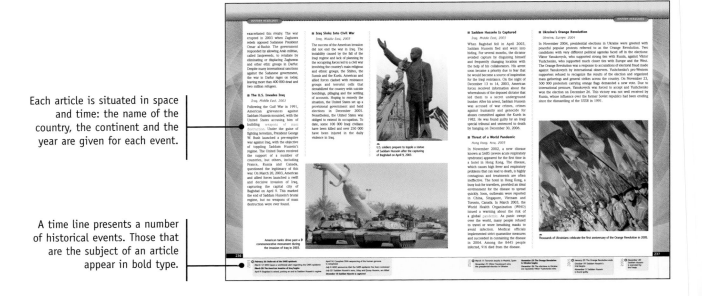

Techniques

The techniques suggested in the program are described in this section. Easy to consult, they present theory and examples drawn from contemporary documents. Additional pages have been added to help you meet the requirements of the Contemporary World program: Watching and Interpreting a Televised Report, Reading and Interpreting a Newspaper Article, etc.

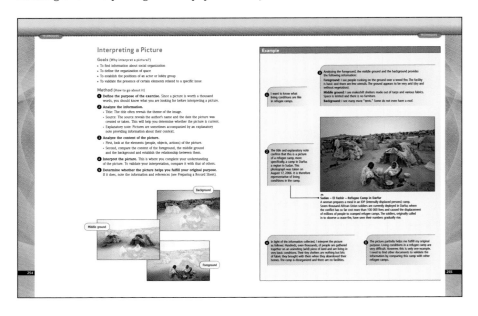

Glossary

The glossary provides definitions of the specific words and terms to understanding the contemporary world.

Index

The index is indispensable for finding information, especially if you are using the Student Book as a reference.

Atlas

The maps provided will help you throughout the research process, whether you are consulting the Student Book, the LES or the media.

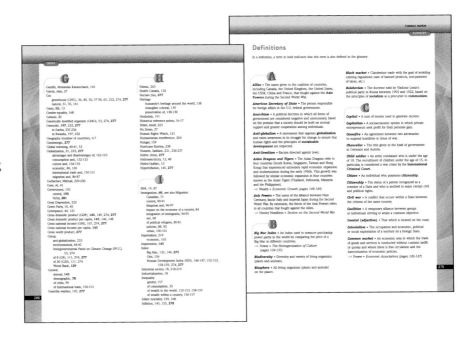

Features

SNAPSHOT

OF TODAY

a How would you define the concept of "governance"?

b Is a world government necessary? Provide an example from the news to support your answer.

This feature has two functions: it enables you to construct an understanding of the concepts in the program and to apply them to current events. In the introductory chapter itself, additional knowledge can be applied in this way.

This feature presents quotes illustrating the points of view of different actors.

SEEN AND HEARD

" To defend and improve the human environment for present and future generations has become an imperative goal for mankind. . . "

Final Declaration of the United Nations Conference on the Human Environment (1972)

THE BIG MAC INDEX

Created in 1986 by the magazine *The Economist*, THE BIG MAC INDEX MEASURES PURCHASING POWER PARITY AROUND THE WORLD. In February 2009, the average cost of a Big Mac was the equivalent of US$3.36 in Canada, US$5.79 in Norway and US$1.83 in China. This index has become a serious tool used by economists. It clearly illustrates the globalization and dissemination of American-style fast food restaurants.

IN BRIEF

This feature presents surprising facts that will make you want to learn more about the topic.

The reproducible sheets in the Teaching Guide will help you develop the two subject-specific competencies. These sheets present documents about news items that can be updated if your teacher so desires.

Each chapter includes two complex tasks called "Learning and Evaluation Situations" (LES).

Connections Between the Student Book and the LES

In the first LES of each chapter, the connection between the Student Book and the reproducible material is clearly explained.

- The structure of the Student Book is repeated in the Performance phase: the titles of the tabs in the Student Book appear in order in the LES.

- At the beginning of each section you must read the corresponding pages in the Student Book. You will find the knowledge you need to construct concepts and knowledge related to the cultural references and the theme.

- Several questions refer to documents or graphic organizers presented in the Student Book.

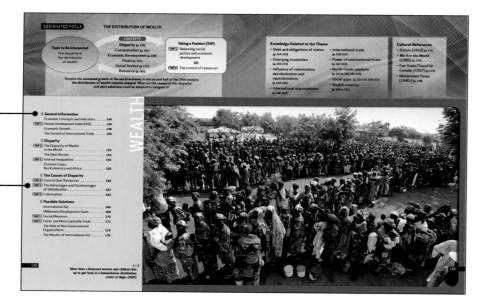

For the second LES, refer to the Student Book for information about the issues, as well as whenever the need arises. The icon (**TAP 1**) indicates the pages related to the first position to be taken and the icon (**TAP 2**), the pages related to the second position to be taken.

The LES in General

Each chapter includes two LES.

The first helps you to develop Competency **1** *Interprets a contemporary world problem.* Case studies reveal the different manifestations of the problem in the world and the varying degrees to which it manifests itself. This LES allows you to apply the theory you have learned and to acquire the knowledge you will need to voice an opinion on the issue.

The second LES, which focuses on Competency **2** *Takes a position on a contemporary world issue,* allows you to take a position on an issue and to consider opportunities for social action. To do so, you need to learn the points of view of the various actors, as well as those conveyed by the media.

Since the media play a key role in the *Immediate* material, the titles of the three phases of learning are drawn from the world of journalism.

PREPARATION PHASE: HOOK

At the beginning of each LES you will do an activity that will help you determine what you already know about the theme. The final task is presented at the beginning of each LES in order to give the learning purpose.

PERFORMANCE PHASE: HEADLINE

For each tab in the Student Book, a summary question allows you to use one of the techniques developed in the program.

A variety of documents (graphs, maps, newspaper articles, cartoons, etc.) are presented to help you understand the problem from every angle. The documents are authentic, helping you to accurately interpret the problem. Each document or series of documents is accompanied by one or more interpretation questions. You will thus have all the tools needed to perform the proposed final task.

The subject-specific competency and the evaluation criterion are specified when the task can be used to evaluate competencies. Space is provided for the teacher to evaluate the subject-specific competencies.

INTEGRATION AND REAPPLICATION PHASE: SPECIAL REPORT OR EDITORIAL

At the end of each LES, a creative final task allows you to demonstrate your understanding of the problem (Special Report) or to take a position on the situation being interpreted (Editorial).

COMPETENCIES AND THEIR KEY FEATURES

Key Features of Competency 1

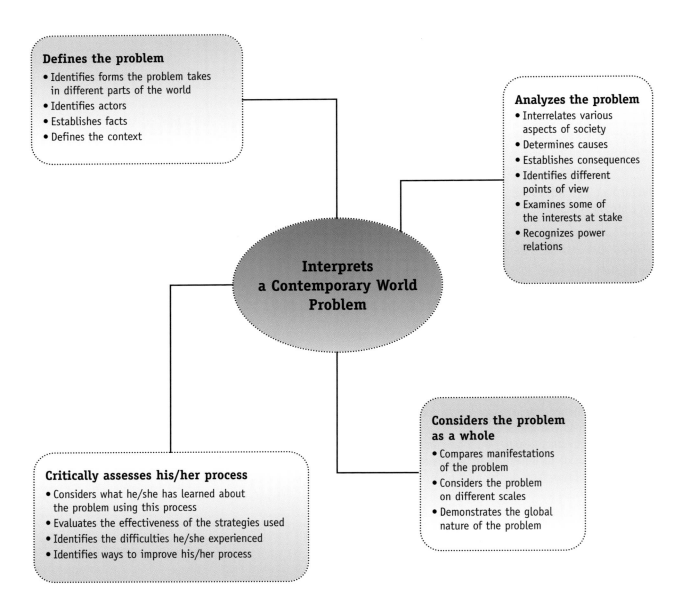

Defines the problem
- Identifies forms the problem takes in different parts of the world
- Identifies actors
- Establishes facts
- Defines the context

Analyzes the problem
- Interrelates various aspects of society
- Determines causes
- Establishes consequences
- Identifies different points of view
- Examines some of the interests at stake
- Recognizes power relations

Interprets a Contemporary World Problem

Critically assesses his/her process
- Considers what he/she has learned about the problem using this process
- Evaluates the effectiveness of the strategies used
- Identifies the difficulties he/she experienced
- Identifies ways to improve his/her process

Considers the problem as a whole
- Compares manifestations of the problem
- Considers the problem on different scales
- Demonstrates the global nature of the problem

Evaluation Criteria
1 Rigour of his/her reasoning
2 Clear overview
3 Critical assessment of his/her process

Key Features of Competency 2

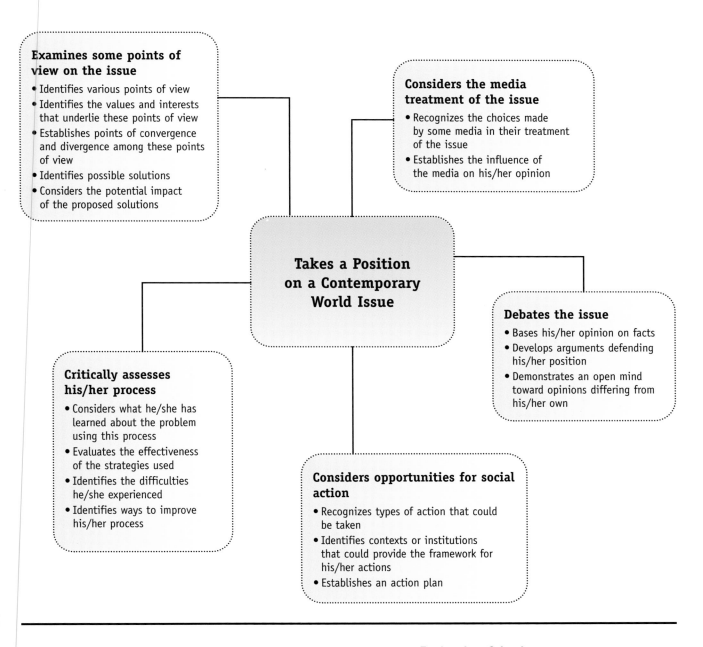

Examines some points of view on the issue
- Identifies various points of view
- Identifies the values and interests that underlie these points of view
- Establishes points of convergence and divergence among these points of view
- Identifies possible solutions
- Considers the potential impact of the proposed solutions

Considers the media treatment of the issue
- Recognizes the choices made by some media in their treatment of the issue
- Establishes the influence of the media on his/her opinion

Takes a Position on a Contemporary World Issue

Critically assesses his/her process
- Considers what he/she has learned about the problem using this process
- Evaluates the effectiveness of the strategies used
- Identifies the difficulties he/she experienced
- Identifies ways to improve his/her process

Debates the issue
- Bases his/her opinion on facts
- Develops arguments defending his/her position
- Demonstrates an open mind toward opinions differing from his/her own

Considers opportunities for social action
- Recognizes types of action that could be taken
- Identifies contexts or institutions that could provide the framework for his/her actions
- Establishes an action plan

Evaluation Criteria
1. Critical distance
2. Expression of a well-founded opinion
3. Critical assessment of his/her process

We live in an ever-changing world. To understand it, you must be an attentive observer, which requires the right observation tools. Since history sometimes provides answers that are essential to understanding our world today, you need to know certain facts and to be aware of past events. You also need to understand

INTRODUCTION

2

both the geographic space within which the current phenomena you are exploring occur and how this space influences and transforms these phenomena.

It is also important to see how these same phenomena can, in turn, have an impact on the geography of a country or region of the world and change it. Your understanding of the contemporary world would not be complete, however, without a look at its political and economic dimensions. Indeed, the political and economic ideologies held by different actors in power have a greater impact than it might seem on the major issues in today's world.

Who
Do You Recognize?

THE CONTINENTS

The distribution of land on our planet has long been determined by the concept of continent, a criterion of physical geography. America, Africa, Eurasia, Oceania and Antarctica are the five recognized continental masses. Certain subcontinents, such as Europe and Asia, were introduced long ago to provide greater definition to these immense land masses.

The continents

ⓐ What is the estimated population of the world today?

ⓑ Why do you think Asia is the most populous region in the world?

ⓒ In your opinion, why do the different regions not have similar population growth?

Note Taking • To correctly interpret the contingency table below, see the methodological sheet on page 265.

World Population Prospects

The evolution of the world population (in millions of inhabitants)

	1950	1975	2000	2025	2050
World	2 535	4 076	6 124	8 011	9 191
Africa	224	416	821	1 394	1 998
Latin America	168	325	251	689	769
North America	172	248	319	393	445
Asia	1 411	2 394	3 705	4 783	5 266
Europe	548	676	729	713	664
Oceania	13	21	30	40	49

Population Division of the Department of Economic and Social Affairs of the United Nations Secretariat, *Trends in Total Migrant Stock: The 2006 Revision*, [On-line], 2008.

SEEN AND HEARD

" According to the 2006 *Revision*, the world population will likely increase by 2.5 billion over the next 43 years, passing from the current 6.7 billion to 9.2 billion in 2050. This increase is equivalent to the size that the world population had in 1950 and will be absorbed mostly by the less developed regions. . .

As a result of declining fertility and increasing longevity, the populations of a growing number of countries are ageing rapidly. Between 2005 and 2050, half of the increase in the world population will be accounted for by a rise in the population aged 60 years or over, whereas the number of children (persons under age 15) will decline slightly. Furthermore, in the more developed regions, the population aged 60 or over is expected nearly to double (from 245 million in 2005 to 406 million in 2050), whereas that of persons under 60 will likely decline (from 971 million in 2005 to 839 million in 2050.) "

Population Division of the Department of Economic and Social Affairs of the United Nations Secretariat, *Trends in Total Migrant Stock: The 2006 Revision*, [On-line], 2008.

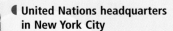

◀ **United Nations headquarters in New York City**

THE REGIONS OF THE WORLD

Following the Second World War, there were just over 70 countries. Today, new criteria take into account human factors, such as culture, economic connections and history. These have contributed to redefining national boundaries by placing greater emphasis on human activities within a given territory.

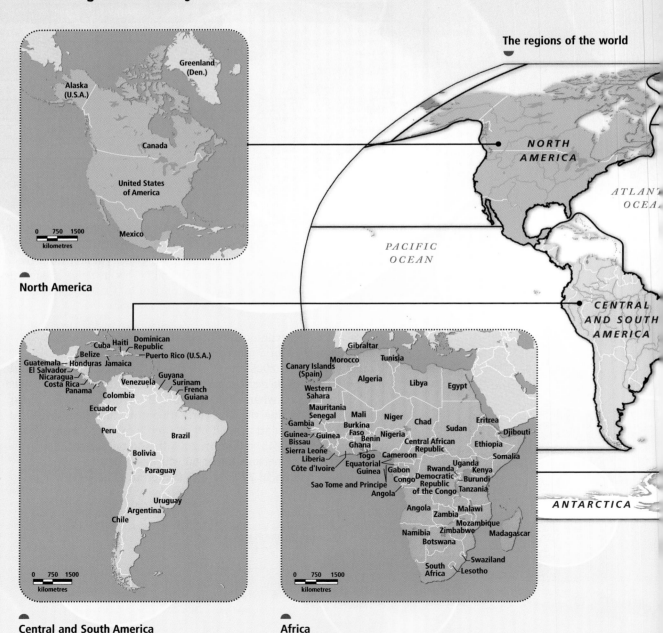

The regions of the world

North America

Central and South America

Africa

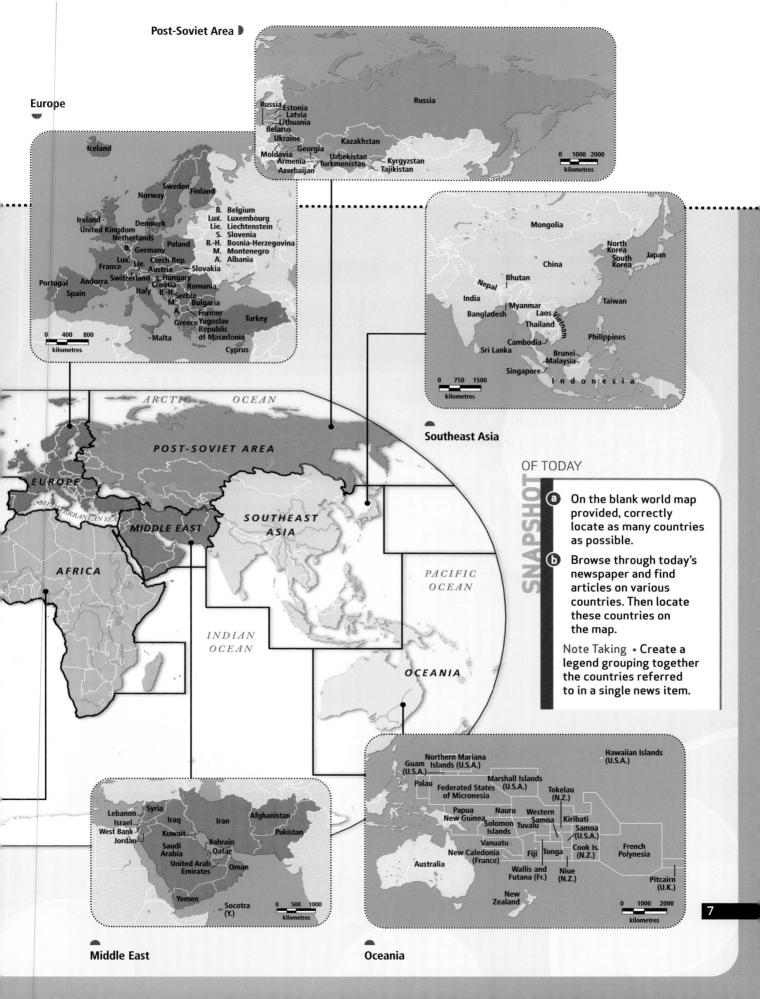

Post-Soviet Area ▶

Europe

Russia
Estonia
Latvia
Lithuania
Belarus
Ukraine
Russia
Moldavia
Georgia
Armenia
Azerbaijan
Turkmenistan
Kazakhstan
Uzbekistan
Kyrgyzstan
Tajikistan

0 1000 2000
kilometres

Iceland

Sweden
Norway Finland

Ireland
United Kingdom
Denmark
Netherlands
B. Germany Poland
Lux. Lie. Czech Rep.
France Austria Slovakia
Switzerland S. Hungary
Andorra Croatia Romania
Portugal Italy B.-H. Serbia
Spain M. Bulgaria
Greece Former
Yugoslav
Republic
of Macedonia
Malta
Cyprus

B. Belgium
Lux. Luxembourg
Lie. Liechtenstein
S. Slovenia
B.-H. Bosnia-Herzegovina
M. Montenegro
A. Albania

0 400 800
kilometres

Mongolia
North
Korea
South
Korea
Japan
China
Nepal Bhutan
India
Bangladesh Myanmar
Laos Vietnam
Thailand Taiwan
Cambodia Philippines
Sri Lanka
Singapore Brunei
Malaysia
Indonesia

0 750 1500
kilometres

ARCTIC OCEAN

POST-SOVIET AREA

EUROPE

MEDITERRANEAN SEA

MIDDLE EAST

SOUTHEAST
ASIA

Southeast Asia

AFRICA

INDIAN
OCEAN

PACIFIC
OCEAN

OCEANIA

SNAPSHOT OF TODAY

ⓐ On the blank world map provided, correctly locate as many countries as possible.

ⓑ Browse through today's newspaper and find articles on various countries. Then locate these countries on the map.

Note Taking • Create a legend grouping together the countries referred to in a single news item.

Lebanon Syria
Israel Iraq Iran Afghanistan
West Bank Kuwait Pakistan
Jordan Bahrain
Saudi Qatar
Arabia
United Arab
Emirates Oman
Yemen Socotra
(Y.)

0 500 1000
kilometres

Northern Mariana
Guam Islands (U.S.A.) Hawaiian Islands
(U.S.A.) (U.S.A.)
Palau Marshall Islands
Federated States (U.S.A.) Tokelau
of Micronesia (N.Z.)
Papua Nauru
New Guinea Western
Solomon Samoa Kiribati
Islands Tuvalu Samoa
(U.S.A.)
Vanuatu Cook Is.
(N.Z.)
New Caledonia Fiji Tonga French
(France) Niue Polynesia
Australia Wallis and (N.Z.)
Futana (Fr.) Pitcairn
(U.K.)
New
Zealand

0 1000 2000
kilometres

7

Middle East

Oceania

DEMOCRACY VERSUS DICTATORSHIP

Today's world and the issues confronting it cannot be fully understood without addressing the political dimension. Politics, namely everything to do with the exercise of power in a society, creates situations, leads to actions and informs certain decisions that move the world forward, and sometimes backward.

When explaining a phenomenon or understanding a problem pertaining to politics, we tend to look at the ideology of the country, party or main actor involved in the issue at hand.

What Is An Ideology?

An ideology is a set of ideas, opinions and beliefs that constitutes a doctrine and influences the behaviour of individuals or communities that adhere to it. Conservatism, political liberalism, economic liberalism, nationalism, socialism, communism, mercantilism, imperialism and feminism are just a few examples of ideologies.

Democracy and dictatorship are two opposing political systems.

Democracy

Democracy is government by all or, according to Lincoln's formulation, of the people, by the people, for the people. In other words, democracy is a political system in which the citizens hold power.

VERSUS

Dictatorship

Dictatorship is a political system in which one person or a small group of people exercise all the power without being restricted by laws or institutions. In other words, dictatorship is a political system in which the people hold no power.

Whether in a democracy or a dictatorship, power is always exercised according to the ideology chosen by the party or person in power. For example, the USSR under Stalin was a dictatorship whose ideology was communism. The United Kingdom under Margaret Thatcher's government was a democracy whose ideology was conservatism. Both of these ideologies, along with many others, will be presented in the following pages.

IN THIS TEMPLE
AS IN THE HEARTS OF THE PEOPLE
FOR WHOM HE SAVED THE UNION
THE MEMORY OF ABRAHAM LINCOLN
IS ENSHRINED FOREVER

◀ **Statue of Abraham Lincoln inside the Lincoln Memorial in Washington**
A symbol of democracy in the United States, President Lincoln abolished slavery, which was legal until the 19th century.
(Text above the statue: *In this temple, as in the hearts of the people for whom he saved the Union, the memory of Abraham Lincoln is enshrined forever.*)

Demonstration in Baghdad, Iraq (2003) ▶
After decapitating the largest statue of Saddam Hussein, Iraqis sang and danced while dragging the head of the statue through the city. As a sign of humiliation, they hit the head with their shoes. Similar demonstrations took place all over Iraq after the downfall of the dictator who had ruled with an iron fist for 24 years.

Political Axis

In France, following the French Revolution in 1789, the concepts of left and right first emerged in political vocabulary. During discussions on limiting royal power, the supporters of change sat on the left side of the room while the supporters of the *status quo* sat on the right side. This is the origin of the distinction between left and right. Since then, these two concepts have become better defined to the extent that they can now be associated with different political ideologies.

LEFT	CENTRE	RIGHT
Parties on the left share or have in common certain values, such as the promotion of social progress and reform, freedom and equality. Left-wing parties generally criticize the established social order and manifest a strong desire to transform it. They are referred to as progressive because of this desire for change. Progressivism is therefore in opposition to conservatism. Those who favoured limiting the king's power following the French Revolution were progressives, as are today's supporters of left-wing ideologies, such as socialism and communism.	The centre is occupied by parties that share or have in common certain values, such as the defence of individual freedoms on the one hand and the redistribution of wealth on the other. Centrist parties generally defend equality and freedom, as well as respect for certain traditions. The centre advocates ideologies that promote a middle ground between progressivism and conservatism, such as liberalism.	Parties on the right share or have in common certain values, such as the defence of traditions and the rejection of rapid change, especially with respect to society and the economy. Right-wing parties generally defend the established social order and manifest a strong desire to preserve it. They are referred to as conservative due to this desire to maintain the status quo. Conservatism is therefore in opposition to progressivism. Those who favoured keeping the king's power intact following the French Revolution were conservatives, as are today's supporters of right-wing ideologies, such as conservatism and fascism.

Nighttime Session, August 4 to 5 (1789) ▶
This drawing by Charles Monnet, engraved by Isidore Stanislas Helman, represents the members of the young French National Assembly hotly debating the issue of the abolition of feudal rights.

9

IDEOLOGIES

Anarchism and Communism

Anarchism ▪ Ideology that defends anti-authoritarian practices. The supporters of anarchism refute the principle of authority and reject any form of constraint. The goal of anarchism is to found a society free of domination, where all individuals participate in managing society and in which all rules and authority are abolished.

Communism ▪ Ideology inspired by the ideas of Karl Marx, who advocated a society without private property and in which all resources, wealth and businesses are nationalized, which is to say, they belong to the State. The goal of communism is to promote common ownership for the benefit of all.

◀ **Cuban stamp (1974)**
Photograph commemorating the meeting in Cuba of two communist leaders. Fidel Castro (Cuba) is on the right and Leonid I. Brejnev (USSR) is on the left.

Demonstration in California (2001)
During negotiations around FTAA in 2001, masked demonstrators marched under the banner of the Black Bloc, an openly anarchist organization that originated in Europe and advocates property destruction as an attack on corporate wealth.

EXTREME LEFT ──────────────── **LEFT**

Socialism and Environmentalism

Socialism ▪ Ideology whose goal is to promote social justice through the elimination of inequalities and, by extension, social classes. Socialism also promotes social progress. *Example:* The French Socialist Party, founded in 1905, is still a part of the French political landscape. It was led by Lionel Jospin from 1981 to 1988 and again from 1995 to 1997. Under the banner of the Socialist Party, Lionel Jospin was the Prime Minister of France from 1997 to 2002, with Jacques Chirac as President, a representative of the liberal right. This was known as a government of cohabitation.

Environmentalism ▪ Ideology whose goal is to take ecological or environmental issues into account in political and economic action, in order to preserve, safeguard or even restore the environment. *Example:* The Green Party of Canada was founded in 1983 to promote the ideology of environmentalism on the federal political scene. During the 2008 federal elections, the Green Party participated for the first time in the televised leaders' debate alongside the Conservative Party of Canada, the Liberal Party of Canada, the New Democratic Party and the Bloc Québécois.

Benito Mussolini addressing a crowd in Rome, Italy

Liberalism

Ideology whose goal is to promote individual freedom and a limited role for the State. According to this ideology, one of the primary roles of the State is to maintain and protect individual freedoms. A distinction is made between political liberalism (protecting individual freedoms) and economic liberalism (limiting State intervention). Certain supporters of liberalism place themselves on the right of the political axis. They are generally supporters of economic liberalism. *Example:* The Liberal Party of Canada, founded at the time of Confederation, on July 1, 1867, claims to represent liberalism. From its inception to 2008, it has had 14 leaders, 12 of whom have occupied the position of Prime Minister of Canada.

Fascism

Ideology inspired by the fascist movement of Benito Mussolini, who rejected socialism, the defence of individual freedoms and liberalism. While the term is used to designate several movements that share these values, it only designates the Italian experience from 1922 to 1945. *Example:* Italian fascism from 1922 to 1945, introduced by Benito Mussolini. Mussolini himself summarized the ideology he founded as: "All within the State, nothing outside the State, nothing against the State."

CENTRE   **RIGHT**   **EXTREME RIGHT**

Conservatism

Ideology that defends traditional values (for example, in Québec, the values advocated by Catholic morality: the sense of family and duty) or that advocates their return. This ideology is in opposition to progressivism, which is generally associated with the left. *Example:* Nicknamed the "Iron Lady," Margaret Thatcher was the first and only woman to lead the British Conservative Party, from 1975 to 1990. She became the prime minister of the United Kingdom in 1979, a position she held until 1990.

◀ **Margaret Thatcher**

OF TODAY

SNAPSHOT

On the sheets provided, you will find examples drawn from the news.

ⓐ Find the dominant ideology represented by each example.

ⓑ Place it on the left-right axis.

Note Taking • As you read the texts, underline the passages you think are important and circle the concepts related to an ideology.

11

Introduction

ECONOMIC SYSTEMS

Politics and economics are closely intertwined. Together, these two disciplines make it possible to study the behaviour and influence of States on current problems and issues. Economics examines State intervention in economic activity, just as political science examines State intervention in the exercise of power.

Economic agents

Countries can be classified into three major categories based on how their economic activities are organized and conducted. These categories are called systems, and their characteristics influence production, relations between different economic agents and the functioning of the labour market.

Just like political ideologies, these economic systems are ideologically driven and can be placed on a left-right axis, based on their characteristics.

EXTREME LEFT

LEFT

Planned Economy

A planned economy is an economic system that advocates the nationalization of the means of production. In this type of economy, the State determines what and how much is produced, as well as who benefits from this production. This system draws on left-wing economic ideologies, with strong State intervention in the economic sphere and little or no room for private enterprise.

Before the end of the Cold War in 1990, the USSR had a planned economy. This system still exists in Cuba today. The State determines production and regulates the labour market. Food stores, among others, belong to the State and are subjected to strict rules. Citizens generally use ration cards to obtain food.

Cubans line up in front of a State store to obtain food
(c. 1991–1994)
At the entrance, a propaganda poster sings the praises of the heroes of the Bay of Pigs in 1961.

The James Bay dam (1991) ▶
The construction of this dam
began in the 1970s.

Mixed Economy

A mixed economy is an economic system in which free enterprise predominates over State intervention. The State nevertheless plays a role, since it regulates, and even nationalizes, certain businesses or resources in order to attain specific economic goals. This system, with its compromise between those of the left and those of the right, draws on centrist economic ideologies. State intervention is not excluded from the promotion of individual economic initiatives.

Québec has a mixed economy. Business and private enterprise are encouraged, but the State plays a major role in the economy. The nationalization of hydroelectricity during the Quiet Revolution in the 1960s is a good example. Today, Hydro-Québec is still State-owned and the sole supplier of hydroelectricity in the province.

CENTRE   **RIGHT**   **EXTREME RIGHT**

Free Enterprise

Bill Gates

Free enterprise is an economic system in which private ownership of the means of production is not only advocated, but strongly encouraged. In this type of economy, the laws of the market (supply and demand) determine what and how much is produced and who benefits from this production. This system, with a predominance of private enterprise in the economic sphere and little or no State intervention, draws on right-wing economic ideologies.

The United States is a good example of the free enterprise system. In fact, private enterprise constitutes the means to achieving the American dream. In a country that adopts this type of economic system, anyone can start a business and become an economic giant. Bill Gates is a prime example. He started a small computer software company at the age of 20, which has since become the world's leading company in that industry.

THE LAWS OF THE MARKET OR SUPPLY AND DEMAND

In free enterprise and mixed economies, the laws of the market, or supply and demand, are crucial. In fact, the price of a good or service is established based on supply and demand.

Supply
Supply is the quantity of a good or service that a producer is ready to sell at a given price.

The laws of supply and demand
By combining supply and demand, or what producers and consumers want, it is possible to set the price of goods and services based on four rules or laws. These are the laws of the market, also known as the laws of supply and demand.

Demand
Demand is the quantity of a good or service that a consumer is ready to purchase at a given price.

Supply Increases While Demand Remains Stable

In the economic market, an increase in supply and stable demand generates a surplus of the good or service offered. This surplus leads to a decrease in the price of the good or service.

Example: In autumn, when apple growers are harvesting their crop, there is an abundance of apples. Consequently, the supply increases. However, in the supermarkets, consumers are not demanding more apples: demand is stable. In order to sell their apples, producers must reduce their prices.

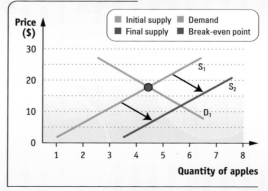

Supply increases

Legend: Initial supply, Demand, Final supply, Break-even point

Price ($): 30, 20, 10, 0
Quantity of apples: 1 2 3 4 5 6 7 8
S_1, S_2, D_1

OF TODAY

SNAPSHOT

On the sheet provided, you will find examples drawn from the news.

Match each of the examples to one of the graphs of supply and demand.

Supply Decreases While Demand Remains Stable

In the economic market, a decrease in supply and stable demand generates a shortage of the good or service being offered. This shortage leads to an increase in the price of the good or service.

Example: During the 1979 oil crisis, the oil supply suddenly dropped in Western countries as a result of the Iranian Revolution. Oil exports dropped dramatically, causing oil prices to skyrocket until 1981.

Supply decreases

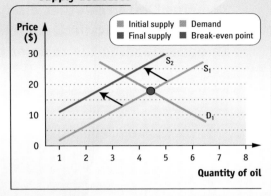

Demand Increases While Supply Remains Stable

In the economic market, an increase in demand and stable supply generates a scarcity of the good or service in demand. This scarcity leads to an increase in the price of the good or service.

Example: Tickets for a rock show in Montréal are sold out in record time. However, some people are able to obtain very high-priced tickets from resale sites on the Internet.

Demand increases

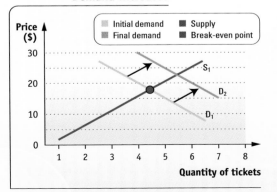

Demand Decreases While Supply Remains Stable

In the economic market, a decrease in demand and stable supply generates a surplus of the good or service in demand. This surplus leads to a decrease in the price of the good or service.

Example: In February, in the middle of winter, the demand for winter tires is low, since car owners have already purchased and installed them. Companies that still have winter tires in stock and want to get rid of them must lower their prices in order to attract customers.

Demand decreases

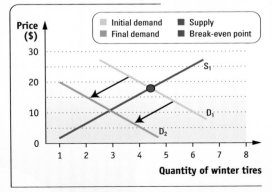

15

HISTORICAL REFERENCE POINTS

An exploration of today's world and its issues requires a look back at history. Combined with the other disciplines in the social sciences (geography, economics, political science, etc.), historical context is an essential ingredient in understanding the roots of the problems and issues facing us today.

Periods as Historical Reference Points

As the discipline evolved, historians developed tools to classify facts and human phenomena in time in order to better analyze and understand them.
One of these tools is the division of the chronology of events into periods, or eras.

The purpose of this division is to establish reference points in order to get a better sense of the chronology of events. These reference points are chosen by historians, who focus on turning points in history, that is, events that lead to major changes within one or several societies. A historical period is made up of a series of events between two historical reference points.

The domination of industrial societies

1914

The world wars

1945

The beginning of the First World War

The end of the Second World War

A man in front of a steel mill in Pennsylvania (1907)

The American military cemetery in Colleville-sur-Mer, France, contains the graves of over 9000 soldiers who lost their lives during the Second World War

Dozens of satellite dishes installed ▶
on the balconies of a building
in Marseille, France (2004)

What Is the Contemporary World?

The contemporary period is probably the most difficult to subdivide because the events are chronologically recent to us. Since we lack the historical distance necessary to objectively define the period, establishing turning points runs the risk of being influenced by our current situation.

Nevertheless, the concept of "contemporary world" is based on the most widespread definition of the concept of "contemporary," in that the events included in the period have a direct impact on the world today.

The Cold War and the emergence of the Third World

1991

The global village

The collapse
of the USSR

UN General Assembly (1954)

THE LEGACIES OF EACH PERIOD (I)

The Domination of Industrial Societies

The turn of the 20th century was marked by the domination of industrialized societies. Through the technical and technological advances spurred by industrialization, these societies gained an advantage over the rest of the world.

However, their domination, both politically and economically, added to the tensions that already existed between Europe's major powers. The democratization of European empires and the birth of nationalism created the conditions necessary to unleash the First World War, bringing the first period to an end.

Scientific and Cultural Legacy of the Period

At the turn of the 20th century, the major European powers dominated the political and economic scene. Through their imperialist policies, they controlled the development of their colonies for their own gain. They invested their capital in exploiting the wealth in the colonies. The dominance of European powers can also be explained by their technological advances.

The century opened with the 1900 Paris World's Fair and continued with major scientific breakthroughs, including Einstein's theory of relativity, which established a fourth dimension, space-time, in 1905. Before the First World War, every Nobel prize had been awarded to European researchers, a testament to the fact that this part of the world was fertile ground for new ideas.

Technical advances led to mass production, especially in Ford automobile plants and, in 1909, to the first crossing of the English Channel by plane. Culturally, this period saw the birth of the film industry with the production of the first films.

The situation, however, was not as rosy as it seemed. The many rivalries that existed between European powers prevented leaders from understanding that their domination was under increasing threat. These rivalries led European countries into the First World War. This unprecedented conflict opened the way for the United States to surpass the European powers.

Ford automobile plant assembly line (c. 1913) ▶
At the beginning of the 20th century, rapid industrialization, as well as scientific and technical advances, allowed the United States to rival Europe. The Ford company, for example, revolutionized mass automobile production with the creation of an assembly line in its Detroit plant.

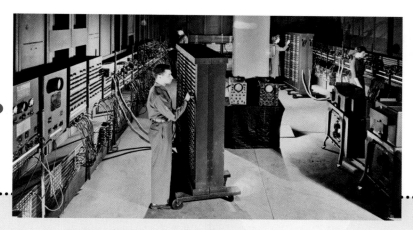

Development of the world's first electronic analog computer (1946) Construction of ENIAC (Electronic Numerical Integrator and Computer) began in 1943.

The World Wars

Unable to preserve their fragile balance, the major European powers entered into an unprecedented conflict, which marks the beginning of this second period. Through alliances and colonial ties, they pulled the entire world into a brutal war.

At the conclusion of the first major conflict, the attempt to establish a new equilibrium was disrupted by the worst economic crisis in history and by challenges to traditional political and economic systems. In this context, the path was cleared for the extreme right-wing ideologies that led to the Second World War.

Scientific and Cultural Legacy of the Period

The period of the two world wars left an indelible mark on societies. The loss of human lives and the economic consequences of these conflicts left deep wounds. However, this period was also marked by major scientific advances and a cultural scene that continues to shape our world today.

In science, Albert Einstein published his theory of relativity in 1916 and received the Nobel Prize for physics in 1921. During this same period, Sigmund Freud developed the field of psychoanalysis, while Pierre and Marie Curie were conducting research on radioactivity. The 1920s were a decade of discoveries: some made daily life easier (frozen foods in 1925), others provided entertainment (television in 1926) and others saved lives (penicillin in 1929). The 1930s saw the worst economic crisis in history, but also generated John Maynard Keynes' new economic theories (State interventionism), as well as advances in transportation, with J.-A. Bombardier patenting the first snowmobile in 1937. On the eve of the Second World War, the first programmable calculator was designed, and despite the conflict that marked the first half of the 1940s, scientific discoveries continued: the theory of the Big Bang (1940); the use of cortisone and the invention of aerosol cans and the stapler (1941); the first controlled atomic chain reaction (1942); the beginning of the construction of the first electronic analog computer, ENIAC (1943); the discovery of DNA (1944); and the invention of the microwave oven (1945).

Culturally, this period was marked by mass consumption during the Roaring Twenties, spurred on by the emergence of buying on credit and stock market speculation. This period also saw the development of cinema as a source of entertainment for a growing part of the population. In addition, the first daily radio shows hit the airwaves in the 1920s.

Albert Einstein, a German Jewish physicist, being sworn in as an American citizen in October 1940 In 1939, Einstein wrote a letter to then US President Theodore Roosevelt that would become the source of the Manhattan Project to build the atomic bomb. In 1945, when Einstein realized that the United States wanted to use the atomic bomb, he wrote another letter to Roosevelt to try to dissuade him. After the Second World War, Einstein advocated for the nuclear disarmament of all nations.

THE LEGACIES OF EACH PERIOD (II)

The Cold War and the Emergence of the Third World

Two superpowers emerged from the Second World War and went on to dominate the world: the United States and the USSR. However, these two powers did not share the same ideology. In fact, their ideas were diametrically opposed, and they engaged in an ideological war that marked this third period.

Another important post-war phenomenon was the demand for independence by the colonies. The colonies wanted to free themselves from their European colonial rulers, which led to a wave of decolonization. This was supported by both the United States and the USSR, each seeing an opportunity to rally new countries to their side. However a number of colonies refused to submit to the domination of a new power, which led to the emergence of the Third World.

Scientific and Cultural Legacy of the Period

Scientifically, the opposing ideologies of the United States, a capitalist country, and the USSR, a communist country, led to the proliferation of arms, in particular nuclear arms. This period also saw the creation of NATO, the North Atlantic Treaty Organization (a collaboration of American and Western European armed forces) and the Warsaw Pact (a Soviet initiative in response to the creation of NATO), which allowed both enemy camps to increase their arms. During this same period, driven by the rivalry between the United States and the USSR, humankind made contact with the moon, first through radar contact (1946), then through a photograph of its hidden face (1959) and later through the first moonwalk (1969). However, scientific development was not limited to the progress spurred on by Cold War rivalry. Among the many legacies of this period, the most obvious one is the computer.

Culturally, the post-war period was marked by new phenomena. One of them, inherited from the inter-war period and the League of Nations, was the creation of the United Nations, which still works to maintain peace around the world today.

In the area of music, this period saw the emergence of musicians who, each in their own way, were hugely influential: Elvis Presley, Jerry Lee Lewis, the Rolling Stones, the Beatles, Led Zeppelin, Black Sabbath, Genesis, the Ramones, Bob Marley, U2, Madonna, Prince and many others. This period also saw the organization of major festivals, such as Woodstock in 1969, a culminating moment for hippie culture. The music television channel MTV was launched in 1981.

After the Second World War, cinema developed rapidly. During this period, Westerns continued to be very popular, and there was a resurgence of musical comedies, with classics like *Once Upon a Time in New York City* and *Singing in the Rain*. It was also a prolific period for epic films like *The Ten Commandments* and *Ben Hur*. The 1970s saw a wave of films about the Vietnam War, while the 1980s entered a new frontier in film, bringing real actors and cartoon characters together on the big screen with movies like *Who Framed Roger Rabbit?*

The Soviet probe *Luna 3* Launched by the USSR in 1959, this probe took the first pictures of the hidden face of the moon.

The fall of the Berlin Wall (1989)
Thousands of Germans gather to celebrate
the end of communism symbolized
by the fall of the Berlin Wall.

The Global Village

The fall of the USSR and the conclusion of the long Cold War marked the end of the third period and the beginning of new power struggles between nations. The United States became the sole economic power and imposed its model around the world.

In an effort to create a balance in the world, particularly with regard to trade, many countries formed economic associations. A growing number of free trade agreements and treaties between countries created a new phenomenon that marks this fourth and most recent period: globalization.

Scientific and Cultural Legacy of the Period

A great many scientific advances were made during this period. Space observation and exploration continued and led to missions that went as far as sending robotic spacecraft to Mars (1997). In the second half of the 1990s, science made great leaps with cloning. The Internet, as we know it today, appeared in the early 1990s. This technological advance revolutionized the world of telecommunications by introducing, among other things, e-mail communication between users of electronic messaging services. This same technology paved the way for mobile communication and the wireless transfer of images, texts and speech. In addition, since the year 2000, global positioning systems, or GPS, have been available to the general public.

Culturally, independent and multicultural films enjoyed an increasingly important place in the world of cinema, with international box-office hits like *Fahrenheit 9/11* and *Amélie*. The seventh art also benefited from advances in HD (high definition) technology.

During this period, the music scene took off with the first wave of grunge and trip-hop, as well as the ever-popular hip-hop, rap and electronic music. Equally, there is no denying the Internet's major cultural role in the distribution of music.

SNAPSHOT OF TODAY

On the sheet provided, you will find important historical events.

a Situate them on a time line.

b Match each event with a theme in the program.

Note Taking • To help you, consult the History Headlines section at the end of the book.

Dolly the sheep (1997)
In Scotland, in 1996, Dr. Ian Wilmut succeeded in cloning the first mammal, Dolly the sheep. In 2007, the first primate was successfully cloned, bringing scientists closer to the possibility of human cloning.

Global
Geography

Global
Politics

Global
Economics

Global
History

Global
Media

Common
Concepts

Introduction

MASS COMMUNICATION

Since the beginning of the 21st century, the dissemination of information has continued to intensify and gain momentum. Media makers bring us the headlines in news and entertainment, painting a picture of the world around us that is based on fact, and sometimes fiction. Of course, they play an important social role in how we perceive the world, from our immediate environment to the four corners of the globe.

? DID YOU KNOW?

Times Square located in the heart of New York City, remains one of the world's major hubs for display media, boasting a multitude of billboards using the latest technologies.

The Transmission of a Message

All communication is based on three essential and inseparable elements: the sender, the message, and the recipient.

The sender
The person who wants to convey information to a recipient

The message
The information itself

The recipient
The person who receives the information

A medium serves as the intermediary in a communications process. The word "media" is the plural form of the Latin word *medium*, which means "middle."

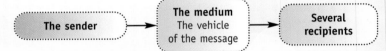

The sender

The medium
The vehicle of the message

Several recipients

A Field in Constant Evolution

The very nature of media is transformed with each new technological advance. Over time, we have gone from print to digital format, not to mention different broadcasting wave formats. The evolution of transmission methods has facilitated the flow of information and ideas. This has led to an extraordinary explosion in the quantity of information available.

Display media: a simple message

Used primarily in advertising, display media continue to be very effective in conveying information, since they are not language-based. A drawing, a symbol or an image can be understood by several societies without having to overcome a linguistic barrier. Today, digital technology transforms static display into dynamic display.

◀ **Times Square**

Print media: up close

Unlike display media, understanding a newspaper requires knowing how to read, as well as understanding the language in which the articles are written. The first newspapers were intended for society's educated elite. As education became increasingly democratized, newspapers began to play a more important role in disseminating information. With the development of photography, newspapers became the media of choice for conveying information to a larger public audience. Today, the press includes all types of newspapers (dailies, weeklies, monthlies), as well as periodicals (magazines and journals).

Radio: instant media

Radio is even more democratic than print media, since it does not require reading skills to understand the message. Listeners simply have to know the spoken language. Radio is a gateway to the world and an important cultural vehicle for the broadcasting of music. Since the transmission of the message is immediate, this type of medium is always current.

? DID YOU KNOW?

In Ramallah, in the Gaza Strip, a radio station opened in 2007 for the purpose of creating a neutral ground for dialogue between Palestinians and Israelis.

Cinema: fact or fiction?

Although today it is considered a lucrative cultural industry, cinema remains a powerful medium where information still enjoys pride of place, particularly in documentary films.

Television: message in a box

Television completely reinvented the media model by simplifying and further distilling the message. Viewers barely need to know the language, since a picture is worth a thousand words. Through satellite communication technology at the beginning of the 1990s, TV entered the "live" era of instant information. It became a valuable source of information, with new 24-hour news channels presenting live images throughout the day from around the world. TV is a powerful industry and a brilliant marketing and entertainment hub.

? DID YOU KNOW?

Russia has over 7000 television stations across the country.

The Internet: high speed versatility

The Internet is the new kid on the block and is just as important as its predecessors. In fact, it has swallowed them up. The Internet uses both spoken and written language, combining images and sound. It can be used live or it can serve as an archive for vast amounts of information. Internet users can receive and send messages, which is revolutionary in itself. As the Internet evolves at lightning speed, other means of mass dissemination must adapt to the realities of the new millennium. Newspapers, radio, television and even cinema must evolve simultaneously as media in their own right and as on-line media.

? DID YOU KNOW?

Norway is one of the world's most connected countries, with nearly 90% of its population having access to the Internet, .

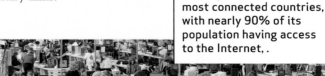

Large computer ▶
trade show in Hamar,
Norway (2006)

MAJOR CHALLENGES FACED BY THE MEDIA

Although the various media are a vital tool for understanding the modern world and its realities, they present their own set of problems. The media world, which has grown dramatically in recent decades, has given rise to many issues today that go beyond borders, bringing up questions about the established order.

In the West, there is concern about increased media consumption, particularly among youth, and its long-term effects. There are also other issues of an international nature that may have a direct impact on the world view we are presented with by all types of media.

The Media's Mission

The media have two basic functions in society:

- to transmit information
- to entertain

The first function relates to the very nature of media, which is to serve as an intermediary in the transmission of a message. While this function is well anchored in society, the concept of entertainment seems to be assuming an increasingly important role for all forms of media.

Many welcome this transition, since it contributes to the growth of culture in society, while others criticize it for reducing the quantity and quality of information available to the population. This reduction has inevitably led to the simplification of media messages addressed to the population regarding major political, economic and social issues.

The Journalist: A Reliable Source of Information

Traditionally, the information presented in the media is primarily the fruit of a journalist's work. The journalist's mandate is to report the facts as objectively as possible. Opinions are reserved for editorials in a clearly indicated section of the newspaper or in television shows on public affairs. On the international stage, press agencies, such as Reuters, Agence France-Press (AFP) and Associated Press (AP), relay information from around the world to various media outlets.

OF TODAY

SNAPSHOT

(a) Find an example of information and an example of entertainment in the media.

(b) Find articles that demonstrate a diversity of reports about the same news item.

(c) Name some public and private media corporations.

Is the Internet a Reliable Source?

With the media explosion in recent years, particularly the development of the Internet as an interactive media, more and more people are becoming "transmitters" of information, as self-proclaimed journalists or editorialists. While many applaud the democratization of information through forums, blogs and amateur video sites, others point to two negative aspects of this new reality:

- The large number of sources makes it difficult to sort through information, with events quickly becoming outdated.

- The technology around media production is now available to a growing number of people, which is gradually creating a gap between information and journalistic principles and ethics.

Media Ownership

Today, we can talk about the media world as an industry in its own right, since corporations are responsible for media production. Like most industries, some corporations are public, while others are private. While private media are more prevalent internationally, it is not uncommon for governments to manage a particular form of media in their own country. In this context, two important issues are raised:

- If a State administers the country in an authoritarian or totalitarian manner, it may adopt the same approach to managing media. In this way, a government can control all or part of the information conveyed to its citizens. For the population, freedom of the press and freedom of expression are at stake. For the rest of the world, the information provided becomes biased.

- While private corporations perform media functions, they must turn a profit to survive.

In recent years, the profit motive has created two phenomena that have also had an impact on the media world: concentration and convergence. It has become common practice for a media corporation to buy a competing corporation. Often, a media outlet buys corporations that work in various production stages. The problem of media ownership is that major media outlets are owned by ever-larger and more imposing corporations, allowing these giants to take control of the industry and choose the information presented to the population.

Awareness campaign on the dangers of reporting from the heart of the Iraqi conflict
Every year, the organization Reporters Without Borders publishes a world press freedom index based on over 50 criteria related to the free flow of information.

Introduction

WHAT DO YOU KNOW?

Five themes are used to study the contemporary world. Each one required the development of a particular concept. These concepts must be used in order to concretely represent the complexity of the issue to which they pertain.

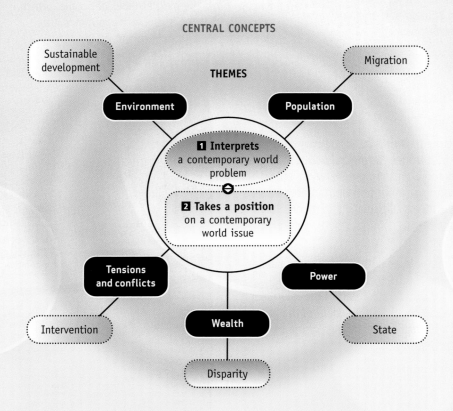

CENTRAL CONCEPTS

Sustainable development

THEMES

Migration

Environment

Population

1 Interprets a contemporary world problem

2 Takes a position on a contemporary world issue

Tensions and conflicts

Power

Intervention

Wealth

State

Disparity

These themes are not isolated. On the contrary, some concepts may be used to analyze any of the realities of today's world. Three concepts are common to the five themes presented:

- **INTERDEPENDENCE**
- **GLOBALIZATION**
- **POWER**

SNAPSHOT OF TODAY

ⓐ Provide a definition of each of the three common concepts.

ⓑ Observe the images and match them with the common concepts.

ⓒ Review each of the definitions if necessary.

26

Description of the photographs

1 Peru's Minister of Foreign Affairs Jose Garcia Belaunde and China's Minister of Trade Chen Deming sign a free trade agreement in 2008 in the presence of their respective heads of State, Peru's President Alan Garcia and China's President Hu Jintao.

2 Nicole Kidman, Australian actress and Goodwill Ambassador for the United Nations Development Fund for Women, presents the report for the 2008 campaign on violence against women in the presence of UN Secretary General Ban Ki-moon.

3 A shoe-shiner works in front of an Internet café in the Egyptian capital, Cairo. Today, more than eight million Egyptians are connected to the Internet, a number that continues to grow each year (2008).

4 In 2005, Italians flocked to Rome for Live 8, the biggest musical event ever organized. This series of shows was presented in 10 cities, across four continents, to promote the "Make Poverty History" awareness campaign, primarily focused on Africa.

5 Clothing labels that show the many different manufacturing countries in the textile industry. This industry remains the economic engine for many countries around the world.

6 In the Turkish capital of Ankara, a young boy casts his father's ballot in the 2007 presidential elections.

7 Demonstrators march in the streets of Manila in the Philippines to protest against the World Economic Forum held in Switzerland. This demonstration was part of an initiative of the World Social Forum, an organization created to serve as a counterweight to the Economic Forum (2008).

DESIGNATED FOCUS ENVIRONMENTAL MANAGEMENT

Topic to Be Interpreted
Economic, political and social choices in environmental management

CONCEPTS

Sustainable Development (p. 47)
Consumption (p. 33)
Dependence (p. 35)
Regulation (p. 55)
Responsibility (p. 51)

Taking a Position (TAP)

TAP 1 The use and consumption of resources

OR

TAP 2 The harmonization of environmental standards

The exploitation and consumption of natural resources have led to major **environmental problems.** **Action** must be taken to ensure their **management**, and economic, political and social choices must be made. Given that this is a **global issue**, the action must be taken on a worldwide scale, particularly through **international agreements**.

ENVIRONMENT

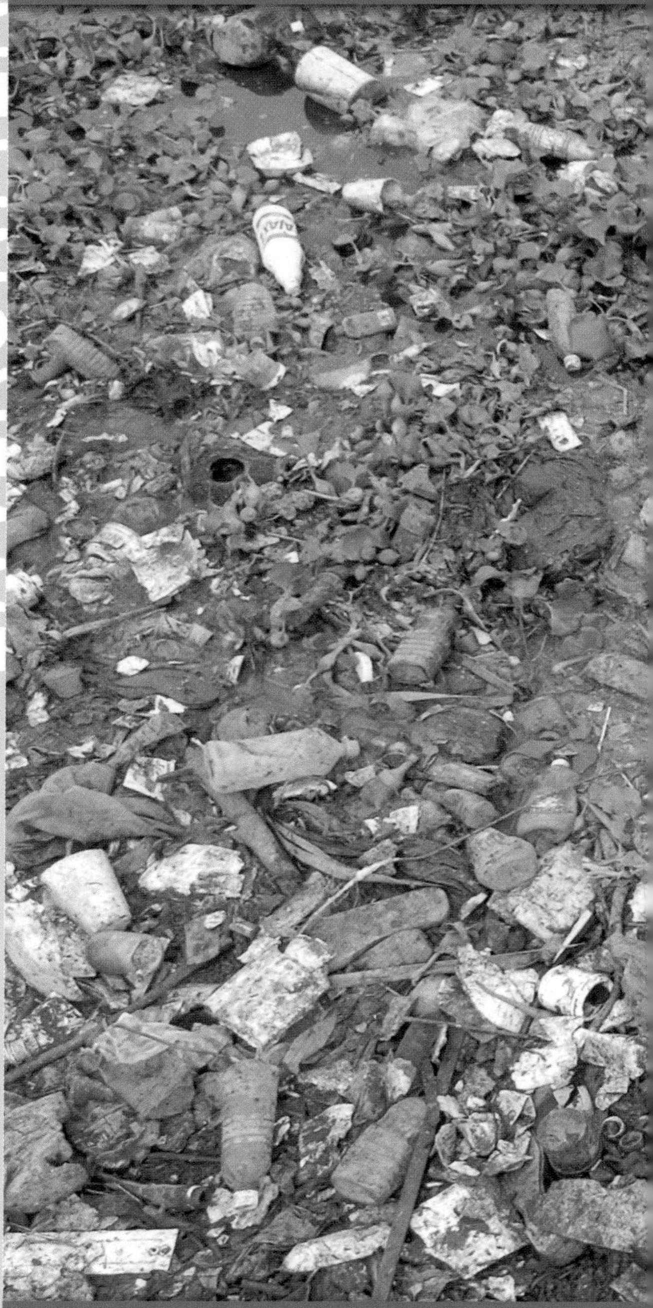

1.1 A little girl playing in a polluted river in the Dominican Republic (2005)

29

Environment

Environmental
Problems

Environmental
Action

International
Agreements

NATURAL RESOURCES

The rise in energy consumption and the production of manufactured goods, as well as the increase in the world's population from one billion in 1800 to 6.5 billion in 2006, have led to the intense exploitation of the planet's natural resources (also called raw materials). Humanity is totally dependent on the planet's resources for its survival and for meeting its basic needs such as food, shelter, water and energy.

Water

While water covers 70% of the Earth's surface, only a small amount is suitable for consumption and irrigation. Each year, approximately 4000 km³ of freshwater is used to meet these needs.

Essential for life, freshwater resources are unequally distributed across the planet. Nine countries, including Canada and the United States, hold 60% of renewable freshwater resources, while arid and semi-arid countries hold a mere 2%. **Around the world, one person in five does not have access to safe drinking water (2002).** Some thirty countries, most located in Africa and South-Central Asia, suffer from a shortage of freshwater, with reserves of less than 1000 m³ per capita.

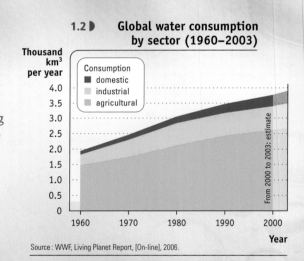

1.2 ▶ **Global water consumption by sector (1960–2003)**

Thousand km³ per year

Consumption
- domestic
- industrial
- agricultural

From 2000 to 2003: estimate

Year

Source : WWF, Living Planet Report, [On-line], 2006.

Forests

Forests cover approximately 4 billion hectares of the Earth's surface. Russia, Brazil, Canada and the United States account for over half of that, while in 64 other countries, forest occupies less than 10% of the territory, particularly in North Africa and West Asia.

Humans exploit forests, transforming wood into furniture, paper, lumber or firewood. Trees are also cut down to create new farmland. **From 2000 to 2005, forests were reduced by an average of 7.3 million hectares a year, or 200 km² a day.**

▲ 1.3
Deforestation in the Amazon (2004)
It is estimated that the Amazon forest, the largest forest in the world, loses the equivalent of one football field every minute.

1.4 ▶
A salmon farm in British Columbia (1990s)
In addition to natural fisheries, aquaculture (fish farming) produced 48.15 million tons of fish in 2005, a volume 30 times greater than in 1960.

Agriculture

Since the 1960s, agricultural production has increased an average of 2.3% per year, outpacing demographic growth. There has been a significant increase in the production of grain, sugar, vegetables, eggs and meat. This growth, however, has been uneven: while it has been high in East Asia and the Pacific, it has been very low in Sub-Saharan Africa. Globally, food consumption has improved and diets have diversified, but there are still **963 million malnourished people around the world (2008).**

▲ **1.5**
Irrigation of a cotton field in California (1998)
In the early 21st century, arable lands cover 1.4 billion hectares, over 275 million of which are irrigated.

Fisheries

Fishing has grown tremendously since the 1960s. Today, over one million trawlers ply the ocean, equipped with advanced electronic probes to locate fish and massive nets measuring up to 300 metres long. **Over a 45-year period, the total volume of fish caught almost tripled, reaching 93.25 million tons in 2005.** Fish constitute an essential food in many countries. For example, in Asia, it represents close to one third of the animal protein consumed by the population.

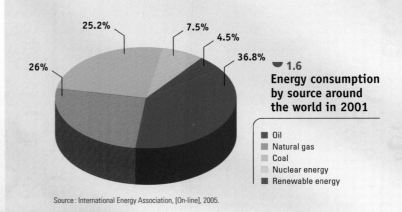

25.2%   7.5%   4.5%   36.8%   26%

▬ **1.6**
Energy consumption by source around the world in 2001

- ■ Oil
- ■ Natural gas
- ■ Coal
- ■ Nuclear energy
- ■ Renewable energy

Source: International Energy Association, [On-line], 2005.

Fossil Fuels

Since the industrial revolution, human development has been based on the use of fossil fuels, that is to say, coal, natural gas and oil. These resources are the result of decomposed flora and fauna that were trapped in the planet's subsoil millions of years ago. **Seventy-five percent of the 80 million barrels of oil processed each day come from about 15 countries, including Saudi Arabia, Russia, the United States, Iran and China.** Developed countries are by far the largest consumers of energy, but developing countries, in particular China and India, are consuming ever-greater quantities. Around the world, one third of this energy is consumed by industry and one quarter by transportation.

31

MASS CONSUMPTION

Since the Second World War, consumption has skyrocketed, particularly in developed countries. Industrialization and technological development paved the way for the mass production of a variety of goods that provide all the comforts of modern living. Mass consumption has been facilitated by increased income and easy access to credit.

Mass Consumption

Over the last few decades, the global population's average income has grown significantly. Between 1980 and 2007, it more than tripled, increasing from $2,760 to $9,852 per year (adjusted for parity). This income drives a consumer society that buys goods and services not only to meet essential needs (food, housing, health, etc.), but also for pleasure and comfort. People buy much more than they need and replace things as trends and technologies change, often before they have truly become outdated or unusable. Bolstered by powerful advertising, capitalist corporations sell anything and everything that can satisfy even the smallest desire, all of it readily available in big-box stores and shopping malls or on the Internet. As a result of economic globalization, market competition and strong demand, prices are generally competitive, at least for populations in developed countries.

Consumerism around the world is...

808 million personal computers in use (2005)

1.34 billion Internet surfers (2007)

2.5 billion radios (2003)

1.4 billion television sets (2003)

73 million motor vehicles produced annually (2007)

100 million portable digital players sold between 2001 and 2007

1 billion automobiles in use around the world (2007)

3.3 billion cellphone subscribers (2007)

500 million to 1 billion plastic bags used each year

ⓐ Based on your reading of these pages and the two preceding pages, how would you define the concept of "consumption"?

ⓑ Do you recognize yourself in this definition?

ⓒ The media often cover issues addressing consumption. Give an example related to the environmental impact of resource consumption.

Unequal Consumption

The planet's inhabitants do not all have the same level of consumption—far from it. In industrialized countries, the gross national income (GNI) per capita was $36,657 per year in 2007, while it was barely $1,173 in the 50 least developed countries. This sort of income gap leads to significant differences in consumer habits. For example, the Canadian population, which numbered 32 million in 2007, spent $31.3 billion that year on clothes and shoes, while Peru's 27 million inhabitants spent $3.6 billion that year on those same items. Household consumption in France in 2005 was $826 billion, while in India it was $385 billion. Yet, India has a population 18.6 times larger than that of France.

If they had the means, most inhabitants in developing countries would consume much like those in wealthy countries, which would spell disaster for the Earth. We would need five or six planets to support the global population if all of the Earth's inhabitants lived like Americans, the world's biggest consumers.

1.7 ▶ Consumption in the United States, China and Nigeria (2007)

	United States	China	Nigeria
Total population	301 621 000	1 319 982 596	147 980 000
Gross national income per inhabitant (adjusted for parity)	US$46,040	US$2,360	US$1,770
Spending on clothes and shoes	US$429.8 billion	US$95.8 billion	US$7.2 billion
Spending on electronic devices (excluding cellphones)	US$162 billion	US$11.8 billion	US$0.4 billion
Spending on alcohol and tobacco	US$205.6 billion	US$31.4 billion	US$2.5 billion
Spending on household goods	US$456.9 billion	US$57.1 billion	US$4.1 billion
Spending on recreation	US$881 billion	US$34.2 billion	US$2.3 billion
Total number of automobiles (per 1000 inhabitants)	824	28	Not available
% phone subscribers (landline and mobile)	139%	69%	28%
% Internet users	73%	16%	6,8%

Sources: World Bank and Euromonitor International, cited in the *New York Times*, [On-line], 2008.

Environmental
Problems

Environmental
Action

International
Agreements

Environment

THE OVEREXPLOITATION OF RESOURCES

Today's exploitation of natural resources exceeds by 25% the Earth's capacity for renewal, as well as exceeding its capacity to absorb the pollution generated by human activity. Within the next few decades, if nothing changes, humanity will be confronted with a planet that has been depleted, especially since the global population is expected to reach close to 9 billion by 2050.

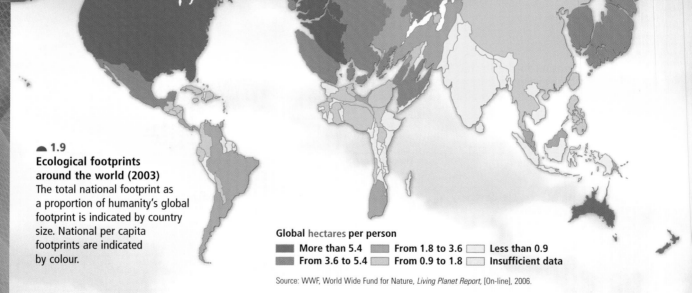

1.8
Representation of the world
This map serves as a reference for the analysis of map 1.9.

1.9
Ecological footprints around the world (2003)
The total national footprint as a proportion of humanity's global footprint is indicated by country size. National per capita footprints are indicated by colour.

Global hectares per person
- More than 5.4
- From 3.6 to 5.4
- From 1.8 to 3.6
- From 0.9 to 1.8
- Less than 0.9
- Insufficient data

Source: WWF, World Wide Fund for Nature, *Living Planet Report*, [On-line], 2006.

The ecological footprint

The World Wide Fund for Nature (WWF) has created an index for estimating the pressure of human activities on the environment, known as the ecological footprint. Calculated in units of area, the ecological footprint measures the area needed to fulfill a person's consumption in terms of cropland, grassland, pasture, fishery and forest. It also includes the area required to absorb the carbon dioxide emitted by the burning of fossil fuels (oil, natural gas and coal). The map of different countries' ecological footprints clearly illustrates the disparity in consumption between developed countries and developing countries.

ⓐ How can the concept of "dependence" be defined in the context of the environment?

ⓑ What is the consequence of dependence today?

Fisheries

Fish and shellfish stocks are being depleted as a result of overfishing and the pollution of the oceans. In 2007, some 1200 species of fish were at risk of extinction, representing 39% of existing species. Many predator fish species, which are less abundant in the oceans, have been overexploited, particularly Atlantic salmon, tuna, herring and cod. In addition, the use of giant fishing nets results in one quarter of all catches being unwanted fish, which are dumped back into the water.

Freshwater

In the 20th century, water consumption increased tenfold. Consequently, the volume of water available each year has decreased from an average of 16 800 m^3 per capita in 1950 to 7300 m^3 in 2000. If demographic growth is taken into account, at the current rate of consumption, this volume is expected to decrease to 5100 m^3 per capita by 2025. Due to the unequal distribution of freshwater resources, 3 billion people will suffer from water stress, meaning they will have less than 1700 m^3 of water available to them per year.

Forests

Over the last few centuries, human beings have destroyed approximately half of the Earth's natural forests. In the United States, close to 90% of virgin forests have been cut down, while Africa has lost 80% of its forests and 50% of Asia's tropical forests have disappeared. Forest exploitation results in far-reaching habitat destruction that threatens not only the survival of hundreds of plant species, but insect and animal species as well.

Soil

While our food needs are expected to triple by 2050, the quality of the soil used for agriculture and raising livestock is deteriorating and the surface area of cultivable land is shrinking. Wind and water erosion carries away 25 billion tons of soil each year. This erosion is accelerated by poor soil management, particularly overgrazing, deforestation and land clearing, which destroys groundcover. Moreover, the overexploitation of land, in regions where little fertilizer is used, depletes the soil's nutrients and reduces its fertility.

Fossil Fuels

At the rate that human beings are consuming fossil fuels, shortages are anticipated in the near future. Given the difficulty of evaluating fossil fuel reserves, experts do not agree on the date when production will peak, after which it will begin to decline. Pessimists predict this peak will occur between 2010 and 2015 for oil and around 2030 for natural gas. Only coal reserves, which are extensive, can be expected to survive for a few more decades, but this is by far the most polluting fuel.

POLLUTION

Rising consumption, urbanization and industrialization lead to pollution that affects all ecosystems, whether water, air or land. Additionally, the increasing amount of garbage produced obliges societies to develop waste management programs to avoid being buried under it.

Waste Management

United States
750 kg/person

Mexico
340 kg/person

Poland
250 kg/person

Since the 1980s, the production of municipal waste has increased faster than the world's population. In industrialized countries, each person produced an average of 580 kg of garbage per year in 2005, representing an increase of 120 kg compared to 1985. This production is uneven, but the most economically developed countries tend to top the list. In rapidly industrializing countries, the rapid growth in waste constitutes a real management problem. For example, in China, since the mid-1990s, the volume of household garbage has increased by 8 to 10% per year and many cities lack adequate waste disposal systems.

Garbage is a source of pollution, particularly when improperly managed. Garbage emits methane, an especially harmful greenhouse gas (GHG). It can also pollute the soil and water tables, since the toxic products in garbage seep into the ground, particularly mercury from batteries and paint lead. As for incinerators, they pump toxic dust and heavy metals into the environment, and the ash they produce—called clinker—can contaminate the soil.

Waste Recycling

Waste can be useful if the energy it produces when burned is captured or sorted and recycled. This type of sustainable management has become more and more common, particularly in developed countries that have the financial means to build the necessary infrastructure. For example, in Western Europe, the recycling rate for paper and cardboard increased from 40% in 1992 to 64% in 2005, while glass recycling increased from 51% to 65% in the same period.

1.10 ▶ Composition of municipal waste (%)

	Canada	South Korea	Mexico
Paper and cardboard	47	24	15
Organic matter	24	28	51
Plastic	3	8	6
Glass	6	5	6
Metals	13	7	3
Textiles and other	8	28	18

Source: OECD, *OECD Environmental Data Compendium*, [On-line], 2008.

INDIGESTIBLE PLASTIC

Plastic decomposes very slowly and breaks down into miniscule particles that birds and marine animals mistake for plankton, one of their food sources. This affects the entire food chain, since plastic is indigestible. According to the environmental organization Greenpeace, THE INGESTION OF PLASTIC KILLS ONE MILLION BIRDS AND 100 000 MARINE MAMMALS EACH YEAR.

IN BRIEF

1.11
**The major garbage patches
in the Pacific Ocean**
Garbage patches in the Pacific Ocean weigh a total of 3.5 million tons. The area of the patch between Hawaii and California is two times greater than that of the State of Texas. The two large garbage patches depicted on the right, whose area has tripled since the 1990s, occupy close to 3.5 million km².

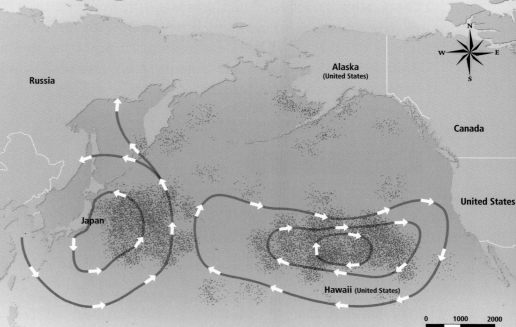

Russia

Alaska
(United States)

Canada

Japan

United States

Hawaii (United States)

0   1000   2000
kilometres

Ocean Pollution

Human activity has had devastating effects on the marine environment and the organisms that live there. Oil tanker wrecks and accidents on oil rigs on the high seas spill thousands of tons of oil into the waters. These black tides coat plankton, birds and marine mammals and pollute beaches. Many other kinds of pollutants pour into the oceans from rivers or are transported through the atmosphere. Fertilizers used for agriculture, rich in nitrogen and phosphates, provide the marine environment with a surplus of nutrients that lead to the proliferation of algae. This phenomenon, called eutrophication, reduces the quantity of oxygen in the water and causes asphyxiation in aquatic environments.

Carried by ocean currents, waste dumped into the ocean is often found far from its point of entry. This is particularly true of plastic, which takes 500 to 1000 years to decompose. In fact, 10% of the hundreds of millions of tons of plastic manufactured each year ends up in the oceans. After floating around for several years, this waste finds its way to one of the two zones in the northeast of the Pacific Ocean. Ocean currents create an enormous vortex that pulls the plastic waste into a whirlpool.

GLOBAL PROBLEMS

The Earth's biosphere functions as a vast dynamic system: each of its elements is in constant interaction with the others. That is why the impact of most environmental problems (pollution, destruction of natural environments, etc.) extends beyond State borders and can affect the entire planet.

Inadequate Measures

Few States completely ignore environmental problems, particularly since they can have serious economic repercussions. Consequently, most countries have developed some regulations, often in the form of legislation, to prevent environmental abuses.

However, these laws only have a limited impact on a global scale because they are applied within the State's territory. For example, a country that regulates its sulphur emissions (a chemical element that causes acid rain) will likely still be affected by toxic precipitation if its neighbours continue to pollute the atmosphere. A lack of environmental coordination can also have negative economic effects. For example, a country that refuses to adopt the same automobile pollution standards as its neighbour may, as a result, lose a market for the automobiles it produces.

SEEN AND HEARD

Protecting One's Neighbours

In 1972, delegates to the first major international environmental conference defined the principles that should govern relations between States with respect to the environment:

" States have, in accordance with the Charter of the United Nations and the principles of international law, the sovereign right to exploit their own resources pursuant to their own environmental policies, and the responsibility to ensure that activities within their jurisdiction or control do not cause damage to the environment of other States or of areas beyond the limits of national jurisdiction. "

Final Declaration of the United Nations Conference on the Human Environment (1972)

1.12 ▶
**Contaminated zone
in the Chernobyl region
of Ukraine (1998)**

Acid rain

The major industrial centres of Germany and southern Europe emit a large quantity of toxic products into the atmosphere. Eventually, these products fall into the lakes and onto the forests of Scandinavia (Northern Europe) in the form of acid rain, with serious consequences for flora and fauna. This phenomenon is also very common in China, as well as in North America, where Eastern Canada is affected by acid rain originating in the United States.

Invasive species

Certain species of exotic animals and plants, that are accidentally or intentionally introduced by humans, proliferate quickly and become major competitors with the local flora and fauna. They contribute to considerably reducing the biodiversity of certain regions. Well-known examples of invasive species include the zebra mussel, Nile perch, *Caulerpa taxifolia*, algae, starlings and domestic cats.

◀ 1.13
Zebra mussels (2005)

International fisheries

The oceans constitute international zones where any country is free to exploit the resources. In 2006, close to 92 million tons of fish were caught in oceans. Some scientists estimate that if fishing continues at its current rate, all stocks will disappear by 2050. Already, the rate of destruction of the big predator fish, like tuna, cod and shark, has surpassed 90%.

The Chernobyl disaster

On April 26, 1986, an accident at a nuclear reactor at the Chernobyl plant, in Ukraine (then part of the USSR), created a massive radioactive cloud. Winds carried the cloud across Europe, contaminating to varying degrees soil, watercourses and vegetation, and the animals that fed off of them. The effects of this disaster were felt as far away as Ireland and northern Scandinavia.

1.14 ▶
**The hole in the ozone
layer above Antarctica
(2000)**

The ozone layer

The ozone layer, located in the upper atmosphere, envelopes the Earth. The bulk of the sun's ultraviolet radiation, which is dangerous to living organisms, is absorbed by the ozone layer. Since the end of the 1970s, the ozone layer has been growing thinner, completely disappearing over the poles during certain seasons. CFCs, a gas that is primarily produced by human activity, is the main cause of this thinning.

Tuna fishing (1989)
▼ 1.15

GLOBAL WARMING

Human activity releases a large quantity of pollutants into the atmosphere. These gases have harmful effects and are causing global warming. Every country, from the richest to the poorest, is affected by this phenomenon, although the effect on the latter is greater, as they have a limited capacity to respond.

As the Planet Heats Up

Since 1850, the planet's average temperature has been steadily rising. According to the vast majority of scientists, global warming will continue and even worsen over the next few decades. The Earth's average temperature is expected to increase by 1.8 to 4 degrees Celsius by the end of the 21st century.

Global warming is primarily caused by the presence in the atmosphere of greenhouse gases (GHGs), which allow solar radiation to pass through, but do not allow the heat emitted from the Earth's surface to escape. There are several different greenhouse gases. Among those produced by human activity are carbon dioxide (CO_2), methane, nitrous oxide (N_2O) and chlorofluorocarbons (CFCs).

Power plants, industry, transportation, agricultural production and the extraction of fossil fuels, namely, coal, oil and natural gas, contribute greatly to GHG emissions into the atmosphere and, ultimately, global warming.

◄ 1.16
Industrial pollution in Russia (1991)

1.17 ►   Temperature increase

Temperature anomaly (°C)

■ Annual average
■ Five-year average

0.6
0.5
0.4
0.3
0.2
0.1
0
−0.1
−0.2
−0.3
−0.4
−0.5
−0.6

1860   1880   1900   1920   1940   1960   1980   2000

Year

Source: Global Warming Art, *Instrumental Temperature Record*, [On-line], 2008.

Al Gore

Former Vice-President of the United States, Al Gore now devotes his time to the fight against global warming. He is the leading voice in the documentary *An Inconvenient Truth*, directed by David Guggenheim. Released in 2006, this film explains the main issues related to global warming. In 2007, in conjunction with the Intergovernmental Panel on Climate Change (IPCC), Al Gore won the Nobel Peace Prize for his work to raise awareness about global warming.

Possible Consequences of Global Warming

Melting glaciers and polar ice caps

Global warming has caused a significant decrease in snow cover around the world. Since the early 20th century, the total area of glaciers has dropped by 50%. Pack ice is particularly affected: many scientists predict that the Arctic's waters will be practically free of ice at summer's end by the second half of the 21st century.

Rising waters

Warmer waters lead to a global increase in the volume of oceans due to the melting of the polar ice caps. It is predicted that sea levels will rise 18 to 59 cm by 2100. This situation is threatening over 30% of the planet's coastal wetlands and considerably increasing the risk of flooding. Cities like Venice, Italy and Dhaka, Bangladesh, are particularly threatened.

Climate disasters on the rise

Heat waves are expected to become more frequent, leading to an increase in health problems and mortality. The intensity of tropical cyclones (hurricanes and typhoons) is also expected to increase. In temperate regions, precipitation will be more frequent and more intense. Conversely, in tropical regions, it will decrease considerably, exacerbating problems of desertification.

Shrinking biodiversity

Climate change is threatening many ecosystems, which affects the planet's biodiversity Certain highly adaptable animal and plant species may see their territories expand, but most species will be negatively affected. Between 20 and 30% of animals and plants may well disappear.

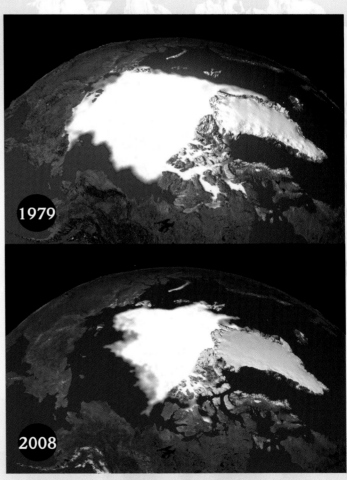

1979

2008

● 1.18
Minimal extension of pack ice

Environmental
Problems

Environmental
Action

International
Agreements

Environment

GROWING AWARENESS

The second half of the 19th century saw the creation of the first nature preservation movements in Western industrial societies. Their actions, however, tended to be isolated. It was only after the Second World War that genuine awareness emerged about the impact of human activity on the environment.

Pioneers

In the 19th century, the Western world became interested in the wealth of nature and saw it as an antidote to life in big, unhealthy industrial cities. In North America and Europe, local movements sprang up to protect natural sites, forests and certain animal species threatened by human activity. In 1872, the world's first national park, Yellowstone, was established in the United States. However, the primary motivation was the desire to study and contemplate nature rather than protect the environment, and naturalists tended to focus on local action.

Post-War Environmental Movement

After the nuclear bombs were dropped on Hiroshima and Nagasaki in 1945, it was clear that humanity had crossed a technological threshold that could threaten the survival of the biosphere. In the context of the Cold War that followed the Second World War, the militarization of science served to heighten this feeling of insecurity. Meanwhile, the scientific community was becoming increasingly alarmed by the explosion of consumer society combined with significant demographic growth around the world.

A number of scientists started to caution humanity about the planet's limited ability to support the accelerating rate of economic development and global population growth. They warned that resources would start running out. Added to this were scientific studies that measured the negative impact of human activity on the environment and its resulting degradation. Starting in the 1950s, a growing number of international conferences and symposia were held on these issues, as scientists became increasingly alarmed by the situation.

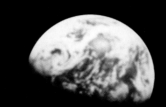

1.19 ▶
The Earth rising above the moon's horizon (1968)
In the 1960s, images of Earth from outer space made our planet look smaller and more vulnerable. They helped raise awareness of the fragility of the Earth.

David Suzuki

A Canadian of Japanese origin, geneticist David Suzuki is renowned for his work as a science communicator and environmental activist. He has hosted a number of radio and television shows, including *The Nature of Things*, written several popular books on the environment and won many prizes. He also co-founded the David Suzuki Foundation, which seeks to protect the environment through science and education.

Provocative Publications

The 1960s saw the emergence of scientific publications that had a major impact and caught the attention not only of scientists but politicians and the general public as well. One example is *Silent Spring*, by American biologist Rachel Carson, published in 1962. Considered the first successful popular work to raise environmental awareness, the book explored the impact of pollution on nature, particularly the effects of pesticides on the environment. It led both to the ban of the pesticide DDT in the United States in 1972 and to a remarkable increase in environmental consciousness.

The first report from the Club of Rome (an international think tank), published in 1972, also shook up the Western world. Entitled *The Limits to Growth*, the report used a computer model that combined five parameters, including natural resources, global population and pollution, to demonstrate the limits of humanity's economic and demographic growth. It argued that if the then current rate of growth continued, natural resources would run out and the Earth would be unable to absorb all of the pollution generated by humanity. The report also predicted a meltdown of the global system during the 21st century. These kinds of publications prompted the ruling class and the population to take measures to prevent an environmental disaster.

1.20

A controlled exploitation zone (ZEC) in Mauricie
In Québec, the provocative documentary *L'erreur boréale* by Richard Desjardins denounced the harmful effects of abusive forest exploitation by the large pulp and paper companies. This film created a stir and prompted the Québec government to establish a commission of inquiry into forest management.

SEEN AND HEARD

" The 'control of nature' is a phrase conceived in arrogance, born of the Neanderthal age of biology and philosophy, when it was supposed that nature exists for the convenience of man. . . . It is our alarming misfortune that so primitive a science has armed itself with the most modern and terrible weapons, and that in turning them against the insects, it has also turned them against the earth. "

Rachel CARSON, *Silent Spring,* 1962

Environmental
Problems

Environmental
Action

International
Agreements

Environment

ENVIRONMENTAL MOVEMENTS

At the same time as the scientific community was diffusing alarming information about the deterioration of the environment, movements were being organized to protect nature, to put pressure on governments and to raise public awareness about environmental problems. Today, there are thousands of these kinds of organizations.

⏷ 1.21
John Muir (1902)

Sierra Club

The Sierra Club, founded by John Muir in San Francisco in 1892, was the first non-governmental organization (NGO) devoted to the protection of nature. Originally, the club focused on investigating and protecting wild areas in North America, particularly those in the Sierra Nevada, in eastern California. Today, the Sierra Club boasts 1.3 million members and has broadened its objectives. In addition to protecting wild areas around the world, it promotes the responsible use of natural resources in order to protect and restore the quality of the environment, using all available legal means to achieve these ends.

Greenpeace

Greenpeace is an independent, non-violent organization that seeks to draw international attention in order to protect the environment. It was created in 1971, when activists boarded an old fishing boat in Vancouver, intending, if possible, to prevent nuclear testing by the United States on Amchitka Island, Alaska. Today, Greenpeace is present in 40 countries and has 3 million members. These members sometimes engage in dangerous activities to achieve their ends, such as infiltrating nuclear testing areas, placing themselves between harpoons and whales or blocking pipes that discharge toxic substances.

Four Greenpeace founders preparing to sail to Amchitka Island (1971)
⏷ 1.22

◀ 1.23
Wangari Maathai

Eco-Terrorism

The eco-terrorist or eco-guerrilla movement refers to various environmental activist organizations that will even go to the point of resorting to violence to protect the environment. For example, eco-terrorists occupy work sites they consider harmful to the environment in order to stop the work or set themselves up on platforms in trees to prevent them from being cut down. The Sea Shepherd Conservation Society, founded in 1977 by Paul Watson, seeks to protect the oceans. Its members board ships engaged in whaling, sealing or shark fishing on the high seas.

The Green Belt Movement

In 1977, Wangari Maathai founded the Green Belt Movement, which works to reforest Kenya in order to prevent soil erosion and preserve the country's biodiversity. Over 30 years, Kenyan women who support the movement have planted more than 20 million trees and developed some 30 000 tree nurseries. In addition, 80 000 jobs have been created, most of them for women. Other countries in Africa, including Ethiopia, Uganda and Zimbabwe, have adopted similar reforestation methods. In 2004, the movement's founder became the first African woman to win the Nobel Peace Prize.

1.25 ▶
Paul Watson aboard his ship, the Ocean Warrior (2000)

Green Parties

In many countries, environmental concerns have led to the creation of political parties devoted to protecting nature and promoting world peace. Most of these political parties call themselves the "Green Party." The first was created in New Zealand in 1972. However, it was only in the 1990s that members of Green Parties started to get elected.

To promote common principles, representatives of 80 Green Parties around the world signed the Global Green Charter in 2001. This charter recognizes six basic principles: ecological wisdom, social justice sustainable development, non-violence, participatory democracy and respect for diversity.

Green Parties have only had a few members elected to parliaments around the world. However, the growing percentage of votes for Green Parties demonstrates that the environment has become a serious issue for voters. Politicians must now address the environment in their political platforms.

◀ 1.26
Indulis Emsis (2004)
In 1993, Indulis Emsis was appointed Latvia's Minister of the Environment, making him the first environmentalist to occupy a ministerial post.

45

WHAT IS SUSTAINABLE DEVELOPMENT?

As the world began to recognize our planet's limited capacity to support economic and demographic growth, a new concept emerged: sustainable development. Widely used today, this term was popularized in 1987 in *Our Common Future*, also known as the Brundtland Report, named after its author.

Sustainable Development According to the Brundtland Report

The concept of sustainable development does not just apply to the environment, as illustrated in this excerpt from the Brundtland Report.

SEEN AND HEARD

" Sustainable development seeks to meet the needs and aspirations of the present without compromising the ability to meet those of the future. Far from requiring the cessation of economic growth, it recognizes that the problems of poverty and underdevelopment cannot be solved unless we have a new era of growth in which developing countries play a large role and reap large benefits.

Economic growth always brings risk of environmental damage, as it puts increased pressure on environmental resources. But policy makers guided by the concept of sustainable development will necessarily work to assure that growing economies remain firmly attached to their ecological roots and that these roots are protected and nurtured so that they may support growth over the long term. Environmental protection is thus inherent in the concept of sustainable development, as is a focus on the sources of environmental problems rather than the symptoms. "

Gro Harlem Brundtland (ed.), *Our Common Future*, Chapter 1, 1987

Gro Harlem Brundtland

Born in Oslo in 1939, medical doctor Gro Harlem Brundtland was Norway's Minister of the Environment from 1974 to 1979, as well as its Prime Minister in 1981, then again from 1986 to 1989 and 1990 to 1996. She also chaired the UN World Commission on Environment and Development from 1983 to 1987 and was Director-General of the World Health Organization (WHO) from 1998 to 2003. In 2004, the *Financial Times* designated her the fourth most influential person in Europe.

Sustainable development is the main concept in this chapter.

ⓐ How would you define this concept?

ⓑ Have you read or heard a news items about projects based on sustainable development?

1.27 ▲

The eco-friendly neighbourhood of BedZED in South London (2007)
Built primarily from recycled materials, BedZED was designed to maximize recycling and reduce energy consumption. The ecological footprint left by a person living in this neighbourhood is half that left by the average Londoner.

The Three Pillars of Sustainable Development

Sustainable development focuses on three main concerns, also referred to as its three "pillars": the economy, society and the environment. The objective of sustainable development is to reconcile these three pillars in order to ensure better distribution and management of resources, the elimination of social and economic inequalities and a healthy environment for future generations.

Ecological development respects the planet's ecosystems, that is to say, the relationships that exist between living beings and their milieu. In its broad sense, it refers to development that respects the environment.

Liveable development refers to production that ensures a level of comfort for individuals, while respecting the environment.

Ecological development respects the planet's ecosystems, that is to say, the relationships that exist between living beings and their milieu. In its broad sense, it refers to development that respects the environment.

Ecological

Liveable

Viable

Sustainable

Social

Economic

Equitable

Social development seeks to improve the quality of life of all individuals living in a community and to reduce the inequalities that exist among its members, whether they relate to economics, hygiene, legislation or other social issues.

Equitable development is a commercial partnership based on respect, which seeks to increase workers' rights and improve their working conditions. It is a practice particularly suited to trade between developed countries and developing countries.

Economic development refers to positive changes (demographic, technical, industrial, sanitary, etc.) adopted in a region. It enriches and improves a population's quality of life.

47

Environmental
Problems

Environmental
Action

International
Agreements

Environment

MAKING CHOICES

Societies must make choices to prevent the degradation of their living environment and to promote sustainable development on Earth. These are difficult choices, since all of the options come with advantages and disadvantages, as well as economic and environmental costs, that must be considered. The issue of energy is a good example. There are several options available: oil, coal, natural gas, geothermal energy, hydroelectricity, solar energy, etc. A number of these potential sources are examined below.

Hydroelectric Energy

This form of energy is produced by the conversion of the flow of watercourses (rivers, waterfalls, etc.) into electricity through turbines and alternators.

Benefits

- Hydroelectricity is a renewable and clean source of energy. It constantly regenerates and produces very few pollutants and greenhouse gases (GHGs).
- The cost of maintaining hydroelectric power plants is relatively low, since these plants are built to last a long time.
- When building dams, components can be integrated that counter the negative effects on the environment, such as "fish ladders" that allow migratory species to swim upstream.

Disadvantages

- Hydroelectricity requires exploitable watercourses, which are unequally distributed on the planet.
- The cost of building a hydroelectric power plant is high.
- The development required to exploit hydroelectric energy, particularly the construction of dams, transforms landscapes and threatens ecosystems. For example, the migration of certain species of fish, such as salmon and eel, is hindered by these dams.
- Building large dams can force populations off their land and flood large areas of agricultural land.

Wind Energy

This form of energy is produced by the wind, which is transformed into electricity by an aerogenerator, such as a wind turbine.

Benefits

- Wind turbines generate clean energy that does not produce any waste.
- This energy is renewable.
- The cost of operating wind turbines is low.
- This energy source is accessible in all countries, regardless of their natural resources.

Disadvantages

- Wind turbines produce noise pollution.
- They alter the natural landscape.
- Their capacity varies, since wind varies and cannot be controlled.

◀ **1.28**

Iceland's Strokkur geyser
Iceland is home to many volcanoes and geysers. Extensive use is made of the energy produced by the Earth's heat. However, the development of this type of renewable energy, known as geothermal energy, is still in its infancy.

Nuclear Energy

This form of energy is generated through the fission of uranium atoms, a process by which atoms are split into smaller particles.

Benefits

- Nuclear energy is a clean form of energy to the extent that nuclear power plants do not emit any greenhouse gases.
- Uranium produces much more energy than oil or coal. Today, one kilogram of uranium produces 50 000 kWh, while one litre of oil produces only 6 kWh.
- The planet's uranium resources are relatively abundant. Estimated at 17 million tons, they could last 300 years based on current consumption levels.
- Countries that use nuclear energy are less dependent on oil-producing countries, many of which are situated in politically unstable regions of the world.

Disadvantages

- Nuclear energy presents the risk of serious accidents resulting in major radioactive fallout. Such fallout has an adverse effect upon both the population and the environment.
- Nuclear waste management is problematic, particularly in the case of the more radioactive waste, which will remain toxic long into the future. Some countries bury nuclear waste several hundred metres underground, in stable geological layers.
- The planet's uranium resources are not unlimited.
- Nuclear power plants could be the target of terrorist attacks in order to acquire nuclear fuel to make atomic bombs.

Solar Energy

This form of energy is produced by the sun's rays, which can be transformed into heat and electricity.

Benefits

- Solar energy is renewable, since it is unlimited.
- This clean energy source does not produce any pollutants or greenhouse gases.
- This energy source is accessible in all countries, regardless of their natural resources.
- Once the systems for producing solar energy are installed, the energy produced is free and maintenance costs are low.
- Solar energy is well adapted to household use and does not require the installation of a centralized system.

Disadvantages

- Manufacturing photovoltaic panels (solar panels) requires advanced technology that is quite costly.
- Since solar installations depend on sunshine, other forms of energy are needed at night and on overcast days or a system to store solar energy is required.
- The technologies developed to resolve these problems are still too costly to be viable.

Environmental
Problems

Environmental
Action

International
Agreements

Environment

PUTTING THE ENVIRONMENT FIRST: THE EXAMPLE OF THE AUTOMOBILE

To be effective, environmental protection and sustainable development require the participation of all members of society and an overall change in lifestyle. Concrete measures must be taken not only by all levels of government, but also by corporations and individuals. Efforts to reduce the pollution caused by automobiles are a good example of action that can be taken to protect the environment.

Individuals

Every person can contribute to reducing pollution emissions by walking, using public transportation, carpooling or bicycling. In addition, automobile owners can buy models with better emission standards, service their engines regularly and reduce their driving speed. Together, all of these small, individual actions can help protect our shared environment.

▲ 1.29
Vélib', a self-serve bicycle system set up in Paris in 2007

Industry

Automobile manufacturers have an important role to play in reducing air pollution. Thanks to the technologies they are developing, manufacturers are producing vehicles that emit lower levels of greenhouse gases (GHGs), thereby responding to the demand of many consumers who want to drive cleaner automobiles.

▲ 1.30
Hybrid car (2003)
A hybrid car combines an electric engine and a combustion engine, which reduces polluting emissions.

Today, automobile manufacturers are designing smaller, lighter and more aerodynamic automobiles that are more fuel efficient. In January 2008, an industrial group in India unveiled an automobile that weighs only 530 kg. Nonetheless, the ideal solution for reducing automobile pollution is electricity. Many companies are investing in the development of powerful batteries that can be quickly recharged and store enough energy for automobiles to travel long distances. The technological obstacles that long prevented the marketing of electrical automobiles are gradually becoming a thing of the past as companies strive to meet the growing demand for cleaner options.

OFFSETTING YOUR CARBON EMISSIONS

IN BRIEF

To offset their greenhouse gas (GHG) emissions, INDIVIDUALS AND BUSINESSES CAN CO-FINANCE SUSTAINABLE DEVELOPMENT PROJECTS AROUND THE WORLD THROUGH ENVIRONMENTAL ORGANIZATIONS. This could take the form of investment in tree planting, the protection of forests or the development of renewable energy sources by installing solar panels or wind turbines, for example. Many of these projects are already being implemented in developing countries.

Municipalities

Cities, where half of the world's population lives, are grappling with major problems caused by automobile pollution. This is why big cities are prioritizing the reduction of this form of pollution by adopting concrete measures to improve the situation. These measures can include developing public transportation, introducing reserved lanes for carpooling, putting up parking lots near subway stations in the suburbs as an incentive, reducing the number of parking spaces on city streets, increasing the cost of parking, developing bicycle paths and using electric or hybrid vehicles for the public transit system.

Regions and Nations

Regions and States can take action to help reduce automobile pollution. They can pass laws that require automobile manufacturers to sell vehicles that respect greenhouse gas emission standards. This is precisely what the European Union did at the end of the 1990s.

Governments can also prohibit the use of leaded gas, a particularly polluting fuel. In addition, they can offer tax breaks to individuals and companies that acquire less polluting automobiles and fund the technological research and development necessary to bring cleaner automobiles to the market. In July 2008, the governments of Israel, France and Portugal signed an agreement with automobile manufacturers for the large-scale development and marketing of electric automobiles on their respective territories.

SNAPSHOT OF TODAY

a How would you define the concept of "responsibility"?

b Find examples in the news of ways to promote environmental regulation.

CITIES WITH CREATIVE SOLUTIONS

IN BRIEF

In London and Milan, access to downtown is an expensive proposition for automobile owners. In Berlin, Cologne and Hanover, the automobiles responsible for higher levels of pollution are outright banned from the city centre. This is enforced through a system of colour stickers used to classify vehicles based on the degree of pollution they emit. In Athens, Seoul and Beijing, a system of alternating traffic has been adopted: AUTHORIZATION TO TRAVEL BY AUTOMOBILE IS PROVIDED ALTERNATELY BASED ON WHETHER AUTOMOBILE LICENCE PLATE NUMBERS END IN AN EVEN NUMBER OR AN ODD NUMBER. In Québec City, visitors can travel between the city's major tourist attractions at no cost on a fully electric Écolobus.

1.31
An Écolobus in Québec City (2008)
On the road since May 2008, Québec City's Écolobuses can run for 12 hours at a cost of only $3.25 to recharge and 3¢ for every kilometre travelled.

ACHIEVING CONSENSUS

Despite the obvious importance of environmental issues, there is often a lag between identifying a problem and its public recognition. Long debates about the real dangers and the scope of the problem can delay any meaningful decision-making.

Using Science and Information to Alert Public Opinion

Due to the scope and complexity of environmental problems, it is often difficult to quickly achieve consensus on solutions. It is not always easy to clearly identify the cause of an environmental problem and to determine if its origin is natural or human. Moreover, environmental concerns do not affect everyone in the same way. Some people are less sensitive to these concerns than others. This may be the case because they have different priorities, conflicting personal interests or insufficient information.

During the 1960s and 1970s, ecologists came to understand that environmental issues would only be taken seriously if they were presented in a credible manner. To achieve this goal, they encouraged the systematic use of scientific research and the widespread dissemination of information.

Many international organizations interested in the environment created scientific programs to collect new data in order to better understand environmental issues, to gather research conducted by other scientific groups and to disseminate information to the general public.

1.32
Seveso disaster in Italy (1976)
In 1976, a chemical plant in Northern Italy released an enormous cloud of toxic gases that caused serious environmental damage. This disaster encouraged the European Union to impose stricter regulations on industrial sites.

1.33 ▶ A few examples of international scientific programs

Scientific programs	Implementing organization	Objective
World Weather Watch (WWW)	World Meteorological Organization (WMO)	Record meteorological observations around the globe and monitor major meteorological events, such as tropical cyclones, etc.
Intergovernmental Oceanographic Commission (IOC)	United Nations Educational, Scientific and Cultural Organization (UNESCO)	Share knowledge and technologies related to oceans and monitor rising sea levels, etc.
World Climate Programme (WCP)	International Council for Science (ICSU) and WMO	Study climate predictability and determine the effects of human activities on the climate, etc.

◀ 1.34

***Exxon Valdez* oil spill (1989)**
EIn 1989, the oil tanker *Exxon Valdez* ran aground off
Alaska, releasing a major oil slick. As a result of this
accident, the United States made major changes to its
safety standards for maritime transport.

The Precautionary Principle

Often, governments and public opinion only focus on
environmental problems when the damage to nature is
apparent and irreversible, for example, following oil spills or the clear-cutting of
forests. Many environmentalists criticize the tendency of the general population
to react to disasters after the fact. Instead, they promote preventive action
whenever possible.

These environmentalists promote the precautionary principle officially adopted
at the 1992 Earth Summit, according to which:

> "Where there are threats of serious or irreversible damage, lack of full
> scientific certainty should not be used as a reason for postponing such
> measures, taking into account that policies and measures to deal with
> climate change should be cost-effective so as to ensure global benefits
> at the lowest possible cost."

In other words, if it is not proven beyond a doubt that an activity or a project
will not cause any damage to the environment, it is best to abstain from it.

The European Union's regulation that restricts the cultivation of genetically
modified organisms (GMOs) due to the lack of knowledge about the long-term
effects is a good example of the precautionary principle.

The Debate About Global Warming and the IPCC

At the end of the 1970s, the World Meteorological Organization (WMO)
was concerned about the global warming trend it saw in its meteorological
statistics. Is the warming of the planet part of a natural climatic process
that we can do nothing about, or is it caused by human activity that can
be controlled through our actions?

To answer this complex question, a neutral scientific organization was
founded in 1988: the Intergovernmental Panel on Climate Change (IPCC).
The IPCC does not conduct its own research. Instead, it compiles all of
the relevant scientific research in order to assemble knowledge from experts
around the world on the issue of global warming. The IPCC's general reports
represent prevailing opinions within the international scientific community.
These reports provide governments and international organizations with
a clear and accurate picture of the situation so they can adopt
appropriate measures.

1.35 ▲
Weather station in Slovakia

Environmental
Problems

Environmental
Action

International
Agreements

Environment

HARMONIZING ENVIRONMENTAL STANDARDS

Since environmental problems affect the entire planet, States have no choice but to work together if they want to be truly effective. They must find ways to coordinate their actions in order to harmonize the standards and mechanisms for environmental management.

Polar bear
The polar bear, designated an endangered species by the IUCN, has become a symbol of the problems caused by global warming
1.36 ▼

Coherent International Action

Every State is free to develop its own solutions to deal with major environmental challenges, but concerted and coherent international action is also needed. This action can take various forms, such as the development of international environmental standards and the signing of international diplomatic agreements.

International Standards

To coordinate international action, it can be useful to develop standards and mechanisms for environmental management that are the same everywhere. This greatly facilitates the exchange of information, a crucial element when assessing the severity of a situation and choosing the best solution.

Some leading international organizations, such as the International Union for Conservation of Nature and various United Nations agencies, can provide objective benchmarks that are acceptable for everyone. These benchmarks are adopted on a voluntary basis, which gives States some flexibility in using them based on their particular needs.

IUCN — THE INTERNATIONAL UNION FOR CONSERVATION OF NATURE

Founded in 1948, the International Union for Conservation of Nature (IUCN) is the leading non-governmental organization devoted to preserving the world's natural heritage. It is best known for its "red list," which classifies the thousands of endangered animal and plant species in the world. Regularly updated, this list is considered one of the most objective references in the field. Many countries refer to this list when developing their own national laws for the protection of plants and wildlife.

The IUCN uses the latest research to classify animals and plants into eight categories.

Extinct
Extinct in the wild
Critically endangered
Endangered
Vulnerable
Near threatened
Least concern
Insufficient data

SNAPSHOT

ⓐ How would you define the concept of "regulation"?

ⓑ Find examples in the news of ways to promote environmental regulations.

International Agreements

International environmental standards can be harmonized by signing international agreements in the form of diplomatic treaties negotiated between States. These treaties require all signatories to adhere to common standards, which they agree to enforce in their respective countries. Usually, this means enacting national laws that restate the terms of the agreement. Given the political and legal constraints that an agreement imposes on each State, this method is less flexible than simply adopting international standards. However, it guarantees better results.

Various Types of Treaties

Signed treaties can be bilateral (between two countries) or multilateral (involving several countries). Some States may even decide to sign on in order to develop a common environmental policy. This is the case with the European Union, which has many environmental agreements that are applicable in all of its countries.

Treaties can cover a broad range of issues. Some focus on specific local problems, such as the Agreement on the Conservation of Small Cetaceans of the Baltic and North Seas, which seeks to protect whales in Northern Europe. Others have a much more general scope, such as the Convention on Biological Diversity, which aims to protect the many forms of life on Earth. Due to their broad scope, these general treaties are often more difficult to negotiate.

◀ **1.37**
The Danube in Budapest, Hungary (2005)

A giant panda
Considered an endangered species, the giant panda has become a major symbol of the need to protect nature. Its natural habitat in China was even classified a world heritage site by UNESCO.
▼ **1.38**

BEYOND BORDERS

IN BRIEF

Environmental problems that surpass the borders of a single country pose a major challenge, since their regulation requires the collaboration of several States. A POLLUTED WATERWAY THAT FLOWS THROUGH SEVERAL COUNTRIES CAN ONLY BE CLEANED UP IF ALL OF THE STATES INVOLVED PLAY A ROLE IN ITS DECONTAMINATION. This can be particularly complicated in the case of a river like the Danube, which is nearly 2900 km long and flows through a dozen European countries. This has required the development of several international treaties to define the rights and obligations of each State in the event of various environmental problems.

Environmental
Problems

Environmental
Action

International
Agreements

Environment

THE UNITED NATIONS EARTH SUMMITS

As an organization that represents almost all States, the United Nations offers a natural framework for developing international solutions to environmental problems. Several major international conferences, known as Earth Summits, have been organized under the leadership of the UN.

First Earth Summit

The United Nations Conference on the Human Environment (also known as the Earth Summit) convened in Stockholm on the initiative of the Swedish government, was the first major international conference on environmental issues. Under the theme of "Only One Earth," it played a major role in raising the world's awareness of environmental problems.

The United Nations Environment Programme (UNEP)

One of the main outcomes of the Stockholm Conference was the creation of the United Nations Environment Programme (UNEP), is the main organization responsible for environmental issues within the United Nations. In collaboration with many partners, it encourages cooperation for the protection of the environment and sustainable development. Its staff offers valuable technical and administrative expertise to develop and manage international agreements on the environment.

World Commission on Environment and Development

Publication of the Brundtland Report, *Our Common Future*

1972

1983

1987

1.39 ▶
Nairobi, Kenya (1989)
The choice of this African city for UNEP's headquarters enables it to be closer to the environmental issues that affect developing countries.

SEEN AND HEARD

" To defend and improve the human environment for present and future generations has become an imperative goal for mankind. . .*"*

Final Declaration of the United Nations Conference on the Human Environment (1972)

1.40 ▶
Indigenous Kayapo man from Brazil (1992)
Many indigenous groups took advantage of the second Earth Summit held in Brazil to present their demands and protest the destruction of the Amazon forest.

Second Earth Summit

Many thousands of people, including over a hundred heads of State, participated in this international conference in Rio de Janeiro, Brazil. The meeting was crowned by success with the elaboration of several declarations of principles and a number of international agreements.

Action 21

Adopted at the 1992 Earth Summit, Action 21 (an action plan for the 21st century) proposes over 2500 recommendations for implementing the principles of sustainable development. It addresses environmental problems, as well as the eradication of poverty and the improvement of health conditions in the world. This voluntary plan can also be applied locally. In fact, several municipalities and communities have already adopted Action 21, more commonly known as Agenda 21.

United Nations Framework Convention on Climate Change (UNFCCC)

Negotiated at the 1992 Earth Summit, this convention, signed by 192 countries (as of 2009), represents the first major initiative to tackle the problem of global warming within the framework of the United Nations. It aims to stabilize the concentrations of greenhouse gases (GHGs) in the atmosphere in order to prevent climatic disturbances. This agreement establishes common goals, but does not include any real action strategies. These strategies must be discussed and approved by additional protocols, such as the Kyoto Protocol signed in 1997.

Kyoto Protocol

Millennium Development Goals

1992 **1997** **2000** **2002**

Third Earth Summit

With more than 60 000 participants, the third Earth Summit, held in Johannesburg, South Africa, was the biggest meeting ever organized by the United Nations. Ten years after the Rio Summit, this conference was intended to further develop the program introduced in 1992 and to take stock of international environmental efforts. Despite the adoption of a general action plan, its success was overshadowed by the American government's decision to not attend.

A RANGE OF AGREEMENTS

The United Nations constitutes an obvious framework for international forums on the environment. However, the specific role of this organization varies considerably. Some agreements may even be negotiated without United Nations' involvement.

The Kyoto Protocol

An example of an agreement signed under the guidance of the United Nations

The Kyoto Protocol was an expression of the will to undertake concrete measures to apply the major principles set out in the United Nations Framework Convention on Climate Change (UNFCCC). After difficult negotiations, which took place in Kyoto, Japan, an agreement was signed on December 11, 1997. The signatories committed to a worldwide 5.2% reduction in emissions of six greenhouse gases (GHGs) by 2012, based on 1990 levels.

The Vienna Convention and the Montreal Protocol

An example of agreements signed by a number of countries and administered by the United Nations

In 1985, the realization that the ozone layer was being damaged by certain gases was the driving force behind the meeting of a number of States, leading to the signing of the Vienna Convention for the Protection of the Ozone Layer. This framework agreement arose out of the need to limit human activities that damage the ozone layer. However, concrete measures to prohibit these dangerous substances were only undertaken within the framework of a complementary agreement, the Montreal Protocol, which came into effect in 1989. Negotiated between governments, the Vienna Convention and the Montreal Protocol were nevertheless administered by the United Nations Environment Programme (UNEP).

The International Convention for the Regulation of Whaling

An example of an agreement independent of the United Nations

Signed in 1946, this convention established an administrative organization, the International Whaling Commission (IWC), responsible for ensuring the preservation of all whale species. In 1986, this Commission imposed a moratorium on whaling that is still in effect. However, some countries still hunt whales for commercial purposes (Norway and Iceland) or scientific ends (Japan), which creates tensions with States that oppose whaling.

1.41
Humpback whale in Antarctica
In 1994, the IWC created a marine reserve around the Antarctic continent where all forms of commercial whaling are strictly prohibited.

1.42
Mural in support of
the Kyoto Protocol in
Montréal (2005)

An International Agreement to Protect a Virgin Territory

Can you imagine a neutral territory where States work together freely to promote science and respect for the environment? No, it is not a utopia, but Antarctica. This cold continent with no permanent population is the only region on the planet that does not have its own government or belong to a country.

Although several States have sought ownership of parts of this territory, their claims were suspended by the adoption of the Antarctic Treaty in 1961. The main countries interested in Antarctica joined forces to make this territory a reserved zone for scientific research where all military activity, particularly nuclear testing, is prohibited.

Originally, the Antarctic Treaty was primarily intended to preserve the continent's neutrality for scientific purposes. However, countries soon realized the importance of protecting this virtually untouched and unique territory from any form of human intervention. Several measures were therefore adopted to protect the Antarctic environment. Together, these conventions and protocols make up the Antarctic Treaty System.

◀ 1.43
Antarctica

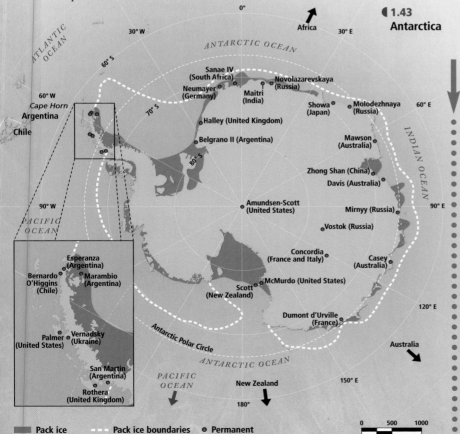

THE ANTARCTIC
TREATY SYSTEM

Main conventions and protocols that form the Antarctic Treaty System:

- *Antarctic Treaty (came into effect in 1961)*

- *Agreed Measures for the Conservation of Antarctic Fauna and Flora (1982)*

- *Convention for the Conservation of Antarctic Seals (1978)*

- *Convention for the Conservation of Antarctic Marine Living Resources (1982)*

- *Protocol on Environmental Protection to the Antarctic Treaty (1998): also known as the Madrid Protocol, this treaty declares Antarctica a natural reserve devoted to peace and science. It prohibits any mining activity that is not scientific in nature.*

Pack ice --- **Pack ice boundaries in the winter** • **Permanent research stations**

0 500 1000
kilometres

59

Environmental
Problems

Environmental
Action

International
Agreements

Environment

MANAGING THE AGREEMENTS

Negotiating an international accord is not merely an exercise in achieving consensus. The parties must also agree on how the treaty will be implemented, in other words, the means by which it will come into effect and how it will then be managed.

From Signing to Implementation

For an international agreement to come into effect, it must first be officially signed by all of the parties interested in complying with the agreement. Signing an agreement must be voluntary: a State cannot be forced to sign a treaty against its will.

Some agreements come into effect upon their signature, but most are first subject to certain conditions.

- International treaties must usually be ratified after being signed, which means that they must be approved by the leaders of the signatory countries. In democratic countries, this generally means that the treaty, like any other law, must be accepted by elected representatives. This prevents leaders from negotiating accords that run counter to the public will.

- Multilateral treaties often contain a clause that specifies that a certain number of countries must ratify the document before it can come into effect.

An example: The Kyoto Protocol

This protocol was supposed to come into effect 90 days after being ratified by a minimum of 55 countries collectively responsible for at least 55% of the world's CO_2 emissions. This objective was attained at the end of 2004 when Russia ratified the protocol, and it came into effect on November 30, 2005, at the conference in Montréal. Nearly eight years elapsed between the time the first signatures were attached to the protocol and its implementation.

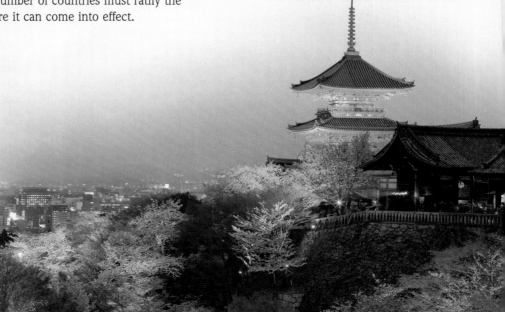

1.44 ▶
The city of Kyoto, where the protocol of the same name was signed (2006)

1.45 ▶
Meeting of the ministers of the environment at the G8 Summit (2007)

Managing a Treaty

After being signed and ratified, a treaty must be implemented. To do so, it is often necessary to create various administrative bodies, such as a central office or an assembly of signatories. These assemblies can be held regularly to assess the treaty's implementation, discuss problems and propose changes, if necessary.

Other organizations can also be created based on the particular needs of each agreement, for example, a scientific or legal committee or an organization in charge of raising international funds to help less wealthy countries implement the convention. All of these groups work together to ensure that the treaty is applied as intended.

An example: The Kyoto Protocol

Since the Kyoto Protocol is part of the United Nations Framework Convention on Climate Change (UNFCCC), the two share several organs: an annual meeting of signatories, a central secretariat in Bonn, Germany, a committee that offers advice on scientific and technological questions and a committee specializing in the implementation process. The protocol also has its own organs to manage certain aspects of the agreement.

The Role of the United Nations Environment Programme

In the case of international agreements on the environment, the administrative organization in charge of managing and implementing a treaty is often overseen by the United Nations Environment Programme (UNEP). The UNEP staff has solid experience in this field and is recognized for its impartiality as a result of its ties with the United Nations. UNEP is therefore responsible for managing a number of international conventions and protocols.

A few organizations that manage treaties under the authority of UNEP:

- Secretariat of the Basel Convention on the Control of Transboundary Movements of Hazardous Wastes and Their Disposal
- Secretariat of the Convention on Biological Diversity (SCBD)
- Secretariat of the Convention on International Trade in Endangered Species of Wild Fauna and Flora (CITES)
- Secretariat of the Convention on the Conservation of Migratory Species of Wild Animals (CMS)
- Ozone Secretariat (Vienna Convention and Montreal Protocol)
- Secretariat of the Stockholm Convention on Persistent Organic Pollutants (POP)

61

PROBLEMS IN IMPLEMENTATION

Given that States can have diverging interests and that most international agreements are based on the good will of its signatories, it can be difficult to implement treaties and make sure that they are respected.

The Refusal to Sign

International agreements are not always the ideal solution to environmental problems, since States often refuse to sign them.

There are a variety of reasons for refusing to sign an agreement: lack of interest, conflicting commitments, preference for an alternative solution, etc. However, economic reasons are the most common. Clearly, a country with a lucrative oil industry will tend to be less inclined to sign an agreement that seeks to reduce global oil consumption.

Furthermore, some States fear losing a certain amount of autonomy if they agree to follow international regulations. As such, the specific interests of any State may stand in the way of the common interests of the planet.

Who's to Blame?

Developed countries, which are highly industrialized, are the source of many environmental problems. Many developing countries feel that they too have the right to build their economies, despite the negative impact on the environment. These countries advocate the "polluter-payer" principle, according to which the parties responsible for producing pollution should also be responsible for correcting the situation.

In practice, however, the collaboration of all States is needed to solve environmental problems. To take this into account, international treaties often apply the principle of "common but differentiated responsibilities." According to this principle, all countries are responsible for the health and well-being of the planet, but some must make greater efforts due to their historical responsibility and their greater financial capacities.

▲ **1.46**
A herd in front of a cement factory in Egypt (1992)
Environmental treaties often provide favourable conditions to less industrialized countries, given their limited responsibility for the current environmental situation and their need to pursue economic development.

1.47 ▶ Number of signatories of several environmental treaties

	Original signatories	Participants in 2009
The Vienna Convention for the Protection of the Ozone Layer (1985)	28	194
Montreal Protocol (1987)	46	194
United Nations Framework Convention on Climate Change (1992)	165	192
Kyoto Protocol (1997)	84	182
Stockholm Convention on Persistent Organic Pollutants (2001)	152	159

Sanctions

Not all countries are able to respect the treaties they sign and ratify. This failure to comply can be the involuntary result of economic problems or unrealistic commitments. These instances tend to be tolerated, with other States providing technical, scientific or financial assistance to the non-compliant party.

Sometimes, however, after being notified of the infraction, a non-compliant country refuses to respect its treaty obligations. Most international agreements stipulate explicitly what steps to follow in this situation. Generally, they recommend the use of diplomacy to try to convince the non-compliant country. The objective is to try to make the country in question understand that they are hindering the will of the majority of States and thereby losing international credibility.

If this intervention does not suffice, the dispute may have to be presented before a pre-determined international authority, such as the International Court of Justice in The Hague, Netherlands. If the non-compliant party refuses to obey the judgment, the international community could decide to apply direct sanctions, such as economic sanctions in the form of commercial penalties imposed on the non-compliant country.

An example: The Kyoto Protocol

The Kyoto Protocol stipulates that countries that fail to respect their commitment to reducing greenhouse gas emissions must make up for this by reducing their emissions an additional 30%. In addition, until the situation has been corrected, they are denied access to the exchange and assistance mechanisms set out in the protocol.

RESULTS

Over the last several decades, there has been a proliferation of national laws and international agreements on the environment. But has all of this legislation actually had a positive impact on the environment? Are the major principles merely wishful thinking or do they actually yield concrete results?

Effective Agreements?

It is difficult to judge how effective the environmental measures taken have been in improving the planet's overall health. In most cases, these measures are just beginning to be implemented. It is therefore too early to tell whether or not they will be successful in the final analysis.

Various criteria can be used to determine their relevance. This makes it possible to evaluate in a strict and concrete manner the role these agreements play in improving environmental conditions. It is also possible to examine their contribution to raising awareness of environmental concerns around the globe. For example, an international conference may not lead to a specific action plan, but it may still play an important role in raising public awareness of a particular environmental problem.

The Environment Overall

The growing importance of environmental issues in international discussions seems to indicate that various environmental policies have had a positive effect. Indeed, before the 1980s, environmental concerns were handled as specific problems, reserved for experts. Since then, however, the environment has become an unavoidable topic of discussion at all international forums, regardless of the main subject being addressed.

Today, trade agreements usually include specific provisions to ensure that environmental standards are respected. This is the case, for example, with the North American Free Trade Agreement (NAFTA), which includes several articles on the harmonization of environmental standards among participating countries.

Today, even warfare is the focus of environmental concerns. We now know that war is often the cause of serious environmental disasters. The Vietnam War is a tragic example. IN AN EFFORT TO FLUSH OUT SOLDIERS HIDING IN THE JUNGLE, THE UNITED STATES SPRAYED MILLIONS OF LITRES OF PESTICIDES ON THE JUNGLES OF VIETNAM. As a result, they destroyed a rich natural environment, poisoned the entire food chain and caused many diseases.

◀ **1.48**
Pesticide spraying during the Vietnam War (1965)

Results: From Failure to Success

A number of international agreements remain little more than expressions of good will with no concrete effect. This is the case with the Convention to Combat Desertification, adopted at the 1992 Earth Summit. Since the signatory States were unable to agree on a clearly defined action plan, desertification continues to spread today. According to UNESCO, nearly one third of the Earth's landmass is now threatened. Each year, deserts continue to expand, reducing the land available for agriculture and threatening surrounding populations.

Although not total failures, certain environmental treaties have also been less than complete successes. This is the case with the Kyoto Protocol. Some signatory countries have made significant efforts to reach the objectives that were set for reducing greenhouse gases, while others have failed to make meaningful inroads. While the situation is slowly improving, there is much room for improvement.

Fortunately, some international treaties have been very successful and have greatly improved environmental conditions on the planet.

The Montreal Protocol is by far the best example. Nearly 20 years after it entered into effect, the 194 signatories, nearly all of the world's States, have markedly reduced their use of gases that destroy the ozone layer. A total ban on the production of these gases is slated for 2010 and many scientists estimate that, as a result of these efforts, the ozone layer should regain its 1980 condition sometime between 2055 and 2065.

Desertification in Mali (2005)
▼ **1.49**

CONCEPTS

Migration (p. 69)
Culture (p. 98)
Relocation (p. 87)
Diaspora (p. 97)
Network (p. 97)
Urbanization (p. 98)

Topic to Be Interpreted
Economic and social changes related to the increase in migration

Taking a Position (TAP)
TAP 1 The management of urban expansion
OR
TAP 2 Migration and the world of work

With the globalization of trade, **world population movements** are increasing.
Regardless of the **reasons for these movements**, they have serious **economic consequences**
and a marked impact on the **societies in question.**

POPULATION

2.1 ▶
A tsunami forces Indonesians
from the province of
Lampung out of their
homes (2004)

Knowledge Related to the Theme

- Demographic change
  (p. 78-79)
- Immigration policies
  (p. 82-83, 90-91)
- International networks
  (p. 73, 96-97)
- Labour policies
  (p. 86 to 89)
- Migration flow
  (p. 74-75, 84-85)
- Parallel economies
  (p. 96-97)
- Urban organization
  (p. 98 to 101)

Cultural References

- Office of the United Nations High Commissioner for Refugees (1951)
  (p. 80)
- Migrinter (1985) (p. 75)
- International Labour Organization, *Declaration on Fundamental Principles and Rights at Work* (1998) (p. 87)
- Jane Jacobs (1916-2006) (p. 101)

MIGRATION: BASIC CONCEPTS

In recent decades, migration has increased markedly. Since 1980, the number of migrants has been growing by 2 to 3 million every year, compared with 600 000 in the 1960s. Yet, the migrant population still represents less than 3% of the world's population.

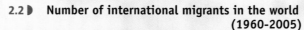

2.2 ▶ **Number of international migrants in the world (1960-2005)**

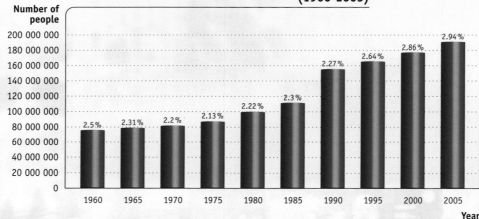

Source: Population Division of the Department of Economic and Social Affairs of the United Nations Secretariat, *Trends in Total Migrant Stock: The 2005 Revision*, [On-line], 2008.

Proportion of migrants in the world's population

Types of migration

permanent ⟺ temporary
legal ⟺ clandestine
local ⟺ international
voluntary ⟺ forced

Immigration
Arrival in a country of individuals who want to live there

Emigration
Departure of individuals who want to live in another country

Net migration

Number of arrivals (immigrants)
– Number of departures (emigrants)
_____
Balance of migration or net migration

Migration is the central concept of this chapter.

(a) How would you define this concept?

(b) Have you seen or read a news item on migration?

◀2.3
Romany from Romania (1990)
Until recently, the Romany (also known as Gypsies) were craftspeople with a nomadic lifestyle.

Nomadic Populations

Although it is becoming increasingly rare, the nomadic lifestyle is still favoured by many peoples. Most nomads herd animals, practising transhumance, that is, the seasonal migration of animals to fresh pastures. They follow precise and long-established itineraries. However, some traditional circuits are now unfeasible because they cross national borders, a practice that has become increasingly difficult. Most nomads must therefore be content with migrating from one region of their country to another.

Profile of Migrants

Age ▪ Most migrants are young, usually between the ages of 20 and 40. Many migrate when they are old enough to work or when they are ready to begin their career, enroll in higher education or start a family.

Gender ▪ Women represent almost half of all migrants (49.6% in 2005). There are slightly more women migrants in developed countries than in developing countries, largely because industrialized countries provide more opportunities.

Civil status ▪ Many of the young men who settle in foreign lands are single, especially those who migrate in search of work. Women migrate more often in the context of family reunification programs. They and their children join their husbands, who have already settled in a foreign country.

Occupation ▪ In recent years, the number of migrating skilled workers has increased, and not only in industrialized countries. However, the women who join their husbands often have fewer work skills.

2.4 ▶
Tuareg shepherds from North Africa (2003)

A RECENT HISTORY OF MIGRATION

Humans have been migrating since the dawn of time. Archaeological finds show that human beings first appeared in Africa, and then dispersed throughout the planet. However, in the contemporary period, the mobility of populations has increased and migration flows have diversified.

2.5
Inspection of immigrants at Ellis Island (1920)
Between 1892 and 1954, immigrants arriving in New York had to disembark at Ellis Island, near Liberty Island, home of the Statue of Liberty. The authorities examined their papers and made sure they were free from contagious diseases before allowing them to enter the United States.

19th Century – Beginning of the 20th Century: Transoceanic Migration

Up until the Great Depression in the 1930s, the major migratory movements were one way, from Europe to the Americas and, to a lesser extent, to Australia and New Zealand. Between 1821 and 1932, more than 50 million Europeans left their countries of origin to settle, for the most part permanently, in the sparsely populated New World. There, the development of vast tracts of land required a large number of workers, and many European countries were overpopulated. These migratory movements helped spread European culture across the planet.

1821   **1900**   **1930**

The Great Depression and the Second World War: Time Out

During the Great Depression in the 1930s and the Second World War (1939-1945), migration died down. During the Depression, the spectacular and generalized rise in the unemployment rate limited the possibilities for a new life in a new country. To limit immigration and protect local jobs, many countries, including Canada and the United States, adopted measures such as quotas and admission criteria based on country of origin and work skills. The Second World War prevented the resurgence of migratory movements, both because populations were mobilized for the conflict and because ocean travel became too dangerous.

2.6
In 1945, American soldiers return home from Europe after two years on the battlefield.

CANADIAN IMMIGRATION

As a British colony, Canada traditionally welcomed British immigrants and other European immigrants. In the 20th century, Canada, like the United States, adopted measures to limit immigration from certain areas of the world, in particular Asia and Africa.

For example, in 1927, Canada received 144 000 immigrants, 60 000 of them from the British Isles. ONLY 2 CHINESE, 4 ARABS AND 13 AMERINDIANS WERE ALLOWED TO IMMIGRATE!

From the Post-War Period to the 1970s: Migration from the South

At the end of the Second World War, there was a resurgence of immigration to the Americas. Between 1950 and 1970, almost 10 million Europeans left the Old World. However, migration primarily flowed northward along the north-south axis. Migrants left developing countries in the South (South Asia, Africa and Latin America) to find jobs in the industrialized countries in the North, which were experiencing significant economic growth.

Finally, between 1945 and 1960, decolonization resulted in major population movements. For example, the partition of British India forced some seven million Muslim Indians to move to Pakistan and six million Hindus to move to India. Then, once independence was achieved, thousands of foreign nationals returned to their mother country.

🔺 2.7
Vietnamese refugees known as "boat people" (1978)
After the United States was defeated in North Vietnam in 1975, more than a million Vietnamese fled the communist regime in makeshift boats.

1945 1950 1970 2000

Since the 1970s: Diversified Immigration

Since the 1970s, new poles of attraction have emerged, directing migration flows along a South-South as well as a North-South axis. In Persian Gulf countries, the oil boom required an abundant labour force from neighbouring Arab countries, as well as from India, Pakistan and Southeast Asia. In South Africa and some West African countries (Nigeria, Côte d'Ivoire, Senegal), development of the mining industry and export crops has attracted many workers from poorer African neighbours.

At the end of the 1980s, the fall of the communist bloc resulted in the appearance of a new East-West axis of migration. Tens of thousands of people from former communist countries emigrated to Western Europe and North America.

Population

A Global
Phenomenon

Reasons for
Migration

Economic
Aspects

Social
Aspects

TRANSPORTATION AND COMMUNICATIONS

The evolution of transportation since the 19th century has had a major impact on migratory movements. People can travel to remote locations increasingly quickly and at a decreasing cost. Passengers' itineraries are becoming more diverse.

Means of Transportation

The ocean liner

Starting in the 1840s, sailing vessels gave way to faster and safer steamships. These ships carried passengers between Europe and the New World and between major cities on the Mediterranean. Passengers could travel from Great Britain to New York in about two weeks.

The railway

The railway appeared in the 1830s, revolutionizing land travel. The use of rails and steam locomotives made it possible to carry more passengers at greater speeds. The railway contributed to increased regional migration, especially in Europe, but rail transportation was also used by international migrants, who could now disperse more easily in a country once they arrived at the port of entry.

The automobile

Invented in the final decades of the 19th century, gas-powered automobiles were being mass produced by the beginning of the next century. The growing demand for automobiles and improvements in production techniques soon led to a decline in prices and a larger market. This means of transportation was flexible and swift, fostering temporary migration within continents and countries.

The airplane

After the Second World War, the airplane, which had until then been used mostly for military purposes, began to transport civilian passengers over long distances. A steep decline in prices, stimulated by competition and growing demand, made air travel accessible to many migrants, especially since the 1980s. This considerably changed the range of receiving countries and the intensity of migration flow. From now on, people could travel anywhere in the world and back.

2.8
The steam train on the Liverpool-Manchester Line in the United Kingdom (end of the 19th century)

A Boeing 747
2.9 ⬇

AIR TRANSPORT

Air transport has become available to the masses in the past 50 years. Some 24 million passengers flew in 1950. Today, the number is almost two billion. Every day, 20 000 airplanes make more than 80 000 flights, the equivalent of ONE TAKE-OFF AND ONE LANDING EVERY SECOND.

The evolution of communications technologies has made migrating easier. Migrants can obtain information about receiving countries much more easily.

Diffusion of Information

In the 19th century, people thinking about emigrating had few sources of information about the countries they were interested in: newspaper ads and articles, advertising posters and propaganda flyers distributed by governments to encourage immigration, letters and telegrams from loved ones who had already emigrated. Then, with the invention of the telephone, it became possible to enter into direct contact with institutions and people in the receiving country, making it easier to plan settling in a new country.

In the 20th century, radio and television provided an opportunity to learn more about the different receiving countries. Documentaries and focus pieces provided information about society, culture and politics in different countries.

Today, the Internet makes migrating much easier. Migrants can find a wealth of information, download administrative forms, remotely rent an apartment, search for a job, etc.

2.10 ⬤
Advertising poster for immigration to Canada in the 1920s

Maintaining Networks

The increased rapidity and quality of communications helps maintain social networks between expatriates and their loved ones in the country of origin. These networks are very useful to migrants. Those who are already settled can provide future immigrants with a wealth of information and help them with the various procedures.

Also, members of a network often take newly arrived immigrants into their homes and help them find jobs and housing.

2.11 ⬧
Late 19th-century telephone

Key Facts

Around 1450 ▪ Johannes Gutenberg invents the printing press
1609 ▪ The first newspaper is printed in Germany
1837 ▪ Samuel Morse invents the electrical telegraph
1876 ▪ Alexander Graham Bell invents the telephone
1895 ▪ The Lumière brothers project the first moving picture in Paris
1906 ▪ The first radio program airs in the United States
1926 ▪ John Baird demonstrates the new television set
1962 ▪ The first telecommunications satellite is launched
Beginning of the 1990s ▪ The Internet becomes available to the public

73

COUNTRIES OF ORIGIN AND COUNTRIES OF DESTINATION

Today, immigrants leave a wide variety of countries of origin for a wide variety of countries of destination. Generally speaking, wealthy countries attract the majority of immigrants, while developing countries provide the majority of emigrants.

Main countries whose net migration is negative (2000-2005)
2.12

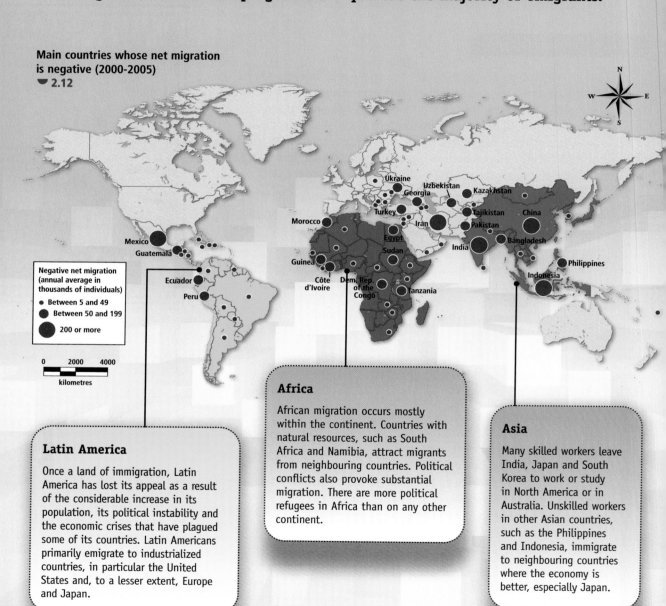

Negative net migration (annual average in thousands of individuals)
- Between 5 and 49
- Between 50 and 199
- 200 or more

0   2000   4000
kilometres

Latin America

Once a land of immigration, Latin America has lost its appeal as a result of the considerable increase in its population, its political instability and the economic crises that have plagued some of its countries. Latin Americans primarily emigrate to industrialized countries, in particular the United States and, to a lesser extent, Europe and Japan.

Africa

African migration occurs mostly within the continent. Countries with natural resources, such as South Africa and Namibia, attract migrants from neighbouring countries. Political conflicts also provoke substantial migration. There are more political refugees in Africa than on any other continent.

Asia

Many skilled workers leave India, Japan and South Korea to work or study in North America or in Australia. Unskilled workers in other Asian countries, such as the Philippines and Indonesia, immigrate to neighbouring countries where the economy is better, especially Japan.

Source: Population Division of the Department of Economic and Social Affairs of the United Nations Secretariat, *International Migration*, [On-line], 2006.

MIGRINTER

Founded in 1985 by Gildas Simon, Migrinter
is a research centre specializing in international
migration. Established in Poitiers, France, it offers
graduate programs and is an important source
of information and publications on migration.

The United States, Canada and Oceania

New World countries attract the most immigrants,
generally for economic reasons. The United States,
38 million of whose residents are foreign-born (2006),
ranks first in the world. The percentage of the immigrant
population in Australia, New Zealand and Canada is also
very high, about 20%.

Main countries whose net migration is positive (2000-2005)
▼ 2.13

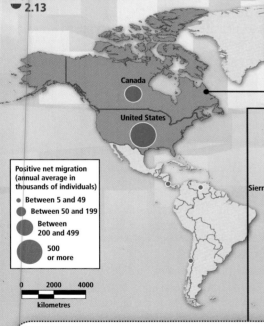

**Positive net migration
(annual average in
thousands of individuals)**

- Between 5 and 49
- Between 50 and 199
- Between 200 and 499
- 500 or more

0   2000   4000
kilometres

Canada · United States · United Kingdom · Germany · France · Portugal · Spain · Italy · Russia · Afghanistan · Saudi Arabia · Chad · United Arab Emirates · Japan · Hong Kong · Sierra Leone · Australia

Europe

Population movements are frequent in the European
community: inhabitants of Eastern countries emigrate
to the West. Also, more than 16 million foreign
nationals from Turkey, North Africa (the Maghreb) and,
to a lesser extent, Sub-Saharan Africa and Asia, live
in Europe. Germany and France receive the largest
numbers of immigrants.

The Middle East

Oil-producing countries attract an abundant labour force from foreign
countries. The more skilled workers come primarily from the West, while
the less skilled come from the Philippines, India, Syria and Egypt. Their
numbers are so high that they constitute the majority of the population
in Kuwait and the United Arab Emirates. They are not encouraged to stay
indefinitely.

75

Source: Population Division of the Department of Economic and Social Affairs
of the United Nations Secretariat, *International Migration*, [On-line], 2006.

TEMPORARY MIGRATION

A hundred years ago, the migrants who crossed the Atlantic usually came to America to settle permanently. Today, thanks to the evolution and accessibility of transportation, the population is far more mobile and temporary migration is on the rise.

Permanent Migration and Temporary Migration

There are many reasons for temporary migration: seasonal jobs, fixed-term labour contracts, business trips, tourism, studies, etc. Temporary migration can last anywhere from a few days to a few years.

The distinction between temporary migration and permanent migration is not always as clear-cut as one might think. Short-term stays sometimes turn into permanent migration. For example, young people who study abroad might take a job in the receiving country or meet someone they want to settle down and start a family with.

It is difficult to precisely measure the level of temporary migration. Short-term labour contracts can be illegal, in which case the number of people involved is impossible to calculate. However, there are government programs to foster the legal hiring of foreign labour. For example, Canada issues visas to thousands of Latin Americans who come to work on commercial farms during the harvest. In 2006, Québec received more than 4000 of these workers, most of them from Mexico.

Student Mobility

2.14
Graduation ceremony at Harvard University (2003)
The universities with the best reputations attract the most foreign students. In 2004, almost 3500 foreign students were enrolled at Harvard University in the United States.

In recent years, student mobility has been growing, especially among graduate students. According to UNESCO, the number of students who do some of their studies outside their country of birth rose from 1.75 million to 2.5 million between 1999 and 2004. A diploma from a foreign country is a valuable asset and is increasingly recognized as such by employers.

The largest contingent of foreign students comes from Asia, in particular from China. However, proportionally speaking, African students are the most mobile: one out of every five graduate students studies abroad. Overall, English-speaking countries welcome the greatest number of students, with the United States in first place, receiving 23% of them.

Canada, like all developed countries, is affected by the internationalization of university studies. In 2006, Canada received 70 000 full-time foreign students and 13 000 part-time foreign students, ALMOST THREE TIMES AS MANY AS IN 1996. A little less than a quarter of these students were Chinese. The rest were mostly from the United States, France and India.

2.15
Retirees in Florida
The term "snowbirds" is often used to refer to Canadians who leave the country in the winter to spend a few months in warmer climates.

Migration of Retirees

With the increase in healthy life expectancy and the implementation of pension plans, a new phenomenon has appeared in developed countries: the migration of retirees. With sufficient financial means and healthy purchasing power, many retirees choose a new home.

Many retirees do not migrate permanently, content to spend a few months a year outside the country. The thousands of Quebecers who leave for Florida, California and Mexico in the winter are a good example. In Florida, there are so many "snowbirds" that you can buy Québec newspapers and the *Caisses populaires Desjardins* has opened three branches there.

The Intensification of Tourism

In recent decades, tourism (vacations and business trips) has increased as never before. According to the World Tourism Organization (WTO), the number of registered international tourists in the world rose from 436 million in 1990 to 903 million in 2007. The WTO estimates that this number will increase by 5.4% yearly to reach 1.6 billion in 2020.

Europe is the most popular tourist destination, attracting more than half of all travellers (54.4% in 2006). Slightly more than half of all international tourists travel for pleasure, while fewer than ⅕ travel for business.

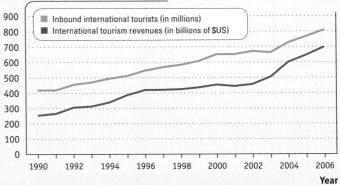

2.16 ▶ **Inbound tourism (1990-2006)**

Legend:
- Inbound international tourists (in millions)
- International tourism revenues (in billions of $US)

Source: World Tourism Organization, *International Tourism Receipt (Euro and $US)*, [On-line], 2008.

MIGRATION AND DEMOGRAPHICS

According to the UN, demographics have an impact on migratory movements in the world. Migrants come primarily from countries with high demographic growth and move to countries with an aging population.

Demographic Growth

Demographic growth expresses the variation of a population over time. It is calculated as follows:

> Natural growth (natality – mortality)
> + Net migration (immigration – emigration)
> ———————————————
> Demographic growth

A negative result indicates that the population is in decline, which is the case in many developed countries. For example, according to the UN, in 2050, the populations of Germany, Italy and Japan will be lower than what they are now. Conversely, the populations of Afghanistan, Burundi and Uganda should triple by 2050.

Aging Population

In addition to seeing their population decline, most developed countries are dealing with an aging population. Since the Industrial Revolution, the mortality rate in these countries has declined substantially thanks to medical developments. Life expectancy has increased in spectacular fashion, reaching 75 years of age at the beginning of the 21st century.

At the same time, fertility rates have plummeted. With an average 1.6 children per woman (2005), developed countries cannot ensure the replacement of each generation. Consequently, the number of young people is falling, while the number of seniors is constantly on the rise.

Demographics and Migratory Movements

In developed countries, the ratio between people in the labour force (ages 15 to 64) to retired people is declining because of the aging population. This means that there are ever fewer workers to pay for the pensions and medical care of aging people, whose numbers are growing. Also, developed countries may find themselves with too few workers in many sectors of their economy. To deal with these problems, they encourage replacement migration, that is, the immigration of individuals of working age.

Conversely, developing countries, whose demographic growth rates are high, are overpopulated and therefore subject to unemployment. Many people emigrate from developing countries to find work and better living conditions. This immigration is often insufficient to counteract the aging population in developed countries. In a few countries, such as Canada, Belgium and Sweden, the number of immigrants received is twice as high as the natural population growth.

Representation of the world

This map serves as a reference for the analysis of map 2.18.

▼ 2.17

Canada
United States
Niger
Brazil
China
India
Japan

Québec

The situation in Québec is similar to that in developed countries. Its population will age in the coming decades because of the low fertility rate (1.62 children per woman in 2007) and the high life expectancy (80.6 in 2007). The number of people over the age of 80 should quadruple by 2050, while the population will begin decreasing around 2031.

Japan

Japan has the oldest population in the world: the average age was 42.9 in 2005. Because of the very low fertility rate (1.27 children per woman) and the very high life expectancy (82.6), Japan's population is both aging and declining. According to the UN, it will decline by 5.5 million by 2050.

World demographic growth (2000-2025)

▼ 2.18

N W E S

Canada
United States
United Kingdom
Germany
Russia
China
Japan
France
Italy
Spain
Turkey
Afghanistan
Mexico
Haiti
Gaza and the West Bank
Syria
Iraq
Iran
Pakistan
Niger
Egypt
Saudi Arabia
Yemen
Philippines
Côte d'Ivoire
Ethiopia
Bangladesh
Vietnam
Nigeria
Dem. Rep. of the Congo
Uganda
Tanzania
India
Brazil
Madagascar
Indonesia
Argentina
Australia

The United States

The United States is one of the few developed countries whose population is growing. The fertility rate, which is slightly more than two children per woman, ensures the replacement of each generation. The country also welcomes the largest number of immigrants in the world, on average 1.2 million per year between 2000 and 2005.

Niger

This underdeveloped West African country has one of the highest fertility rates in the world, women having on average 7.19 children (2005). Its population is also one of the youngest in the world: the average age is 16. The population of Niger will almost quadruple by the year 2050.

Estimated population in 2025, in millions
.100
.50
.10
.1

Time it takes for the population to double, in years		Rate of annual demographic growth as a % between 2000 and 2025
less than 30	more than 2.30	
between 30 and 49	from 1.41 to 2.30	
between 50 and 69	from 1 to 1.40	
more than 70	from 0 to 0.99	
	less than 0	

79

Source: Population Division of the Department of Economic and Social Affairs of the United Nations Secretariat, *World Population Prospect: The 2006 Revision*, [On-line], 2007.

POLITICAL REFUGEES

Many immigrants do not leave their country by choice. War or an unstable, life-threatening political situation forces them to leave their homes and request the protection of a foreign country. These people are considered refugees.

What Is a Refugee?

The Office of the United Nations High Commissioner for Refugees defines a refugee as anyone who meets one of the following conditions:

- A person who is outside the country of their nationality or habitual residence.

- A person who has a well-founded fear of being persecuted for reasons of race, religion, nationality, membership of a particular social group or political opinion.

- A person who is unable, or owing to such fear, unwilling to avail themselves of the protection of that country or to return to it.

Refugee protection is guaranteed under the 1951 Geneva Convention relating to the Status of Refugees and by the 1967 Protocol relating to the Status of Refugees. Signatory countries to these international agreements (more than 147 in 2008) agree to grant right of asylum to refugees and not to deport them to a country in which they fear persecution.

2.19
Kurdish refugees on their way from Iraq to Turkey (1991) In 2007, an estimated 50% of refugees were women and 45% were under the age of 18.

1982
10 319 000

1984
10 728 000

1986
12 634 000

1988
14 347 000

1990
17 396 000

1992
17 838 000

Rwandan refugees (1994) Some Rwandans found refuge in a Tanzanian camp during the Rwandan civil war.

2.20

The Office of the United Nations High Commissioner for Refugees (UNHCR)

The Office of the United Nations High Commissioner for Refugees (UNHCR) is the main international organization responsible for refugees. It was set up in 1950 by the United Nations General Assembly to meet the needs of the many European refugees created by the Second World War. Its mandate was subsequently broadened to include all international refugees and all people displaced within their own country. The UNHCR sees to it that refugees are well treated and helps them either return home or integrate into a new country. The UNHCR's exceptional work has earned it the Nobel Peace Prize on two occasions, in 1954 and in 1981.

Tenzin Gyatso, the Dalai Lama

Tenzin Gyatso, the Dalai Lama, is one of the most well-known political refugees. China's occupation of Tibet in 1950 led many Tibetans to leave their country. Tenzin Gyatso, Tibet's spiritual leader, followed the movement in 1959 because he feared reprisal from China for the revolt among the Tibetan people. He fled to India, where he leads a government in exile. Today, approximately 100 000 Tibetans live in India, and thousands of others have immigrated elsewhere in the world.

The Plight of Refugees

The vast majority of people fleeing war or political unrest find refuge in a neighbouring country. Most want to be repatriated to their country of origin as soon as possible. In some cases, this is either impossible or it would take far too long, so some refugees decide to settle elsewhere. They are then integrated into the society of the country that welcomed them or moved to another country that accepts them as refugees. They can then obtain citizenship in their new country.

2.21 ▶ Refugees and people displaced internally, by region (2006)

Region	International refugees	People displaced within their country
Africa	2 607 600	5 373 000
Asia	4 537 800	3 879 100
Europe	1 612 400	542 200
Latin America and the Caribbean	40 600	3 000 000
North America	995 300	–
Oceania	84 000	–
Total	9 877 700	12 794 300

Source: UNHCR, *Statistical Yearbook 2006 – Trends in Displacement, Protection and Solutions*, [On-line], 2007.

People fleeing war are not always able or willing to leave their country. They become refugees in their own homeland.

1994
754 000

1996
13 357 000

1998
11 480 900

2000
12 129 600

2002
10 594 100

2004
9 559 100

2006
9 877 700

2.22 ◀
The number of international refugees, by year
Source: UNHCR, *The 1951 Refugee Convention: Questions & Answers*, [On-line], 2007.

Refugee Camps

When a conflict results in the displacement of populations, refugee camps are usually set up. These camps meet basic needs: a place to sleep, sanitary facilities, food and medical care. These installations are usually intended for short-term use, housing refugees until they are able to return home. When their stay is prolonged, living conditions in the camps can become very difficult because of epidemics, unsanitary conditions and violence.

81

Population

FAMILY REUNIFICATION

Many States recognize the right of immigrants to live with their family. They make it easier for spouses, parents and children to live together. Many immigrants, therefore, are people who come to join family members who have already settled in a new country.

Family reunification: A classic case

▼ 2.23

A first family member, usually the husband or father, immigrates to a new country to find work. Once he is settled, he begins taking steps so that his wife and children can join him.

An immigrant who wants his family to join him must meet specific conditions that vary from country to country.

In general, the receiving country requires that the immigrant obtain legal status, such as citizenship or permanent residence.

The applicant must also demonstrate that he can support the people he wants to bring over so that they will not become dependent on the State. He therefore agrees to provide financial support and to assist them in integrating into the new society.

When all the necessary steps have been taken and the conditions have been met, the other family members are allowed into the country.
Soon, the family is reunited.

CLIMATE REFUGEES

In a few years, a consequence of global warming will be a new type of immigrant: the climate refugee. According to United Nations estimates, THE NUMBER OF CLIMATE REFUGEES COULD REACH 150 MILLION BY 2050. Some countries, such as Tuvalu in the Pacific, may even have to be completely evacuated because of rising water levels.

◀ 2.24
Earthquake in Iran (1990)

Who Is Eligible?

Family members who are eligible for reunification vary from one country to the next. For example, a citizen or permanent resident of Canada who is at least 18 years old can sponsor the following foreign nationals under the family reunification program:

- spouse, de facto spouse or partner aged 16 or over

- parents

- grandparents

- dependent children

- children under the age of 18 who will be adopted

- single brothers, sisters, nieces, nephews or orphaned grandchildren under the age of 18

- if there is no one who meets the above criteria, any relative

28.4%   2.9%

4.5%   64.2%

▼ 2.25
Family reunification in Canada (2006)

- ■ Spouses and partners
- ■ Sons and daughters
- ■ Parents and grandparents
- □ Other

Source: Citizenship and Immigration Canada, *Facts and Figures 2006 – Immigration Overview: Permanent and Temporary Residents,* [On-line], 2007.

Women and children do not necessarily make up the vast majority of candidates for family reunification. For example, in Canada, women represented 60% and children under the age of fifteen represented 10% of those eligible for family reunification in 2006.

Another Reason for Migration: Natural Disasters

Natural disasters can cause population displacement. Episodic events, such as hurricanes, earthquakes, tsunamis, floods and volcanic eruptions can force people out of their homes for a time. Most often, these people return home once the danger has passed. However, other events can have permanent consequences, forcing the population to emigrate definitively.

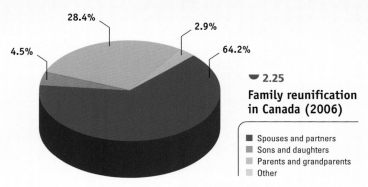

◀ 2.26
Floods in New Orleans after Hurricane Katrina (2005)

A Global
Phenomenon

Reasons for
Migration

Economic
Aspects

Social
Aspects

Population

TOWARD WEALTHY COUNTRIES

Receiving countries and countries of origin differ demographically and economically. Most migrants leave poor countries to find work in industrialized countries where the economy is flourishing.

The Economy and Migration Flows

For developing countries, the departure of a segment of the population is a solution to the problems of overpopulation and unemployment. In these countries, where true industrial and commercial structures are nonexistent, the level of production is insufficient to provide work for the entire population.

Since there is no employment insurance, people without work have no income and consume little, which causes a decline in the already weak national production. To escape from this vicious circle, many choose to leave their country to seek better living conditions abroad. Most of these people have few occupational skills.

The Impact of Migration on the Economy

In addition to helping solve the unemployment problem in developing countries, migration has a positive effect on their economies. According to the World Bank, 60% of migrants send money to their country of origin. In 2007, fund transfers to developing countries were estimated at US$240 billion. However, this situation can create a dependency for developing countries.

The arrival of unskilled labour fills the need created by the aging population in the receiving countries. Moreover, migrants hold precarious and poorly paid jobs that are unappealing to native residents. In the medium and long terms, immigration has a positive effect on economic growth, since migrants consume goods and pay taxes in the receiving country.

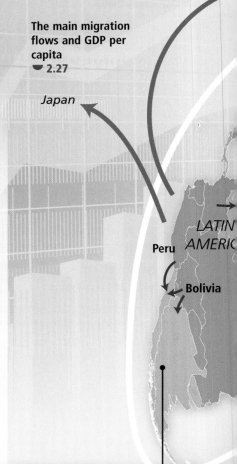

The main migration flows and GDP per capita
▼ 2.27

Japan

LATIN AMERIC

Peru

Bolivia

Latin America

Attracted by the American dream, thousands of Latin Americans have migrated to the United States. In 2000, they represented 70% of the foreign nationals in the United States, and more than half of those are from Mexico. Countries with better economies, such as Costa Rica, Paraguay and Venezuela, also attract migrants.

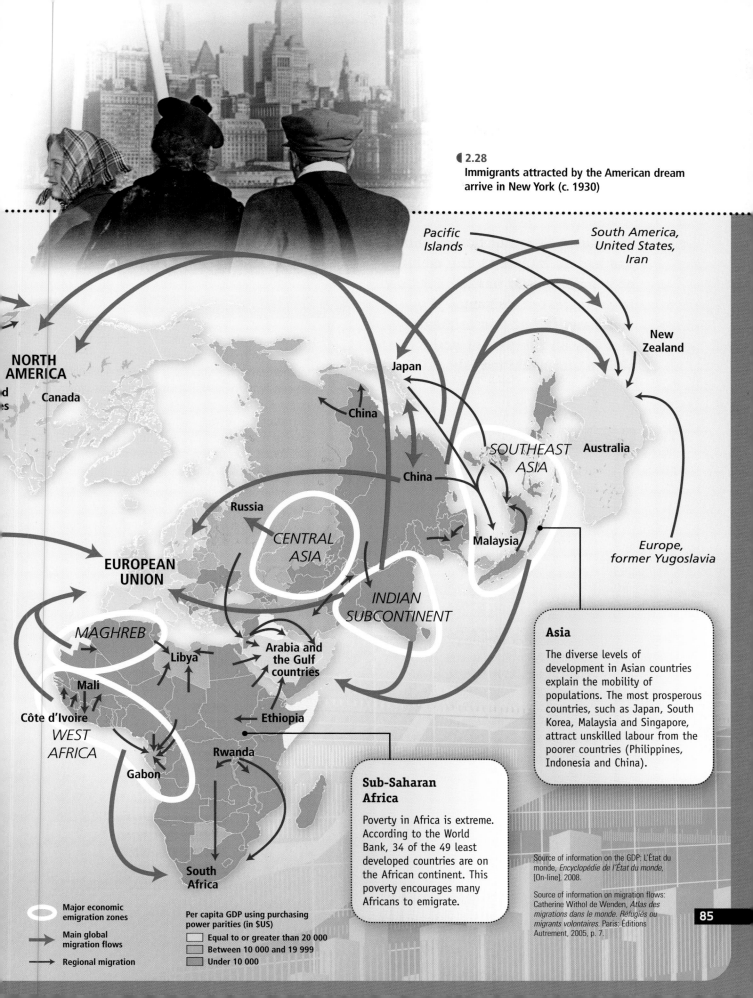

Immigrants attracted by the American dream arrive in New York (c. 1930)

Pacific Islands

South America, United States, Iran

New Zealand

NORTH AMERICA

Canada

China

Japan

SOUTHEAST ASIA

Australia

China

Russia

Malaysia

CENTRAL ASIA

EUROPEAN UNION

Europe, former Yugoslavia

INDIAN SUBCONTINENT

MAGHREB

Libya

Arabia and the Gulf countries

Asia

The diverse levels of development in Asian countries explain the mobility of populations. The most prosperous countries, such as Japan, South Korea, Malaysia and Singapore, attract unskilled labour from the poorer countries (Philippines, Indonesia and China).

Mali

Côte d'Ivoire

WEST AFRICA

Ethiopia

Gabon

Rwanda

Sub-Saharan Africa

Poverty in Africa is extreme. According to the World Bank, 34 of the 49 least developed countries are on the African continent. This poverty encourages many Africans to emigrate.

South Africa

○ Major economic emigration zones

→ Main global migration flows

→ Regional migration

Per capita GDP using purchasing power parities (in $US)

☐ Equal to or greater than 20 000
☐ Between 10 000 and 19 999
☐ Under 10 000

Source of information on the GDP: L'État du monde, *Encyclopédie de l'État du monde*, [On-line], 2008.

Source of information on migration flows: Catherine Withol de Wenden, *Atlas des migrations dans le monde. Réfugiés ou migrants volontaires.* Paris: Éditions Autrement, 2005, p. 7.

85

MIGRATION AND GLOBALIZATION

The globalization of the economy has had an impact on the mobility of populations. It has led not only to an increased exchange of merchandise but also to greater mobility on the part of both skilled and unskilled labour.

The Globalization of the Economy

In recent decades, the global economy has changed, with the development of international trade, the deregulation of financial markets, lower freight transportation costs, the availability of information in real time and the creation of economic free trade zones such as North America (NAFTA) and the European Community (EC).

The globalization of the economy has substantially increased international competition. In newly industrialized and developing countries (such as Taiwan, Singapore and South Korea), salaries are much lower than in developed countries. The cost of goods and services is lower and more difficult for companies in developed countries to compete with.

Relocation and Subcontracting

To remain competitive, many companies move their factories or subcontract part of their production to countries where labour is cheaper. This occurs especially in the manufacturing sector, as illustrated in the European example (see graph below). However, the service sector is increasingly affected by relocations and subcontracting. For example, many call centres have been transferred to other countries, where labour is cheaper.

This phenomenon does not only affect unskilled jobs. Many countries with developing economies, such as China and India, have both a significant technological capacity and a skilled labour force willing to work for less money.

2.29 ▶ Job losses in the European Union in 2005 attributable to relocations, by sector

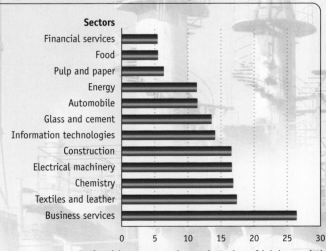

Source: Organisation for Economic Co-operation and Development, *Offshoring and Employment: Trends and Impacts*, [On-line], 2007, p. 94.

▲ 2.30
A call centre in Bangalore, India (2004)

INDIA, A COMPUTER POWER

Each year, India trains 250 000 computer engineers. This skilled labour force, often English-speaking, attracts a number of foreign companies, which PAY SALARIES FOUR TO FIVE TIMES LOWER THAN IN NORTH AMERICA OR EUROPE. For example, in 2007, one multinational, the largest computer company active in India, had 53 000 employees in that country alone.

SNAPSHOT

OF TODAY

a How would you define the concept of "relocation"?

b Give an example of relocation.

c Have you seen an example of relocation in the news recently?

Impact on the Mobility of Populations

Multinationals that relocate their production centres do not relocate all of their employees. However, many managers and technicians volunteer to serve abroad, often with fixed-term contracts. Also, the opening of a new production centre often results in regional migration. In developed countries, the job losses related to such relocations can also cause workers, now unemployed, to migrate to find work.

International Regulation of Labour

To be more competitive, some companies attempt to both increase productivity and lower production costs, showing little concern for their employees' working conditions, often hiring children and illegal immigrants, whom they underpay. To prevent this, and to guarantee respect for basic human rights, the International Labour Organization (ILO), which had 182 member States in 2008, has established basic principles and rights that are binding upon governments of member countries and employers in those countries

SEEN AND HEARD

"Adopted in 1998, the International Labour Organization, *Declaration on Fundamental Principles and Rights at Work* is an expression of commitment by governments, employers' and workers' organizations to uphold basic human values—values that are vital to our social and economic lives.

These principles and rights are:

- freedom of association and the effective recognition of the right to collective bargaining

- elimination of all forms of forced or compulsory labour

- effective abolition of child labour

- elimination of discrimination in respect of employment and occupation "

Source: ILO, About the *Declaration on Fundamental Principles and Rights at Work*, 1998.

BRAIN DRAIN

The globalization of markets is causing fierce competition between countries attempting to attract the most educated and skilled workers. A growing number of the intellectual elite in fields such as medicine, engineering and computer science are emigrating each year. This is referred to as brain drain.

Causes

Several factors motivate the intellectual elite to emigrate. In less developed countries, educational opportunities and advanced training are often limited. Many students leave their country to get a better education or to gain access to technologies that are not readily available in their home country.

Many then decide to remain in the receiving country because of the high unemployment rate and difficult working conditions in their country of origin. They prefer to settle where their career prospects are better.

Developed countries increasingly recruit skilled labour from abroad. Economic growth requires a growing number of specialized workers, and the local labour force is insufficient to meet the need. Many governments have adopted immigration policies that attract and foster the integration of this intellectual elite.

However, there are still many obstacles, such as the recognition of diplomas and degrees. Many immigrants learn that their occupational qualifications are not recognized by the receiving country and are forced to repeat a part of their studies.

Emigration of postsecondary graduates (2000)
The countries shown here are those with at least five million inhabitants. Many microstates, which are especially affected by this phenomenon because of their small population, could also have been included.
2.31 ▼

Haiti
83.6%

Salvador
31%

0   1000   2000
kilometres

DEMAND FOR THE INTELLECTUAL ELITE

IN BRIEF

BRAIN DRAIN IS NOTHING NEW. The emperor Charlemagne (c. 742-814) surrounded himself with the best minds in Europe in order to foster a rebirth of culture and education in his empire: the Englishman Alcuin, the Italian Peter of Pisa, the Spaniard Theodulf of Orleans, etc.

Consequences

The consequences of brain drain are still poorly understood because so few studies have been conducted on the topic. The impact of the phenomenon varies, depending largely on the particular situation in each country. Industrialized countries that already have a large skilled labour force are far less affected than less developed countries.

The most optimistic researchers point out that skilled immigrants can facilitate the transfer of technology and knowledge to their country of origin, thereby making it possible to raise the level of education there. This labour force may also have a positive impact on the economy in their country of origin by sending money and by helping to set up networks for the exchange of ideas, merchandise, etc.

Others note, however, that not all these emigrants return home and their skills are often permanently lost to their country of origin as a result. That is why some international organizations, such as the United Nations Conference on Trade and Development (UNCTAD), lobby for the circulation of skills rather than their exodus.

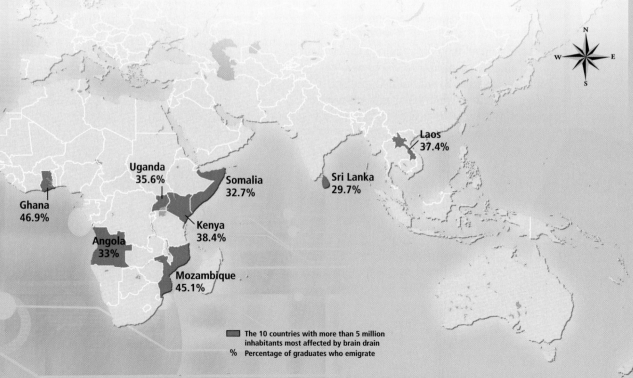

Laos
37.4%

Uganda
35.6%

Somalia
32.7%

Sri Lanka
29.7%

Ghana
46.9%

Kenya
38.4%

Angola
33%

Mozambique
45.1%

> The 10 countries with more than 5 million inhabitants most affected by brain drain
> % Percentage of graduates who emigrate

Source: Caglar Ösden and Maurice Schiff (eds.), *International Migration, Remittances and Brain Drain*, [On-line], 2006, p. 176.

CROSSING BORDERS

States are surrounded by borders that prevent free circulation between countries. Travellers must meet government requirements to cross a border and obtain the right to stay in a country legally. These regulations allow States to control immigration to their territory.

Legal Rules

Each country establishes its own rules for receiving foreign nationals. Generally speaking, people from countries with which diplomatic relations are good are more likely to be accepted than those from countries with whom relations are poor. In the latter case, additional conditions may be imposed, such as the need to obtain a special visa. People considered undesirable may even be forbidden entry into the country.

Usually, foreign nationals can only stay in a country for a limited time. Also, they do not benefit from all the rights afforded the native population. For example, a visitor who has only a tourist visa is not entitled to work. Immigrants who want to become full-fledged citizens must meet the receiving country's conditions and guidelines.

Opening of the border between Poland and Germany (2007)
Hundreds of people celebrate the expansion of the Schengen Area.
▼ 2.32

◀ **2.33**
Passport
A passport is an identification document needed to cross most international borders.

◀ **2.34**
Visa
In addition to a passport, many countries require a visa. There are different types of visas: for tourists, workers, students, etc.

Borders

Borders play a number of roles. They can serve as a barrier against armed invasion. They make possible the control of the transportation of merchandise and the collection of taxes and customs duties. Finally, they facilitate the close monitoring of immigration, since all foreign nationals who enter a country must cross the border at an authorized point of entry. This allows the authorities to ensure that travellers meet all the required criteria.

◀ **2.35**
The Berlin Wall in 1962

A Closed Border: The Berlin Wall

States use different methods to control their borders. Some erect walls, like the Berlin Wall, to prevent the free circulation of individuals.

After the Second World War (1939-1945), Germany was divided in two: a capitalist State in the West and a communist State in the East. Situated in East Germany, the city of Berlin was itself divided in two. To prevent the population of East Berlin from fleeing to West Berlin, where economic and political conditions were better, in 1961, the communist authorities decided to build a huge wall. Some 155 kilometres long, the wall completely surrounded West Berlin. Closely guarded, the barrier was almost impassable until 1989. The fall of the communist regime and the reunification of the two Germanies in 1990 led to its destruction.

Open Borders: The Schengen Area

Some countries tighten border controls, while others relax them to facilitate the circulation of individuals. The creation of the Schengen Area in Europe is a good example of open borders.

The Schengen Area is a borderless territory created by the signatories to the Schengen Agreement. The agreement, which bears the name of the tiny village on the border of France, Germany and Luxembourg where it was signed in 1985, provides for the gradual elimination of borders between the member States, as well as the harmonization of visa policies with extensive police cooperation to prevent arms and drug trafficking. At the end of 2008, the Schengen Area included 25 European countries and allowed the free circulation of more than 400 million individuals.

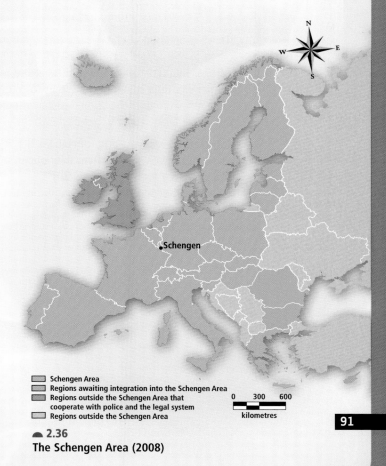

Schengen

☐ Schengen Area
☐ Regions awaiting integration into the Schengen Area
☐ Regions outside the Schengen Area that cooperate with police and the legal system
☐ Regions outside the Schengen Area

0   300   600
kilometres

🔺 **2.36**
The Schengen Area (2008)

CLANDESTINE MIGRATION

The vast majority of immigrants who settle in a new country follow the rules of the receiving State. Some, however, do not. Their stay is therefore considered illegal, which forces them to lead secret lives.

Characteristics of Clandestine Migration

It is very difficult to estimate the scope of clandestine migration. Because of the irregularity of their situation, illegal immigrants are usually very discreet. It is estimated, however, that the number of illegal immigrants has been on the rise since the mid-1970s, especially in the more developed parts of the world, such as Europe and North America. In 2006, there were an estimated 22 to 44 million illegal immigrants in the world. This represents only 10 to 20% of all immigrants.

The phenomenon of clandestine immigration is directly linked to the adoption of increasingly strict immigration policies. Immigrants who do not meet the receiving country's criteria sometimes attempt to settle illegally. Some cross the border at non-designated points, while others use false papers to get past customs.

However, the vast majority of clandestine immigrants cross the border legally. Most often, they obtain a visa for a short stay, such as a tourist visa, which gives them the right to stay in the country for a certain time, but then they do not leave. They stay in the country and become illegal immigrants.

2.37 ▶ Immigrants in the United States (2005)

Number of people

- 40 000 000 — 76%
- 30 000 000
- 20 000 000
- 10 000 000 — 24%
- 0

Clandestine immigration | Legal immigration

Source: Jeffrey S. Passel, *Estimates of the Size and Characteristics of the Undocumented Population*, [On-line], 2006.

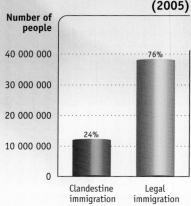

2.38 ▶
The Mexican-American border (1993)

A CLOSELY GUARDED BORDER

According to estimates, THERE ARE MORE THAN 12 MILLION ILLEGAL IMMIGRANTS IN THE UNITED STATES, the greatest number in the world. Most of these immigrants are from Mexico, the neighbouring country that shares a 3000 kilometre border with the United States. To counter this substantial migration flow, the American government is increasing border surveillance, using cameras, more frequent patrols, barbed wire and walls.

2.39
Tijuana, Mexico (1994)
Illegal immigrants await transportation to Los Angeles, in the United States.

Illegal immigrants who make it to their destination are not home free. They must find work to survive, despite the fact that their mere presence in the country is illegal. If the authorities discover them, they can be arrested and deported to their country of origin.

Between 1990 and 2006, the French government deported more than 190 000 illegal immigrants.

Each year, an estimated 2000 people die trying to get to Europe by boat.

ATLANTIC OCEAN

EUROPE

Illegal immigrants use a variety of means to cross the border. Some attempt to cross the sea on poorly built and overloaded boats. Others travel for many days, hidden in freight containers aboard ships or trains, at risk of dying of starvation or asphyxiation.

To avoid getting caught, illegal immigrants take difficult and little-travelled routes. Many die from sunstroke or dehydration trying to cross the Sahara Desert in North Africa.

MEDITERRANEAN SEA

Morocco

Canary Islands (Spain)

SAHARA DESERT

Libya

Niger

There is an entire trade built around clandestine immigration. Unscrupulous individuals think nothing of charging phenomenal amounts to help people cross the border illegally. Many smugglers rob or abandon their clients without resources or allow them to be caught by the authorities.

Sudan

AFRICA

The routes taken by illegal immigrants change in response to the level of border surveillance.

0   400   800
kilometres

2.40
Clandestine immigration routes: Africa to Europe

Of the many who try to immigrate illegally, few succeed. Most of them are discouraged by the difficulties of the trip, the high cost and the many dangers involved.

WELCOMING MIGRANTS

Immigrants carry their cultural baggage with them: language, religion, cuisine, traditions, ways of thinking and acting, etc. They must learn to reconcile their culture with that of the new country in which they have decided to live. Some governments encourage immigrants to assimilate quickly, while others urge them to preserve their culture.

Monument to Multiculturalism, Toronto 2.41 ▼

Integrating Immigrants

Each country has its own policy for integrating immigrants, based on different models.

The melting pot ▪ This expression was long used to describe the American policy for integrating immigrants. According to this model, combining different cultures in a melting pot would result in the appearance of a new, homogeneous culture. Today, most researchers are questioning this model because of its oversimplification and idealism.

SEEN AND HEARD

❝ . . . so in this continent—asylum of all nations—the energy of Irish, Germans, Swedes, Poles, and Cossacks, and all the European tribes – of the Africans, and of the Polynesians – will construct a new race, a new religion, a new state, a new literature. . . ❞

Ralph Waldo Emerson, American philosopher and poet (1845)

Segregation ▪ According to this model, immigrants should maintain their own culture without making an effort to participate in that of the receiving country. They are also encouraged to live apart from the rest of society. This model is especially popular in xenophobic societies that do not want to integrate immigrants.

SEEN AND HEARD

❝ We don't want to start a war between Bahrainis [citizens of Bahrain] and foreigners, but these [foreign] workers should have special places. ❞

Murtadha Bader, Manama Municipal Council chairman, Bahrain, a Persian Gulf country (2004)

Interculturalism ▪ Proponents of interculturalism tolerate, even encourage, cultural diversity, but they do not offer all cultures an equal place. They promote a dominant shared culture. This model reflects Québec's policy for the integration of minorities.

2.42 ▲
**Students in a multiethnic
school in London (2006)**

SEEN AND HEARD

" Québec interculturalism institutes French as the common language of intercultural relations; cultivates a pluralistic orientation that is concerned with the protection of rights; . . . places special emphasis on integration and participation; and advocates interaction. "

Gérard Bouchard and Charles Taylor, co-chairs of the Commission on Accommodation Practices (2008)

Multiculturalism ▪ Proponents of multiculturalism consider that all cultures should be treated equally and that efforts should be made to preserve them. According to this model, the combination of all cultures forms a sort of "cultural mosaic" that can contribute to the development of a common identity. This is the model officially adopted by Canada.

SEEN AND HEARD

" Every ethnic group has the right to preserve and develop its own culture and values within the Canadian context. To say we have two official languages is not to say we have two official cultures, and no particular culture is more 'official' than another. "

Pierre Elliott Trudeau, Prime Minister of Canada (1971)

Assimilation ▪ According to the assimilation model, immigrants should completely give up their culture in order to adopt that of the receiving country as quickly as possible. Different cultures are rejected in favour of a single dominant culture deemed superior. Societies that adopt this model are generally relatively closed to immigration.

SEEN AND HEARD

" . . . refuse the settlement on our soil of the Muslim masses who will not be assimilated. Loyal to Republican principles, we must organize the departure of immigrants who cannot or will not be assimilated into the national community. "

Henry de Lesquen, president of the Club de l'Horloge, a French extreme right organization (2002)
[Free translation]

From Immigrant to Citizen

Immigrants who want to settle in a new country must take several steps before becoming full-fledged citizens. They must usually begin by obtaining the status of permanent resident, which gives them the right to stay indefinitely in the country and to work there.

Governments decide whether they will grant this status based on certain criteria. For example, some governments prefer immigrants from particular cultures or countries of origin. Other criteria include the financial situation, languages spoken, level of education, occupational skills and the absence of a criminal record.

After obtaining the status of permanent resident, immigrants can take further steps to be naturalized. To do so they must meet additional conditions, usually including having lived in the country for a certain number of years, having mastered one of the country's official languages and having some knowledge of the country's culture.

DIASPORAS

Members of a given community living abroad tend to gather together and to maintain a strong sense of community. They maintain close ties with their country of origin, regardless of the reasons why they left it. They also form a vast network referred to as a diaspora.

An International Network

Immigrants who settle in a new country remain attached to their country of origin. They still have friends, family or professional contacts there. Many of them hope to return home one day.

These ties with the country of origin can last several generations, especially since immigrants often teach their children their language, religion and customs. Descendants of migrants thus continue to cultivate a sense of belonging to their ancestors' country of origin.

A diaspora is made up of all the people who share a common ethnic identity and who continue to maintain ties based on this identity. These ties make it possible to establish international networks that can take different forms: trade relations, fund transfers to the country of origin, economic mutual aid, cultural exchanges, etc. The members of a diaspora often form associations to defend their collective interests.

The major diasporas are Jewish, Irish, Italian, Chinese, Armenian, Turkish and Lebanese. Older diasporas tend to disappear over time, as emigrants integrate into the population of their new country.

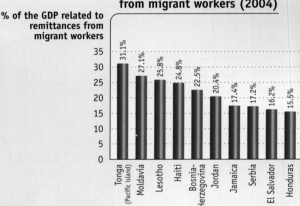

2.43 ▶ **The 10 countries most dependent on remittances from migrant workers (2004)**

% of the GDP related to remittances from migrant workers

- Tonga (Pacific island): 31.1%
- Moldavia: 27.1%
- Lesotho: 25.8%
- Haiti: 24.8%
- Bosnia-Herzegovina: 22.5%
- Jordan: 20.4%
- Jamaica: 17.4%
- Serbia: 17.2%
- El Salvador: 16.2%
- Honduras: 15.5%

Country

Source: The International Bank for Reconstruction and Development/The World Bank, *Global Economic Prospect: Economic Implications of Remittances and Migrations*, 2006, [On-line], 2006, p. 90.

Diasporas and Remittances

By helping preserve immigrants' identity, the diaspora plays an important cultural role. It also plays an economic role. Emigrants living in wealthy countries often send money to their families back home. These remittances can be considerable. For example, in 2007, Indian migrants sent more than US$27 billion back to India. The economic health of many small countries depends in large part on these remittances, as can be seen in the graph above.

(a) How would you define the concept of "diaspora"?

(b) Name a diaspora other than the Jewish diaspora.

(c) How would you define the concept of "network"?

THE IRISH DIASPORA

Throughout history, mass emigration has resulted in the development of diasporas. For example, historians estimate that BETWEEN 45% AND 85% OF THE POPULATION OF IRELAND LEFT THE COUNTRY IN THE MID-19TH CENTURY. Today, an estimated 80 million descendants of these emigrants represent more than 13 times the current population of Ireland.

The Jewish Diaspora: An Example

The Greek word *diaspora* means "dispersion." At first, the term referred to the dissemination of the Jews throughout the world in antiquity. By extension, it is now used to designate the dispersion of any people or community. The Jewish diaspora is one of the most ancient: many Jews were deported from Israel to Persia (now Iran) in 722 BCE. After the Roman conquest of Palestine in the first century BCE, large numbers of Jews began leaving the region.

Two branches of the Jewish people developed: the Sephardim in North Africa and Spain, and the Ashkenazim, first in Western Europe, then in Eastern Europe and Russia. Victims of oppression and racism, many Jews settled in the New World. After the horror of the Holocaust in the Second World War, the State of Israel was created in 1948. Many Jews from around the world settled in the new State, but the Jewish diaspora is still one of the largest.

2.44 ▶ **The Jewish diaspora (2007)**

Country	Population
Israel	5 393 000
United States	5 275 000
France	490 000
Canada	374 000
United Kingdom	295 000
Russia	225 000
Argentina	184 000
Germany	120 000
Australia	104 000
Brazil	96 000
Ukraine	77 000
South Africa	72 000

Jews in the world (2007)
▼ **2.45**

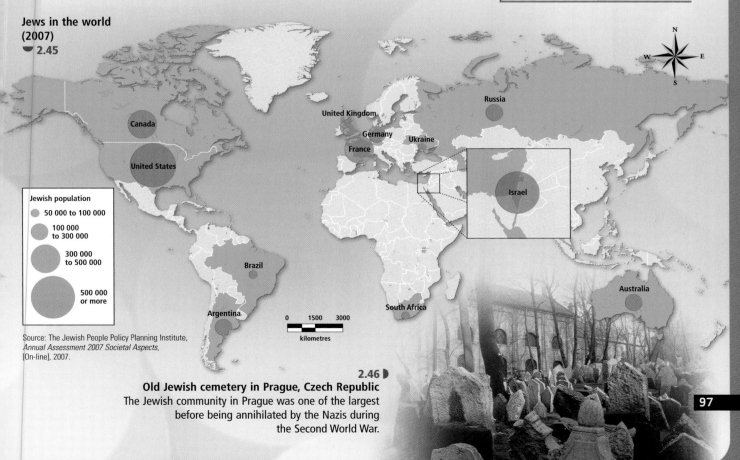

Jewish population
- 50 000 to 100 000
- 100 000 to 300 000
- 300 000 to 500 000
- 500 000 or more

Source: The Jewish People Policy Planning Institute, *Annual Assessment 2007 Societal Aspects*, [On-line], 2007.

0 1500 3000
kilometres

2.46 ▶
Old Jewish cemetery in Prague, Czech Republic
The Jewish community in Prague was one of the largest before being annihilated by the Nazis during the Second World War.

URBAN EXPANSION

Urbanization and migration are closely related. The establishment and growth of cities is a process largely attributable to the influx of people from neighbouring rural areas. As well, international immigrants usually settle in cities.

A Century of Urbanization

The 20th century was marked by an extensive process of urbanization. In 1900, barely 13% of the world's population lived in cities. In 2005, almost half (49%) of the planet's 6.5 billion inhabitants lived in urban areas.

The most developed countries are usually the most urbanized. For example, in North America (including Mexico), almost 80% of the population lives in cities. The world urbanization rate should therefore continue to increase in the coming years because of the economic growth of the least developed countries.

SNAPSHOT OF TODAY

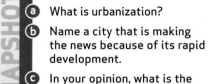

a   What is urbanization?

b   Name a city that is making the news because of its rapid development.

c   In your opinion, what is the connection between migration and culture?

d   Give an example drawn from the news.

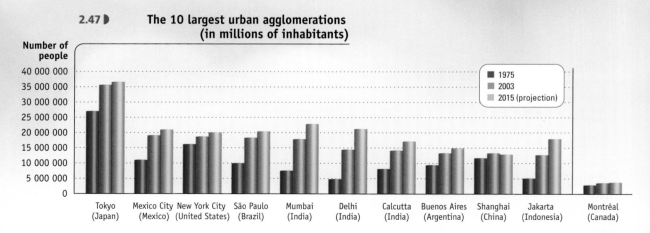

2.47 ▶ **The 10 largest urban agglomerations (in millions of inhabitants)**

Number of people

- 1975
- 2003
- 2015 (projection)

Tokyo (Japan) · Mexico City (Mexico) · New York City (United States) · São Paulo (Brazil) · Mumbai (India) · Delhi (India) · Calcutta (India) · Buenos Aires (Argentina) · Shanghai (China) · Jakarta (Indonesia) · Montréal (Canada)

Source: Population Division of the Department of Economic and Social Affairs of the United Nations Secretariat, *Urban Agglomerations 2003*, [On-line], 2004.

Not only are there more cities, the cities are larger. In 1950, 80 cities had a population of more than one million, and only one, New York City, had a population of more than 10 million. Fifty years later, almost 400 agglomerations have more than one million inhabitants; 19 of them have more than 10 million inhabitants.

2.48
Satellite image of the Earth at night
The points of light show the locations of cities. The more dense patches of light indicate industrialized urban areas.

Growing Cities

As the world's population moves to urban areas, the Earth's cities are growing as never before in terms of both population density and surface area. For example, the population density in the Marine Lines district of Mumbai, India, is 114 000 inhabitants per square kilometre. In some highly populated areas, cities are growing so fast that they are merging with each other, forming what are called megalopolises (from the Greek *mega*, "big," and *polis*, "city"), or megacities. For example, on the east coast of the United States, you can travel from Boston to Washington without ever leaving the urban landscape. More than 55 million people live in this megalopolis, known as "Bos-Wash."

Multiethnic Cities

The case of São Paolo, Brazil

Because they receive a large number of immigrants, cities are often much more multiethnic than rural areas. The case of São Paolo, Brazil, one of the largest agglomerations on the planet, is a good example. Founded in the 16th century by a Portuguese religious order, São Paolo soon became home to European colonists and African slaves. By the end of the 19th century, immigration began increasing and diversifying. Between 1880 and 1980, the city received 2.5 of the 5.5 million immigrants to Brazil. Today, São Paolo has between 90 and 100 different ethnic groups, including the largest Japanese community outside Japan.

2.49 ▶ The main ethnic groups in São Paolo (2008)

Ethnic groups	Population
Ethnic groups	6 000 000
Portuguese	3 000 000
Africans	2 000 000
Arabs (Lebanese and Syrians)	1 000 000
Germans	400 000
Japanese	326 000
Chinese	120 000
Jews	70 000
Spaniards, Bolivians, Greeks, Koreans	50 000 and more

Source: Governo de Estado de São Paolo, *Memorial do Imigrante*, [On-line], 2006.

The numbers include immigrants and their descendants.

2.50 ▲
View of São Paolo, Brazil

MIGRATION TO THE CITY

The vast majority of immigrants settle in cities. Their arrival contributes substantially to urban growth. Their diversity enriches the cultural landscape. However, their integration is not always easy, and they are often the city's poorest inhabitants.

Ethnic neighbourhoods

Immigrants who arrive in a new city often settle near their compatriots. That is why, over time, ethnic neighbourhoods develop in a community. These enclaves make it easier for immigrants when they arrive, but they can also make it harder for them to integrate into the rest of society.

Downtown

Immigrants often settle near industrial and commercial centres. These densely populated areas have often been abandoned by more affluent residents, who now live outside the city and commute downtown to work.

2.51
Downtown Tokyo

Affluent neighbourhoods

Affluent neighbourhoods are often found outside the centre of the city. They are less densely populated and contain more green spaces. Except for the most wealthy, immigrants do not usually settle in these neighbourhoods when they arrive.

Shantytowns

Located at the periphery of a city, shantytowns house the poorest residents, newly arrived immigrants in particular. These very densely populated neighbourhoods often have no electricity, running water or sewer systems. Also, garbage collection is often unavailable.

2.52
North American suburb

2.53
Shantytown in Mumbai

" Like people, cities have personalities. Each represents a unique mix of history and natural setting, cultural patterns and lifestyles. Some are ugly yet attractive, others beautiful but dull. Under such circumstances, modelling and theorising about cities is risky, if even possible. "

Ignacy Sachs, Polish naturalized French economist (1988)

2.54 ▲
Chinatown, Philadelphia

2.55 ▶
Jane Jacobs

Urban Planning

Some people promote precise, detailed urban planning. Others believe that we should allow the different neighbourhoods in a city to develop freely, in order to preserve a human dimension. Jane Jacobs (1916-2006), an American urban planner who immigrated to Canada at the end of the 1960s, held the latter view. Her work *The Death and Life of Great American Cities* is one of the most important works on urban planning.

The Impact of Urban Immigration

The mass arrival of immigrants in a city can create problems. The newly arrived immigrants, usually poor, must find housing. They often settle in overpopulated and underprivileged neighbourhoods, such as shantytowns. These urban areas often develop in a disorganized fashion, and municipal authorities must ensure the implementation of viable infrastructures. Moreover, the influx of immigrants can cause an increase in the unemployment rate if the available labour exceeds the number of jobs offered. In some cases, the presence of a large population of immigrants can cause concern among the local population and result in racial tensions.

The Attraction of the City

Immigrants mostly settle in cities because of their economic importance. The chances of finding a job are greater in cities than in rural areas. Also, cities offer better access to commodities and services. For example, they usually have more schools and health care institutions. It is also easier for immigrants to integrate into an urban population, which is already large and diverse. Generally speaking, immigrants appear to be attracted to the city lifestyle.

Shantytown in Jakarta (1995)
Shantytowns are a type of uncontrolled urban development.
▼ **2.56**

CONCEPTS

State (p. 105)
International Law (p. 119)
Governance (p. 107)
Integration (p. 127)
Sovereignty (p. 105)
Standardization (p. 135)

Topic to Be Interpreted
The redefinition of
the powers of states

Taking a Position (TAP)

TAP 1 The capacity of states
to take action

OR

TAP 2 The sovereignty of states
and economic or political
associations

In the context of globalization, States are signing an increasing number of international agreements.
This had led to the **redefinition of their political, economic and cultural powers**, which they must now
share at the international level.

POWER

3.1 ▶
Ban Ki-moon,
the UN Secretary General,
during the 63rd UN General
Assembly at the headquarters
in New York City (2008)

Knowledge Related to the Theme

- Cultural, economic and environmental policies
  (p. 122-123, 128-129, 134-141)
- Economic zones
  (p. 126-127)
- Globalization of markets
  (p. 122-125, 130-131)
- International and multilateral agreements
  (p. 112-113, 126-127)
- International institutions
  (p. 106-113, 138-139)
- Multinational firms
  (p. 130-131)
- Political alliances
  (p. 112-117)
- Pressure groups
  (p. 120-121)

Cultural References

- United Nations (1945)
  (p. 106-109)
- G6 Summit (1975)
  (p. 111)
- Maastricht Treaty (1992)
  (p. 115)
- Dongjiang Free Trade Port Zone (2006)
  (p. 123)

WHAT IS A STATE?

States are the main actors in international relations. They play a major role in most international exchanges. Their powers have a direct impact on most human activities, although they are not absolute. These powers are limited by theoretical principles and practical realities.

The Powers of States

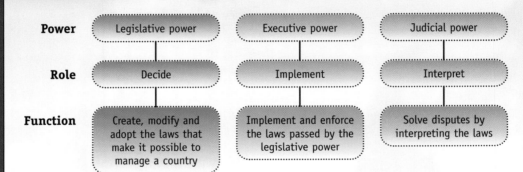

Power	Legislative power	Executive power	Judicial power
Role	Decide	Implement	Interpret
Function	Create, modify and adopt the laws that make it possible to manage a country	Implement and enforce the laws passed by the legislative power	Solve disputes by interpreting the laws

The three powers are exercised differently depending on the State. For example, under an authoritarian regime, the head of government can hold legislative, executive and judicial powers at the same time. In a democracy like Canada, these powers are divided among several institutions that are largely independent of one another.

State powers are also subject to several constraints.

3.2
Reichstag Palace, the seat of Germany's Parliament

External relations (with other countries)

International law stipulates that States cannot freely interfere in the internal affairs of other States. They are free, however, to try to convince or influence them through dialogue, promises or threats. For example, in 1986, the United States imposed significant trade sanctions on South Africa in order to pressure it to change its apartheid laws.

Internal affairs (within a country)

In theory, States are free to exercise their powers over internal affairs. In practice, this power is subject to certain limits. States often impose their own constraints through laws adopted by governments. For example, many countries have a written constitution that determines how they should be governed, as well as the limits on government power. Moreover, other States may directly or indirectly influence the policies of another State.

HOW MANY STATES ARE THERE?

Based on the main criteria defined by international law, IN 2009, THERE WERE MORE THAN 193 INTERNATIONALLY RECOGNIZED SOVEREIGN STATES, 192 of which are members of the United Nations (the Vatican has observer status, but is not a full member). A dozen other countries, such as Taiwan, Kosovo and the Palestinian Territories, function like sovereign States, but have not yet been recognized internationally.

The Main Attributes of a State Based on International Law

Territory

All States must be able to assert exclusive rights over a territory. This territory includes an area of land delimited by borders, as well as any lake or watercourse within those borders. In addition, according to international law, States exercise exclusive authority over the seas and oceans that border their coastline up to a distance of 12 nautical miles (22.2 km). A State's airspace extends vertically up to 80 km.

Population

A State can only exist with a human component, that is, a population. This can include a certain number of foreigners, but must be composed primarily of individuals holding the nationality of the State.

Government

A State must possess a system of government that can exercise authority and power over its territory. This government must also be able to represent the State on the international scene. Each State can determine the structure of its system of government (unitary, federal and confederal) and the nature of its political system (presidential, parliamentary, constitutional or absolute monarchy, military dictatorship, etc.).

International legal personality

A State must possess an international legal personality, a recognized status that allows it to hold rights and obligations in the international arena. This legal personality allows the State to distinguish itself from its government. Consequently, when there is a change of government in a country (which frequently occurs in democracies following an election), the State itself continues to exist and to be recognized internationally.

Sovereignty

Each State exercises full sovereignty over its territory. In other words, it holds all and exclusive authority and power. Under international law, no State has the right to interfere in the internal affairs of another State.

International recognition

This criterion is not indispensable to the existence of a State, but it greatly facilitates its participation in international affairs. A State that is not recognized by other countries is usually condemned to isolation and decline.

OF TODAY

 Reading these pages, how would you define the key concept of the chapter, namely, the "State"?

b In your own words, define the concept of "sovereignty."

c Provide an example from the news of State sovereignty.

3.3 ▲

The Capitol, the seat of legislative power in the United States

THE UNITED NATIONS

During the 19th and 20th centuries, international exchanges—
economic, political, social and cultural—grew exponentially.
The United Nations (UN) was born out of a desire to help regulate
these exchanges by introducing a form of permanent
international cooperation.

The Origin of the United Nations

A precursor: The League of Nations

Founded in 1920, the League of Nations sought to
maintain peace and stability around the world in
order to avoid a recurrence of the horrors of the
First World War (1914–1918).

- **Its major weakness:** It was not a universal
  organization. The United States, in particular,
  never joined, and the League never had more
  than 58 members at any given time.

- **Its limited success:** The League of Nations
  was only able to solve a few minor conflicts.
  Its ultimate failure came with the outbreak
  of the Second World War (1939–1945).

A new international organization: The UN

While the Second World War was raging, the leaders
of the countries allied against the Axis Powers met to
lay the foundation of a new, more effective
international organization: the United Nations.

- **Founding charter:** In the spring of 1945, the
  constitutive charter of the new organization was
  signed by 51 States. The United Nations officially
  opened its doors on October 24, 1945.

- **Headquarters:** Completed in 1952, the UN's
  headquarters are located in New York City. It houses
  the UN's main agencies, in particular, the General
  Assembly and the Security Council.

SEEN AND HEARD

The Charter of the United Nations

The United Nations is a universal organization, which means it is open to all countries that
accept and implement the principles of its Charter. The UN is not a global government, and
each member State retains its full sovereignty. The United Nations does, however, encourage
international cooperation in a number of areas.

" The Purposes of the United Nations are:

1. To maintain international peace and security. . .

2. To develop friendly relations among nations based on respect for the principle of equal
   rights and self-determination of peoples. . .

3. To achieve international cooperation in solving international problems of an economic,
   social, cultural, or humanitarian character, and in promoting and encouraging respect
   for human rights and for fundamental freedoms for all without distinction as to race, sex,
   language or religion. . . *"*

Article 1 of the Charter of the United Nations

ⓐ How would you define the concept of "governance"?

ⓑ Is a world government necessary? Provide an example from the news to support your answer.

◀ 3.4
UN headquarters in New York City

Secretariat

The Secretary General heads the entire United Nations bureaucracy. This person is responsible for the proper functioning of the organization and often mediates international conflicts. The person appointed to this position must demonstrate absolute political neutrality, which makes the choice very difficult. The General Assembly appoints the Secretary General, on the Security Council's recommendation, for a renewable five-year mandate.

Security Council

The Security Council is composed of 5 permanent members who have *veto* power (China, United States, France, United Kingdom and Russia) and 10 non-permanent members who are elected for 2-year terms. The Council is responsible for maintaining international peace and security, using armed force if necessary. Its decisions are binding.

The main agencies of the United Nations
◆ 3.5

Trusteeship Council

This agency is responsible for protecting and administering certain territories that are not yet autonomous. It has been inactive since 1994, when the last territory placed under its trusteeship, the Pacific islands of Palau, gained independence.

General Assembly

Composed of all of the member States (192 in 2009), the General Assembly is a forum for discussion where each State can express its point of view. The Assembly can issue non-binding resolutions, which are essentially recommendations. During voting, each State has one vote. The most important issues (peace, budget, admission of new members) must be adopted by a two-thirds majority.

Economic and Social Council (ESC)

The ESC is the UN agency responsible for economic, social and cultural issues, as well as those related to education, health and human rights. It is comprised of 54 member States elected by the General Assembly for a 3-year mandate. Its recommendations are non-binding.

International Court of Justice

Headquartered in The Hague, Netherlands, the International Court of Justice rules on international disputes that are brought before it. All member States can bring their grievances before the court, however, they must respect the rulings of its 15 judges from various countries, elected by the General Assembly and the Security Council.

Specialized institutions

In addition to its six primary agencies, the United Nations has a number of specialized institutions in all areas.

THE UNITED NATIONS SYSTEM

The United Nations system includes a number of commissions, programs, funds, specialized agencies, research institutes and associated organizations related to all aspects of international cooperation. Here are just a few of the most important.

Economics

International Labour Organization (ILO)
Headquarters: Geneva, Switzerland
Founding date: 1919
Objective: Develop policies that promote decent work, taking into account the point of view of governments, employers and workers.

International Monetary Fund (IMF)
Headquarters: Washington, DC, United States
Founding date: 1945
Objective: Encourage international monetary cooperation and ensure global economic stability.

World Bank Group (WB)
Headquarters: Washington, DC, United States
Founding date: 1945
Objective: The five institutions that form the World Bank Group fight poverty by offering advice and financial support to States in economic difficulty.

Security

United Nations High Commission for Refugees (UNHCR)
Headquarters: Geneva, Switzerland
Founding date: 1950
Objective: Ensure the international protection of refugees.

International Atomic Energy Agency (IAEA)
Headquarters: Vienna, Austria
Founding date: 1957
Objective: Promote the development of nuclear energy for peaceful purposes and limit its military applications.

Department of Peacekeeping Operations (DPKO)
Headquarters: New York City, United States
Founding date: 1992
Objective: Coordinate the various United Nations peacekeeping operations, led by multinational forces (Blue Helmets).

3.6 ▲
United Nations Blue Helmets (1995)

Culture and Education

United Nations Educational, Scientific and Cultural Organization (UNESCO)
Headquarters: Paris, France
Founding date: 1945
Objective: Encourage collaboration between nations in fields of education, science, culture, communications and information.

United Nations University (UNU)
Headquarters: Tokyo, Japan
Founding date: 1973
Objective: Encourage international university research on the major global issues of human survival, development and welfare.

▲ 3.7
V. Narry Kim, winner of the 2008 Women in Science prize
This prize is awarded jointly by UNESCO and a French industrial group.

Environment

United Nations Environment Programme (UNEP)

Headquarters: Nairobi, Kenya

Founding date: 1972

Objective: Promote international cooperation on the environment.

Development

United Nations Children's Fund (UNICEF)

Headquarters: New York City, United States

Founding date: 1946

Objective: Improve conditions for children around the world. Its primary fields of action are education for children of both genders, vaccination, the protection of children from violence, exploitation and abuse, the promotion of the health of newborns and fighting AIDS.

United Nations Conference on Trade and Development (UNCTAD)

Headquarters: Geneva, Switzerland

Founding date: 1964

Objective: Encourage the development of international trade so that it is equitable for all countries.

United Nations Development Programme (UNDP)

Headquarters: New York City, United States

Founding date: 1965

Objective: Main organization responsible for the United Nations' development projects. Its main areas of intervention are the fight against poverty, the prevention of humanitarian crises, the sustainable management of resources and the promotion of democracy.

3.8
A UNICEF worker cares for a child in Zaire (1994)

Health

Food and Agricultural Organization of the United Nations (FAO)

Headquarters: Rome, Italy

Founding date: 1945

Objective: Achieve food security for all by improving agricultural productivity, access to food and the living conditions of rural populations.

World Health Organization (WHO)

Headquarters: Geneva, Switzerland

Founding date: 1948

Objective: Contribute to achieving the highest level of health possible for all of the peoples of the world.

World Food Programme (WFP)

Headquarters: Rome, Italy

Founding date: 1963

Objective: Provide food assistance to people suffering from famine.

3.9
Food crisis in Haiti (2008)
Haitians share food sent by the WFP.

Justice

International Criminal Court (ICC)

Headquarters: The Hague, Netherlands

Founding date: 2002

Objective: Prosecute individuals accused of serious crimes, including genocide, war crimes and crimes against humanity.

Transportation and Communications

International Telecommunication Union (ITU)

Headquarters: Geneva, Switzerland

Founding date: 1865

Objective: Encourage international cooperation in the development of telecommunications.

International Civil Aviation Organization (ICAO)

Headquarters: Montréal, Canada

Founding date: 1947

Objective: Develop civil aviation standards to improve the safety of international air transport.

International Maritime Organization (IMO)

Headquarters: London, United Kingdom

Founding date: 1948

Objective: Develop international maritime regulations and prevent marine pollution.

Politics   Economics   Culture

INTERNATIONAL SUMMITS

The various United Nations agencies provide a useful framework for international cooperation. However, many States feel the need to develop other strategies for exchange and collaboration that are better adapted to their particular needs. International summits are a good example of this.

Discussions on an International Scale

States have long organized international gatherings involving a number of countries in order to discuss particular problems. In the decades following the Second World War, certain meetings began to be held on a regular basis and developed into more structured events, such as the G8. These international summits nevertheless continue to be very flexible, adapting to particular situations and needs. Unlike international organizations, they do not have a permanent and independent administration.

Meetings on a Smaller Scale

The United Nations General Assembly allows each country, regardless of its size or wealth, to express itself, while international summits bring together a smaller number of States that have common interests. These conditions make it easier to discuss issues and reach agreements. Summits are an opportunity to discuss current topics, as is the case at the G8 summits, or particular themes, as is the case at the Paris Club meetings. As complex as they are, these meetings remain simply forums for discussion. The decisions arrived at are not binding and the participating States are free to decide whether or not to pursue them.

◀ 3.10

Top: **Meeting of the G8 leaders in Russia (2006)**

Bottom: **LG8 summits are often met with demonstrations against the government policies of member countries (2003)**

THE JUNIOR 8 (J8)

Since 2005, UNICEF has organized an annual JUNIOR 8, OR J8, SUMMIT, A PARALLEL SUMMIT TO THE G8, FOR YOUNG PEOPLE BETWEEN THE AGES OF 13 AND 17. Student delegations from the eight member countries of the G8, as well as a dozen participants from developing countries, meet for one week to discuss the thematic issues addressed by the official G8 Summit. Following deliberations, the youth delegates issue a written declaration, which is presented to the heads of State attending the G8.

A Few Examples of International Summits

Group of 8 (G8)

Who? ▪ The G8 brings together eight of the most economically powerful countries. These States alone represent approximately two thirds of the gross world product (GWP), even though they are home to less than 15% of the world's population.

When? ▪ To deal with the economic problems that arose at the beginning of the 1970s, a first summit of leading nations brought together Germany, the United States, France, Italy, Japan and the United Kingdom in 1975. Canada joined the group the next year, followed by Russia in 1998.

Why? ▪ The G8 is a discussion forum for analysis and deliberation on pressing international issues, such as the economy, defence, education, development and the environment. The particular themes change each year.

How? ▪ Each year, the leaders of the G8 countries meet for two or three days in one of the member countries. Other countries or international organizations may also be invited.

Members of the G8
Canada, France, Germany, Italy, Japan, Russia, the United Kingdom and the United States
🔻 3.11

Group of 20 (G20)

Members of the G20
Argentina, Australia, Brazil, Canada, China, the European Union, France, Germany, India, Indonesia, Italy, Japan, Mexico, Russia, South Africa, Saudi Arabia, South Korea, Turkey, the United Kingdom and the United States
3.12 🔻

Who? ▪ The G20 includes the industrialized member countries of the G8, 11 other countries with emerging economies and a representative of the European Union. Together, these participants represent over 90% of the gross world product, approximately 80% of international trade and two thirds of the global population.

When? ▪ The G20 was created in 1999 to deal with the financial crises of the 1990s.

Why? ▪ The G20 is above all a forum for economic consultation. It is more representative than the G8, since it takes into account the economic weight of several countries undergoing major growth, such as China, Brazil and India.

How? ▪ The G20 summits are held annually and bring together the finance ministers and central bank directors of the member States. Special meetings that bring together the heads of State can also be organized.

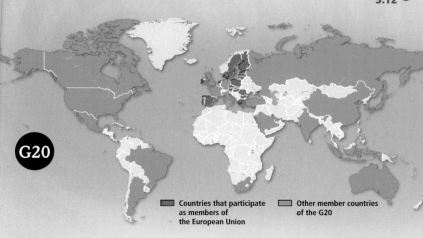

Countries that participate as members of the European Union ▢ Other member countries of the G20

INTERGOVERNMENTAL ORGANIZATIONS

To bolster their capacity to act, most independent States associate with other countries in some way. This collaboration can take the form of signed treaties, informal meetings (for example, during international summits) or adherence to structured intergovernmental organizations.

Strength in Numbers

3.13 📷
Meeting of the leaders of the Commonwealth of Independent States (CIS), a regional group of countries that once belonged to the USSR (2000)

Today, there are many intergovernmental organizations with varying degrees of specializations. Some, like the United Nations, have a universal mission, while others only bring together States from a certain region within the framework of specific activities (military, economic, cultural, etc.).

States that belong to these organizations enjoy certain advantages. Members of a given group usually enjoy privileged relations with each other and can take advantage of certain predetermined benefits. For example, the members of a military alliance lend their support if an enemy attacks one of them, while those who belong to an economic group may benefit from preferential tariffs when trading with each other. With these advantages come obligations. For instance, States agree to partially delegate their sovereign power to the organization they belong to.

CANADA ON THE INTERNATIONAL SCENE

Canada participates in many intergovernmental organizations, including:

- United Nations
- Commonwealth of Nations
- International Organization of the Francophonie (OIF)
- Organization of American States (OAS)
- North Atlantic Treaty Organization (NATO)
- North American Free Trade Agreement (NAFTA)
- Organization for Economic Cooperation and Development (OECD)
- World Trade Organization (WTO)
- Asia-Pacific Economic Cooperation (APEC)

IN BRIEF

3.14 📷
The Prime Minister of Canada, Stephen Harper, in front of the flags of the member countries during the Francophonie Summit (2008)

International Organization of the Francophonie (OIF)

Who? ▪ This organization is comprised of 56 member States and governments for which the French language holds a special status.

When? ▪ Founded in 1970.

Why? ▪ To increase cooperation among countries with a francophone culture.

How? ▪ The OIF has several specialized bodies and organizes the Francophonie Summit every two years to discuss the economy and international politics.

Commonwealth of Nations

Who? ▪ This organization is comprised of 53 States that used to belong to the British Empire.

When? ▪ Founded in 1926.

Why? ▪ To promote democracy, human rights, peace and free trade.

How? ▪ The Commonwealth of Nations has several specialized bodies and organizes various activities, including the Commonwealth Games every four years and the Commonwealth Heads of Government Meeting every two years to discuss the economy and international politics.

Two examples of cultural intergovernmental agencies ▼ 3.15

◼ The Francophonie
◼ The Commonwealth of Nations

0 1500 3000
kilometres

Various Types of Intergovernmental Organizations

Security organizations

Military alliances represent the oldest type of intergovernmental organization. Other security organizations seek instead to restrict the use of certain types of arms in order to increase security around the world.

Economic organizations

Most intergovernmental organizations are keenly interested in economic issues, some exclusively so.

Regional organizations

The United Nations is a universal organization, however, there are many regional intergovernmental organizations that seek to improve cooperation among neighbouring countries on various levels (political, social, economic, cultural, environmental, etc.).

Cultural organizations

States cooperate due to their cultural affinities. These cultural links can be based on a shared history, language or religion.

113

THE EUROPEAN UNION (I)

Europe has long been a politically divided continent. Some 50 countries coexist between the Atlantic Ocean and Russia's Ural Mountains. However, since the end of the Second World War, Europeans have gradually developed a feeling of collective identity and shared interests. This development has led to the gradual emergence of the European Union. This confederation of independent States is one of today's most advanced political associations.

A Precursor: The Marshall Plan

At the end of the Second World War, Europe was in shambles and its economy destroyed. With the beginning of the Cold War, the United States wanted a quick recovery in order to combat communism more effectively. It organized a vast financing operation, known as the Marshall Plan. Between 1948 and 1952, the United States invested close to $13 billion to bring stability to the countries of Western Europe.

The Treaty of Rome and the Founding of the European Economic Community (EEC)

The EEC pursued European economic integration by joining the European Coal and Steel Community (ECSC). It allowed for the development of a customs union (completed in 1968) and a common market for all agricultural and industrial production. Customs duties between member countries were gradually removed and a shared foreign trade policy was established. This led to a large increase in trade among the countries of the EEC.

1945   1947   1952   1955   1958   1962   1965   1967

1952

Member countries of the ECSC

3.16 ▲

The Creation of the European Coal and Steel Community (ECSC)

Six European countries (France, Germany, Italy, Belgium, Netherlands and Luxembourg) laid the foundation for an economic union by consolidating their production of coal and steel. The production of these two commodities is of symbolic importance, since they are vital to economic development ... and arms production.

SEEN AND HEARD

" . . . any war between France and Germany becomes not only unthinkable, but materially impossible. "

Robert Schuman, French Minister of Foreign Affairs (1950)
[Free translation]

3.17 ▶
European Union building in Brussels (2007)
Most institutions of the European Union are headquartered in Brussels (Belgium), Strasbourg (France) or Luxembourg (Luxembourg). Brussels is home to some of its most important agencies, including the Council of the European Union and the European Commission, making it the informal capital of Europe.

The Common Agricultural Policy (CAP)

CAP is the oldest community policy of the European Union. It seeks to promote European agricultural production through subsidies and measures that protect it from foreign competition. Other countries have sharply criticized the policy as unfair competition with respect to their own agricultural producers.

The Maastricht Treaty and the Founding of the European Union (EU)

The Maastricht Treaty led to the creation of the European Union (EU), a political and economic union of the States of the European Economic Community (EEC), with broader powers in the areas of foreign policy, security, justice and internal affairs. Within the EU, the EEC was replaced by the European Community (EC), which was given a broader objective: to establish an economic and monetary union between member countries through the free circulation of goods, services, money and people.

The Maastricht Treaty stipulates that individuals possessing the nationality of one of the member States of the Union also become European citizens. This citizenship allows them to freely circulate and work in any country of the Union, benefiting from that country's social rights. They can also vote in elections for the members of the European Parliament and exercise their right to vote during municipal elections in the country where they reside.

1973 1975   1981   1985 1986   1993 1995

1st Expansion

After lengthy discussions, Denmark, Ireland and the United Kingdom joined the EEC.

2nd and 3rd Expansions

Greece joined the EEC in 1981, followed by Spain and Portugal in 1986.

Merger of the European Communities

The ECSC, EEC and European Atomic Energy Community (Euratom) centralized their administrations.

3.18 ▶

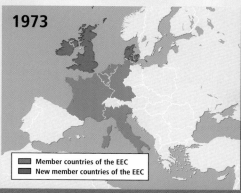

1973

Member countries of the EEC
New member countries of the EEC

◀ **3.19**

1986

Member countries of the EEC
New member countries of the EEC

THE EUROPEAN UNION (II)

THE EURO
A COMMON EUROPEAN CURRENCY

The European Union proposed a monetary union to its members, which would involve the use of a common currency. This measure would facilitate trade between member countries and strengthen regional economic integration. However, participants would lose a part of their economic sovereignty, which explains why some countries, like the United Kingdom and Denmark, have so far refused to join the euro area, despite its undeniable success.

Launching the Euro

The first bills and coins began to circulate in 2002 and quickly replaced the national currency of a number of countries. In 2009, the euro area was comprised of 16 member countries of the European Union and several others plan to adopt this currency.

2004

Member countries of the EEC
New member countries of the EEC

▲ 3.21

Major Expansion

Ten new States joined the European Union: the islands of Malta and Cyprus, as well as eight countries from Eastern Europe. In 2007, Romania and Bulgaria also joined.

1995   1999   2004 2005   2010

4th Expansion and the Schengen Accords

Austria, Finland and Sweden joined the European Union. The same year, the Schengen Accords, which removed border controls between the signatory countries, came into effect. Since 1997, all member countries of the European Union have been obliged to participate in the Schengen Accords, with the exception of Great Britain and Ireland, which were given special status.

1995

Member countries of the EEC
Countries that joined to form the EU

▲ 3.20

The Constitutional Question

To render the Union more efficient and simpler to manage, efforts are underway to adopt a European constitution. However, negotiations are difficult, and several treaties have only managed to reform existing institutions without creating a new constitution. In 2009, discussions are ongoing.

3.22 ▶
European Union flag

The great expansion of 2004 constituted a major eastward extension of the European Union's borders. Some countries along the current border of this political association may now be interested in joining the group. In fact, Turkey has already shown interest. However, at this point the debate surrounding the modalities for integrating this densely populated Islamic country (72 million inhabitants) is ongoing.

The European Union in 2009
- Area: 4 324 782 km²
- Population: Close to 500 000 000
- Member States: 27
- Official languages: 23
- Total GDP (in 2007): US$14,430,000 million
- GDP per inhabitant (in 2007): US$32,700

▼ **3.23**

The European Union is both a *transnational* organization, bringing together independent States, and a *supranational* organization, having created a new level of government above those of the member countries. The European Union possesses its own powers and institutions that are similar to those of a State.

The European Parliament ▪ Approves and controls

Since 1979, the European Parliament has been composed of members elected by universal suffrage for a period of five years. Each country elects a number of members that varies depending on its population. The Parliament cannot propose laws, but rather offers its opinion on those advanced by the Council of the European Union. Depending on the issues presented, these opinions can be merely consultative, or they can constitute necessary approval for passing laws. The Parliament also exercises control over the European Union's budget and the functioning of its other institutions.

The Council of the European Union ▪ Decides

Also known as the Council of Ministers, this agency studies bills from member States or the European Commission and decides whether or not they will be passed. The Council brings together ministers from the governments of each State, who defend the interests of their respective countries and try to reach compromises. The ministers involved change depending on the issue at hand. When voting, the number of votes each State has varies based on the size of its population.

The European Commission ▪ Proposes and implements

The 27 commissioners (one per country) who sit on this body are responsible for proposing laws for the entire European Union. Once the Council and Parliament have accepted these laws, the Commission implements them. It also oversees the enforcement of treaties and manages the European Union's budget. As such, it has very broad powers.

JUSTICE AND INTERNATIONAL LAW

Most conflicts between States are resolved through diplomacy, with discussions and agreements carried out directly between the countries involved or with the help of other countries playing the role of intermediary. In some cases, however, diplomacy does not lead to an acceptable solution for both parties. Rather than resorting to war, it is possible to turn to arbitration by international institutions.

International Law

A certain number of rules govern relations between States.

Clearly defined rules

Some of these rules are clearly explained in international treaties that are signed by numerous States, for example, the United Nations Convention on the Law of the Sea or the Geneva Convention on Prisoners of War.

Established practices

Other rules of international law are not so formally defined. Rather, they are longstanding, established practices, for example, the right of a State to defend itself if attacked, or basic moral principles, such as the prohibition of crimes against humanity (genocide, slavery, torture, piracy and wars of aggression).

The limitations of international law

No global power can impose its laws on every country on the planet. The application of international law depends in large part on the willingness of States to respect it. Some countries voluntarily do so, while others adamantly defend their sovereignty, the right to act when they see fit. The United States, China and Israel, for example, refuse to have their soldiers judged by international tribunals for war crimes.

Nevertheless, States exercise significant pressure on each other to respect their commitments and obligations. A country that rejects the basic rules of international law will quickly find itself isolated and will have to deal with the consequences: it could be subject to diplomatic sanctions (the withdrawal of ambassadors, for example), economic sanctions (an embargo) or even military sanctions imposed by other countries.

◀ 3.24
Statue of Justitia, the Roman goddess of justice

INTERPOL

International tribunals are not the only organizations that encourage cooperation among States in terms of justice. Interpol is an institution that seeks to improve collaboration among the police forces of various States. IN PARTICULAR, INTERPOL FIGHTS INTERNATIONAL CRIMES, SUCH AS DRUG TRAFFICKING, TERRORISM, MONEY LAUNDERING AND ORGANIZED CRIME.

International Tribunals

In an effort to prevent conflicts between States from degenerating into war, an international legal system has evolved since the Second World War. Several treaties now include clauses to create special international tribunals. For example, the United Nations Convention on the Law of the Sea has led to the creation of the International Tribunal for the Law of the Sea to resolve maritime conflicts. Regional tribunals have also been created to solve problems between neighbouring States, for example, the Court of Justice of the European Communities or the Caribbean Court of Justice in the case of Caribbean countries.

The United Nations and International Law

Certain United Nations organizations, like the General Assembly or the Security Council, also have powers that allow them to intervene in international conflicts. The United Nations' most important judicial organization, however, is the International Court of Justice (ICJ).

Only States can solve their disputes before the ICJ. Questions of international law related to individuals, such as those accused of crimes against humanity, are tried by another tribunal, the International Criminal Court. A growing number of States are turning to the ICJ, and they must agree to abide by the court's rulings. If they do not respect the rulings, the United Nations Security Council can decide to intervene, although this is very rare.

SNAPSHOT OF TODAY

ⓐ How would you define the concept of "international law"?

ⓑ Have you seen anything in recent news about international law?

🔺 3.25
The Peace Palace, in The Hague, Netherlands, which houses the International Court of Justice (ICJ) (2006)

NON-GOVERNMENTAL ORGANIZATIONS

Over the last few decades, citizen groups that work independently of their governments have come to occupy an ever-greater place on the international stage. The associations they create to defend particular causes are known as non-governmental organizations (NGOs). They are playing an increasingly important role in international relations.

Characteristics of NGOs

They must be formed by citizens working on a voluntary basis and must have no ties to any government.

They are non-profit organizations.

3.26
Grain distribution by Doctors Without Borders during a famine in Niger (2005)
Many NGOs work directly in the field to help the populations whose interests they defend.

NGO Actions

Given the influence NGOs can have on governments, intergovernmental organizations and even multinationals, they enjoy significant political weight. NGOs use a wide variety of means to achieve their goals.

Mobilize and sensitize

To mobilize public opinion and sensitize leaders to the causes they defend, NGOs conduct research, disseminate information, organize demonstrations and other public events, conduct lobbying activities, carry out public relations campaigns, raise funds, etc.

NGOs as consultants

Not only do NGOs serve as consultants in their area of expertise within States or intergovernmental organizations, a number also serve as consultants within various specialized institutions of the United Nations.

In the field

Many NGOs are active in the field, where they carry out a variety of projects.

THE WORLD ECONOMIC FORUM
AND THE WORLD SOCIAL FORUM

Governments are not the only ones to use international summits to discuss issues and express points of view. Members of civil society, such as NGOs, also organize major international events. The annual World Economic Forum (WEF), a gathering of business leaders, political leaders, intellectuals and media personalities in Davos, Switzerland, is a good examples of this. The forum is an opportunity for participants to discuss major global issues.

However, many question the effectiveness and democracy of this posh and very exclusive forum. Another international movement, the World Social Forum (WSF), has been created to allow NGOs from around the world to meet and offer a different point of view. Here, participants meet to find solutions that will help to change the world in positive ways.

3.27 ▶
Davos, Switzerland (2005)
Each year, major security measures are put in place in order to welcome the guests of the World Economic Forum and keep the many demonstrators at a distance.

A Broad Range of NGOs

NGOs work in many different fields, including health, humanitarian projects, the environment, economics, etc. Some NGOs are national, which means that they work in a single country, while others are international and work in many different countries.

A few examples of international NGOs and their missions

Political or economic NGOs
- **Transparency International (TI):** fights government corruption around the world
- **Association for the Taxation of Financial Transactions to Aid Citizens (ATTAC):** promotes democratic monitoring of financial institutions and markets in order to promote development

Human rights NGOs
- **Amnesty International:** carries out actions to prevent and to bring an end to human rights violations, including violations of political, social, cultural and economic rights
- **Reporters Without Borders:** fights laws that restrict freedom of the press and defends journalists who are persecuted or imprisoned for their work
- **Human Rights Watch:** documents human rights violations in order to draw international attention to these cases
- **World Organization Against Torture:** fights torture, summary executions and any other cruel and inhumane treatment

Environmental NGOs
- **Greenpeace:** protects the environment through educational campaigns, research and the promotion of emerging ecological solutions
- **World Wide Fund for Nature (WWF):** protects biodiversity around the world, promotes sustainable development and fights pollution

Humanitarian NGOs
- **International Committee of the Red Cross:** protects and assists the victims of armed conflicts
- **Oxfam International:** fights poverty and injustice around the world
- **Doctors Without Borders:** offers emergency medical assistance to populations at risk

121

PROTECTIONISM VERSUS FREE TRADE

States play a key role in the economy. Through their policies, they regulate and shape the economy in order to strengthen it and promote its growth. They also influence international trade by opening or closing their borders to trade with other countries, depending on what seems to be the most profitable.

Protectionist Policies

Protectionism is an economic policy adopted by a State to protect either its national production and its businesses or a sector of its economy. In industrializing countries, protectionism serves in particular to protect emerging industries, allowing them to develop safeguarded from foreign competition and to position themselves on the market. Protectionist measures can take various forms and can affect the quantity, the price or the quality of the country's imports or exports.

3.28 ▶ Types of protectionist measures

Tariff barriers Taxes and customs duties that a State imposes on imports or exports.	
Ad valorem tariffs	Tax or customs duty representing a percentage of the value of an imported or exported good.
Specific tariffs	A per unit, fixed amount applied to imported goods, regardless of the total value of these goods.
Non-tariff measures Protectionist measures other than customs duties.	
Quotas	Limits on the quantity of an imported good, either by establishing a maximum number of units of the imported good or by establishing the maximum value beyond which a given good is prohibited from entering the national market.
Standards	The development of health, security or environmental standards that must be respected by imported goods. This makes it possible to control the quality of products and to limit the entry of certain products onto the national market.
Export subsidies	Subsidies granted by the State to national corporations to allow them to compete on the international market.
Administrative procedures	Implementation of burdensome administrative measures (customs clearance for merchandise, requirement of import permits, etc.) designed to discourage importers.
Country of origin	The obligation to indicate the product's country of origin. This measure is intended to foster a sense of nationalism among consumers who often prefer to buy domestic products.

The La Rochelle port in France (2001)
In the time of New France, the La Rochelle port was one of the most important colonial trade centres. Ships entering the port were monitored and had to pay a port tax that was set on the basis of the types of products imported and their place of origin.

Free Trade

What is free trade?

Free trade is an economic policy based on the free circulation of goods and services. The opposite of protectionism, this system of international trade eliminates tariff barriers and non-tariff measures that hinder free international trade. Free trade expands economic markets and increases business opportunities for corporations. Foreign competition stimulates overall corporate productivity and, based on the logic of the laws of the market, leads to lower prices.

Free trade theory

According to free trade theoreticians, this economic policy should lead to specialized production in each country or region. Each nation should come to produce goods that give it a competitive advantage, based on the resources available in its territory. This will allow it both to sell its goods on the market at advantageous prices and to purchase goods that it does not produce at competitive prices. In the long term, free trade should promote overall economic development.

FREE TRADE ZONES

Free trade zones are geographic areas where industrial activities enjoy tax advantages. Merchandise that enters or leaves these zones or is warehoused there is not controlled or subject to customs duties. States use free trade zones to encourage foreign investors to set up factories and to stimulate international trade.

For example, in 2006, China began construction of its largest free trade port zone, the Dongjiang zone, in Tianjin, northeast China. With an area of 30 km², this zone includes materials distribution and processing areas, service areas and docks.

China's main free trade zones (2008)
3.30

Russia

Mongolia

China

India

Tianjin • Dalian •

Qingdao •

Zhangjiagang •

Shanghai •
Ningbo •

Fuzhou •

Xiamen •
Shantou •
Guangzhou • Shenzhen •
Zhuhai • Hong Kong

Haikou •

Myanmar   Vietnam

Laos

North Korea

South Korea

Japan

Taiwan

PACIFIC OCEAN

0   300   600
kilometres

INTERNATIONAL TRADE

There is nothing new about international trade. In antiquity, the Egyptians, Greeks and Romans developed vast trade networks with foreign nations.

Historical Perspective

Over the last two centuries, international trade has intensified as a result of both the development of means of transportation and increased production. Trade relations between countries have also evolved toward greater trade liberalization, a phenomenon that affects the entire planet today.

🔺 **3.31**
A farm in Italy (1998)
Starting in the 1980s, the issue of agricultural trade caused tensions between the United States, which wanted to liberalize it, and the European Union, which wanted to protect it.

The Beginning of Trade Liberalization

In 1860, the world's first major industrial power, Great Britain, signed a trade treaty with France, marking the beginning of a process of commercial trade liberalization in Europe. Up until 1929, most industrialized countries imitated Great Britain, and international trade rose dramatically, even though protectionist measures were not completely abandoned.

After the Second World War

In an effort to avoid a repeat of the economic instability of the 1930s, Western governments decided to work together. In 1944, in Bretton Woods, United States, 44 States gathered to establish an international monetary system. Three years later, 23 countries signed the General Agreement on Tariffs and Trade (GATT), opening an era of free trade that persists to this day.

1860 1900 1929 1945 2000

Economic Crisis and the Second World War

The economic crisis of 1929 caused an unprecedented collapse of production, wages and prices throughout the industrialized world. States moved to protect their national markets, erecting tariff barriers. The United States led the way in 1930, imposing a 40% tariff on all imports. Other nations quickly followed suit, causing international trade to plummet.

DSB THE DISPUTE SETTLEMENT BODY

- At its inception, the WTO established a permanent body to solve trade disputes between member nations. The decisions arrived at by the experts who make up the DSB must be respected by the nations involved, unless there is a consensus among the members affected to reject a ruling.

- Between its creation and January 2009, the DSB received 390 complaints, mostly from developed countries. The United States has been the most often accused (27%), while Canada received only 15 complaints between 1995 and 2002 (4%).

The Basic Principles of GATT and the WTO

- **Reciprocity:** each nation accords trade concessions in order to benefit from those offered by other countries.

- **Non-discrimination:** the benefits accorded to one nation are automatically accorded to all signatories of the agreement.

- **Limited obstacles:** customs duties are the only permissible trade barrier.

- **Consolidation of customs duties:** signatory countries cannot increase customs duties once they have been established through negotiation.

- **National treatment:** imports must receive the same treatment as comparable domestic products.

- **Escape clauses:** in certain specific cases, countries can be authorized to protect themselves. For example, developing countries benefit from special treatment that allows them to protect their emerging industries.

General Agreement on Tariffs and Trade (GATT)

Who? ■ At its inception, the General Agreement on Tariffs and Trade (GATT) was signed by 23 countries. Renewed periodically, there were 120 signatory countries in 1994.

When? ■ It came into effect on January 1, 1948.

Why? ■ GATT serves as a framework for multilateral negotiations that seek to reduce tariff barriers and obstacles to international trade.

How? ■ There have been eight rounds of trade negotiations that have dramatically reduced customs duties among signatory countries. A number of areas, including agriculture, textiles and services, are not covered by GATT.

World Trade Organization (WTO)

Who? ■ 112 GATT signatory countries established the World Trade Organization (WTO) following extensive negotiations, known as the Uruguay Round (1986–1994). In July 2008, the organization had 153 member States.

When? ■ The WTO headquarters opened its doors in Geneva on January 1, 1995.

Why? ■ The WTO is a permanent institution that seeks to manage multilateral trade agreements (including GATT).

How? ■ It is responsible for gradually extending free trade to additional areas of activity, particularly agriculture, services, textiles and intellectual property. It also seeks to dismantle non-tariff barriers that hinder trade, particularly export subsidies.

WTO member countries
▼ 3.32

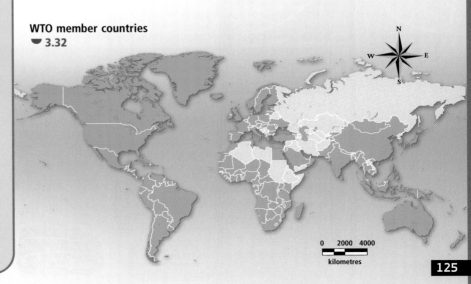

0   2000   4000
kilometres

ECONOMIC ASSOCIATIONS

Regional economic agreements multiplied in the second half of the 20th century. While these economic partnerships would appear to run counter to the principles of GATT and the WTO, escape clauses have allowed for their development.

Regional Unions

With growing globalization of the economy, many countries are seeking to recreate protected economic markets, most often with neighbouring partners. They sign free trade agreements in order to encourage the economic and social development of their regions and, in some cases, to promote political stability. The 1980s saw an increase in the number of regional unions, while the emergence of new industrialized countries like South Korea, Singapore, Mexico and Indonesia created new hubs of competition and the world entered an economic crisis. During its first 10 years of existence, from 1995 to 2005, the World Trade Organization (WTO) ratified 206 economic integration agreements. Almost all of the member States of the WTO participated in one or more of these agreements.

The Stages of Economic Integration

The various international trade agreements do not all lead to the same degree of economic integration. There are successive stages of integration, as described in the table below. This model, largely inspired by the integration process of the European Community, shows how, at each stage, States lose a little of their independence in decisions affecting their commercial policies in favour of the economic integration zone.

3.33 ▶ The stages of economic integration

	1 Free trade zone	**2** Customs union	**3** Common market	**4** Economic and monetary union
Removal of customs tariffs and quotas on the trade of goods and services	X	X	X	X
Common external tariffs with respect to third countries		X	X	X
Elimination of obstacles to the free circulation of goods, services, capital and labour			X	X
Harmonization of economic policies			X	X
Harmonization of monetary and fiscal policies (taxes)				X

Source: D. Éthier, *Introduction aux relations internationales*. Montréal: Presses universitaires de Montréal, 2006

NORTH AMERICAN TRADE

Under NAFTA, trade between the member States has tripled. Every day, merchandise valued at US$2.5 billion is traded among its partners. THIS IS EQUIVALENT TO OVER $10 MILLION AN HOUR.

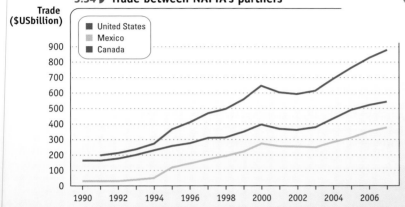

3.34 ▶ Trade between NAFTA's partners

Trade ($USbillion)

Legend:
- United States
- Mexico
- Canada

Source: Statistics Canada, U.S. Department of Commerce and the Secretariat of the Economy Mexico, [On-line], 2009.

North American Free Trade Agreement (NAFTA)

Who? ▪ NAFTA is a free trade agreement between Canada, the United States and Mexico.

When? ▪ Signed in 1992, NAFTA came into effect on January 1, 1994. It replaced the Free Trade Agreement (FTA) that had existed between the United States and Canada since 1989.

Why? ▪ NAFTA's objectives include eliminating customs barriers and facilitating the trade of goods and services among the three signatory countries. This agreement also liberalizes investments and financial services among these countries.

How? ▪ NAFTA gives North America some of the characteristics of a common market. However, the States do not impose the same customs tariffs on the other countries and preserve their full independence in terms of economic policy.

Results ▪ With a total production of US$16,200 billion in 2007, North America is the second largest free trade zone in the world after the European Union.

Major economic associations
3.35

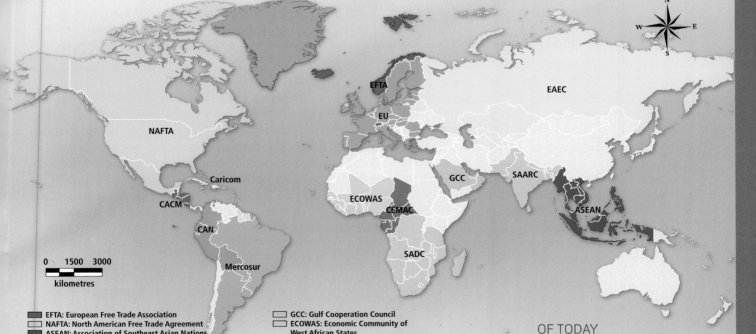

- EFTA: European Free Trade Association
- NAFTA: North American Free Trade Agreement
- ASEAN: Association of Southeast Asian Nations
- SAARC: South Asian Association for Regional Cooperation
- CAN: Andean Community
- Caricom: Caribbean Community
- GCC: Gulf Cooperation Council
- ECOWAS: Economic Community of West African States
- EAEC: Eurasian Economic Community
- CEMAC: Central African Economic and Monetary Community
- CACM: Central American Common Market
- Mercosur: Southern Common Market
- SADC: Southern African Development Community
- EU: European Union

OF TODAY

SNAPSHOT

Define the concept of "integration."

127

INTERNATIONAL FINANCE

International financial transactions have grown exponentially since the end of the Second World War. More than ever, capital circulates from country to country. Control over this exchange of money has become a major issue for States. Should it be given free rein or regulated?

The Evolution of International Finance

A new global economic system

At the end of the Second World War, 730 delegates from 44 States gathered in Bretton Woods, United States, to develop a new global economic system. They hoped to achieve a more efficient coordination of State financial policies in order to facilitate international trade and to create a solid framework for rebuilding the countries devastated by the war.

Bretton Woods Accord

The Bretton Woods Accord was signed on July 22, 1944. The main elements of this new economic cooperation were the creation of institutions like the International Monetary Fund (IMF) and the International Bank for Reconstruction and Development (IBRD), as well as the establishment of a fixed exchange rate for all currencies based on the American dollar. This fixed exchange rate brought greater stability to the global economic system, but limited the freedom of governments that wanted to influence the value of their currency.

A glorious three decades and the demise of Bretton Woods

For close to 30 years, the Bretton Woods system worked well and helped to rebuild the economies of Europe and Japan, while continuing to enrich the United States. In the early 1970s, the global economic situation began to deteriorate. In 1971, several countries abandoned the fixed exchange rate in favour of greater freedom of action, which marked the end of the Bretton Woods Accord.

Market liberalization

The move toward economic liberalization, that is to say, reduced regulation, continued through the 1980s and 1990s. Its advocates argue that financial markets function better when they are left untouched. Other economists argue that State intervention is necessary to preserve the stability of the international economic system and to ensure equitable trade. The debate on this issue rages on.

3.36 ▶
The Canadian delegation at Bretton Woods (1944)

John Maynard Keynes

Considered one of the most influential economists of the 20th century, John Maynard Keynes (1883–1946) played a key role in developing the Bretton Woods Accord. He favoured active State intervention in economic affairs. Keynesianism, the economic theory inspired by this man, opposes economic liberalism, which advocates State disengagement.

IMF THE INTERNATIONAL MONETARY FUND

Created in 1945 under the Bretton Woods Accord, the IMF has 185 member States. This institution, integrated into the United Nations system, is responsible for ensuring the stability of the international economic system. The IMF intervenes in financial crises by lending money to countries in difficulty. These loans are conditional, however, on the adoption of economic reforms aimed at stabilizing and liberalizing the economy of the borrowing country. This condition is sometimes criticized, because it limits the sovereignty of the borrowing countries, which are forced to comply with conditions imposed by an international organization.

3.37 ▶
IMF headquarters in Washington, D.C. (2008)

Exchange Rate

How many euros is a Canadian dollar worth? How many yens can be purchased with a pound sterling? At the time of the Bretton Woods system (1944–1971), this value was fixed, but today it depends primarily on supply and demand. A currency's exchange rate, its value in relation to another, is constantly re-evaluated in order to reflect its availability and popularity. Investors generally prefer strong currencies that have a stable value subject to only minor fluctuation.

THE WORLD BANK GROUP

The World Bank Group is a group of international financial institutions led by the International Bank for Reconstruction and Development (IBRD). Founded in 1945 under the Bretton Woods Accord, the role of the bank was to help fund the reconstruction of countries devastated by the Second World War. Today, it lends money to governments and corporations in developing countries. Like the IMF, the World Bank Group provides loans that are conditional on the adoption of administrative and structural reforms.

◀ **3.38**
World Bank headquarters in Washington, D.C. (2008)

129

MULTINATIONAL CORPORATIONS

Multinational corporations are essential to the globalization of the economy. They are responsible for a major portion of global production and sell goods and services around the world. Over the last few decades, the number, the labour force and the sales figures of these corporations have all undergone phenomenal growth.

Reasons for the Creation of Multinationals

Multinational corporations (also called transnational corporations) are large-scale businesses established in several countries. Productive affiliates (or subsidiaries) are established abroad for a number of reasons:

- to achieve greater proximity to the primary resources needed for production
- to circumvent protectionist measures implemented by States that limit international trade transactions
- to find external markets for their products, particularly when competition becomes more intense in their home country
- to pay lower production costs than in their home country

Multinationals and States

Transnational corporations are extremely powerful: some of them manage sums of money comparable to the revenue of an entire State. In 2007–2008, the federal government of Canada managed $244.5 billion in revenue, which is less than the sales figures of the largest multinationals (see the table on the right). Through their lobbying efforts, multinationals influence State policies, since they employ millions of people and invest enormous sums of money in the countries where they are established. Governments therefore use a variety of incentives, including free trade zones, to attract these corporations.

States cannot completely control the activities of these transnational corporations. Present in many countries simultaneously, these corporations create their own economic space and exploit, for their own gain, the differences that exist between the social and environmental laws of various States.

Several international organizations have tried to regulate their activities, particularly the International Labour Organization (ILO), however, there is nothing that requires multinationals to respect the principles of international organizations.

◢ 3.39
La Grande-3 generating station in Northern Québec
Many States have nationalized some of their natural resources in order to own and manage these resources and prevent them from falling into the hands of multinationals. Québec did this in 1963 with the creation of Hydro-Québec.

THE FIRST MULTINATIONAL CORPORATION

Founded in 1602, the Dutch East India Company is considered the first multinational corporation in history. Established primarily in Indonesia, India, China, Japan and South Africa, it was the largest European company created during the colonial era to exploit the wealth of Asia. Two centuries later, it had approximately 4700 ships, transported over one million Europeans and EMPLOYED UP TO 150 000 PEOPLE AT ONE TIME.

3.40 ▶
Dutch engraving (1682)
The market in Batavia, the Dutch East India Company's commercial capital, in the 17th century.

Multinationals in Numbers

- According to the United Nations Conference on Trade and Development (UNCTAD), in 2006, there were **79 000 multinational corporations** controlling **790 000 subsidiaries**. In 1993, there were **37 000** controlling **175 000 subsidiaries**.

- In 2007, multinational corporations rung in **US$31,000 billion** in sales, a 21% increase from the preceding year.

- Approximately **two thirds of international trade** is conducted by multinational corporations.

- In 2007, multinational corporations employed approximately **82 million people**.

3.41 ▶ **The world's top 10 multinational corporations ranked by sales in US$million (2006)**

Corporation	Home country	Industry	Sales	Number of employees
❶ **Exxonmobil Corp.**	United States	Petroleum	365,467	82 100
❷ **Wal-Mart Stores**	United States	Retailing	344,992	1 910 000
❸ **Royal Dutch/Shell Group**	United Kingdom Netherlands	Petroleum	318,845	108 000
❹ **British Petroleum Co.**	United Kingdom	Petroleum	270,602	97 100
❺ **Toyota Motor Corp.**	Japan	Automobile	205,918	299 394
❻ **Chevron Corp.**	United States	Petroleum	204,892	62 500
❼ **Total**	France	Petroleum	192,952	95 070
❽ **ConocoPhillips**	United States	Petroleum	183,650	38 400
❾ **General Electric**	United States	Electrical and electronic equipment	163,391	319 000
❿ **Ford Motor Co.**	United States	Automobile	160,123	283 000

Source: UNCTAD, *World Investment Report*, [On-line], 2008.

GLOBAL PRODUCTION AND CONSUMPTION

Governments cannot legislate the agricultural methods and manufacturing processes of products from abroad. However, they can regulate production in their own territory, control the quality of products that enter their territory and adopt voluntary international production standards.

National Monitoring Organizations

Even if they sign free trade agreements with other countries, States can ban the entry of certain products if they do not meet quality standards. To inspect the quality of products that are sold in their territory, States have monitoring agencies, such as the Food and Drug Administration in the United States, the *Agence française de sécurité sanitaire et des produits de santé* in France and Health Canada here at home. In 2007, in many countries (including Canada), these agencies removed toothpaste imported from China and South Africa from the market because it contained *diethylene* glycol, a substance used as antifreeze and as a solvent.

International Standards Organization (ISO)

Who? ▪ The International Standards Organization (ISO), brings together the representatives of 159 countries.

When? ▪ Founded in 1947, this non-governmental organization is based in Geneva, Switzerland.

Why? ▪ Its mandate is to develop technical rules and production methods to be used in industry and trade internationally. These standards, called ISO standards, guarantee the quality of goods and services offered by companies that are certified by national standardization committees.

How? ▪ Over 200 technical committees are responsible for establishing these standards, each in a particular field: paint, textiles, plastics, steel, photography, leather, etc. These standards are voluntarily adopted by industries and businesses.

3.42 ▶ The best-known ISO standards

Standard	Title	Description
ISO 9001	Quality management systems	Quality requirements for the design, development, production, installation and after-sale services of a product or service
ISO 14001	Environmental management systems - Environmental protection	Control and continually improve a company's environmental performance

CODEX
ALIMENTARIUS

Created in 1963, the Codex Alimentarius is a compendium of food standards and practices which, while not mandatory, is recognized by 180 countries.

The Codex Alimentarius standards have a solid scientific basis that is internationally recognized in various fields, including food chemistry and food technologies. For example, they establish the acceptable maximum limits of pesticide or veterinary drug residues that foodstuffs can contain without posing a health risk.

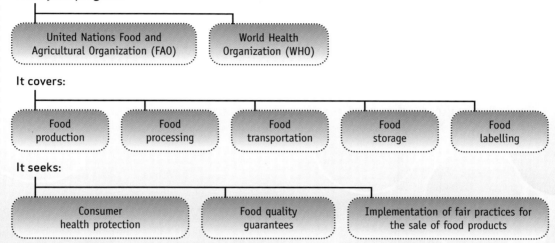

It is a joint program:

- United Nations Food and Agricultural Organization (FAO)
- World Health Organization (WHO)

It covers:

- Food production
- Food processing
- Food transportation
- Food storage
- Food labelling

It seeks:

- Consumer health protection
- Food quality guarantees
- Implementation of fair practices for the sale of food products

THE CHINESE CONTAMINATED MILK SCANDAL

3.43

Chinese scientists test milk samples (2008)
In September 2008, the Chinese government took many milk products off the market in order to conduct comprehensive tests.

The membership of a State in the Codex Alimentarius Commission does not always prevent food scandals. In 2008, in China, powdered baby milk from two major companies was contaminated with melamine, causing serious kidney problems in thousands of children. THREE HUNDRED THOUSAND BABIES WERE HOSPITALIZED, AND AT LEAST FOUR BABIES DIED.

Following the scandal, the person responsible for national food quality control resigned and Chinese authorities sent out over 1600 sanitation teams to monitor the country's milk industry. Despite this, several countries, including the European Union, suspended their imports of Chinese products containing powdered milk. In November 2008, the United States opened its first Food and Drug Administration inspection office in China in order to inspect foods and drugs produced there.

IN BRIEF

THE HOMOGENIZATION OF CULTURE

Over the last few decades, economic globalization and the development of communications technologies have led to the homogenization of culture. From Tokyo to Amsterdam, Buenos Aires to Casablanca, we increasingly find the same clothing, films, songs, restaurants and even cars.

Languages

English, the international language

English is the most studied language in the world and the most commonly used in international exchanges. In many economic sectors, English is the prevailing means of communication. Most of the scientific research is published in this language, whether it be in the fields of medicine, chemistry or engineering. English also dominates the Internet: 68% of data is in English (2000).

However, English is not the most spoken language in the world, since there are fewer native English speakers than Mandarin (Chinese) speakers.

Mandarin: The language of the 21st century?

If the trend continues, specialists predict that China will economically dominate the planet in the 21st century. The use of Mandarin is becoming a prerequisite in the business world. In fact, China has adopted a veritable international language and cultural policy. By 2020, it plans to have established 1000 Confucius Institutes around the world devoted to the dissemination of Chinese culture and the teaching of Mandarin. In October 2008, there were already 292 of these centres operating in 78 countries.

Countries where English is an official language
3.44 ▾

0   2000   4000

kilometres

After reading
the last four pages,
how would you define
the concept of
"homogenization"?

THE BIG MAC INDEX

Created in 1986 by the magazine *The Economist*, THE BIG MAC INDEX MEASURES PURCHASING POWER PARITY AROUND THE WORLD. In February 2009, the average cost of a Big Mac was the equivalent of US$3.36 in Canada, US$5.79 in Norway and US$1.83 in China. This index has become a serious tool used by economists. It clearly illustrates the globalization and dissemination of American-style fast food restaurants.

The Influence of Foreign Cultures

The domination of American culture

American culture has imposed itself around the world through film, music, fast food, clothing labels and its model of consumerism. Some people refer to this phenomenon as cultural imperialism.

- Of the five singers who have sold the most albums around the world, four of them are from the United States: Michael Jackson, Frank Sinatra, Elvis Presley and Bing Crosby.

- In 2007, American movies took in $26.7 billion at the box office, of which $17.1 billion was generated outside the United States. In Europe, in 2005, American movies represented 71% of box office sales.

- In China, KFC (Kentucky Fried Chicken) is the most popular fast food chain. In 2007, there were 2140 KFC restaurants in 406 cities. That year, Yum! corporation, which owns the KFC trademark, opened more than one restaurant a day in China. Its ultimate goal is to open 15 000 KFC restaurants across the country.

- In 2006, according to the ranking of the United Nations Conference on Trade and Development (UNCTAD), 21 of the 100 largest multinationals in the world were from the United States.

Replica of the Statue of Liberty, overlooking Rainbow Bridge, a suspension bridge over Tokyo Bay 3.45 ▼

Other influential cultures

The United States is not the only country to disseminate its culture and lifestyle around the world. For example, Japanese culture has spread to a number of countries. Restaurants serving sushi, a typical Japanese dish, are popping up everywhere, including hundreds in Québec. Japanese animation and comic strips (mangas) are prized by millions of people and translated into a number of languages. For example, 250 million copies of the 42-volume *Dragon Ball* series have been sold (2006), surpassing the famous *Tintin* series.

French culture also has a major presence in the world, particularly in terms of gastronomy, wine and fashion design.

THE PROTECTION OF CULTURES

The homogenization of culture through globalization is cause for concern. The range of cultural expression around the world is considered a precious heritage that belongs to all of humanity. Many States and international organizations are taking steps to protect cultural diversity and encourage artistic production.

Protecting Languages

According to UNESCO, over 3000 languages spoken around the world are in danger of disappearing by the end of the century, because there are too few speakers left to ensure their transmission. As a result, many governments are adopting concrete measures to protect their linguistic heritage.

For example, in 1992, the Council of Europe adopted the European Charter for Regional or Minority Languages, which has been ratified by 25 countries (2008). This charter seeks to have regional or minority languages in Europe recognized as expressions of cultural wealth. It also aims to promote their use in private and public life and to support their preservation through language courses.

Supporting Artistic Creation

Many States, particularly in developed countries, provide significant support to the cultural and artistic sectors: cinema, television, radio, theatre, dance, music, museums, book publishing, etc.

In Québec, government agencies like the *Conseil des arts et des lettres du Québec,* the *Société de développement des entreprises culturelles du Québec* and the *Fonds du patrimoine culturel québécois* provide grants to artists.

Without this support, the cultural life of many countries would be much less dynamic and possibly even overwhelmed by foreign productions, particularly from the United States. One method for preventing this invasion is to impose content quotas on radio or television so that a significant portion of this content comes from national production. This is the approach taken by the Canadian Radio-television and Telecommunications Commission (CRTC).

3.46 ▶

French actor Fabrice Lucchini in the film *Molière* (2006)
In France, the *Centre national de cinématographie* takes a percentage of the sale of all movie tickets and invests it in the writing, creation or dissemination of French-language works.

> *A language is a monument that is as respectable if not more so than a stone monument. Each culture represents an invaluable asset in human wealth. Every people has a capital of beliefs and institutions that represents an incomparable experience for all of humanity.*

Claude Lévi-Strauss
[Free translation]

◀ **3.47**
Signpost in Old Montréal (2005)

Cultural Exception

With the globalization of exchanges, States are under pressure to liberalize their cultural sector within the framework of the World Trade Organization (WTO) or other international economic agreements. Some States, particularly the United States, believe that government subsidies to the film, television, music, publishing or theatre industries violate free trade principles. Nonetheless, many States do not share this view and consider cultural goods and services to be vehicles for values and identity, not simply commercial goods.

THE CHARTER
OF THE FRENCH LANGUAGE

In Québec, in order to protect the status of the French language on a continent that is overwhelmingly anglophone, the government adopted the Charter of the French Language (Bill 101) in 1977. Since then, French is the only official language in Québec and must be prioritized in all areas of community life, particularly at work, in government services and on signs. In addition, children from immigrant families are required to attend French schools.

The Convention on the Protection of Cultural Diversity

To ensure the effective protection and promotion of cultural diversity, numerous States, including Canada and France, have worked for the adoption of an international convention. This convention, prepared under the guidance of UNESCO, was adopted in October 2005 and came into effect in March 2007. Canada was one of the first to ratify it.

The Convention's main principles are:

Principle of sovereignty

> *States have, in accordance with the Charter of the United Nations and the principles of international law, the sovereign right to adopt measures and policies to protect and promote the diversity of cultural expressions within their territory.*

Principle of the complementarities of economic and cultural aspects of development

> *Since culture is one of the mainsprings of development, the cultural aspects of development are as important as its economic aspects, which individuals and peoples have the fundamental right to participate in and enjoy.*

UNESCO, *Convention on the Protection and Promotion of the Diversity of Cultural Expressions*, 2005.

UNESCO AND THE PRESERVATION OF HERITAGE

The United Nations Educational, Scientific and Cultural Organization (UNESCO) seeks to build universal peace by promoting cooperation among nations through education, science, culture and communication. This institution steers a number of programs devoted to the protection of cultural diversity and its manifestations around the world.

Humanity's Heritage Around the World

UNESCO seeks to protect hundreds of sites around the world, because they possess outstanding value for humanity. In 2008, 878 natural and cultural sites were on the World Heritage List as a result of their historical, cultural, geographic or natural value for humanity.

Some of the cultural or natural sites are on a special list: the List of World Heritage in Danger. UNESCO has deemed these sites in danger due to natural disasters, war, urbanization or mass tourism, or because they require major restoration work.

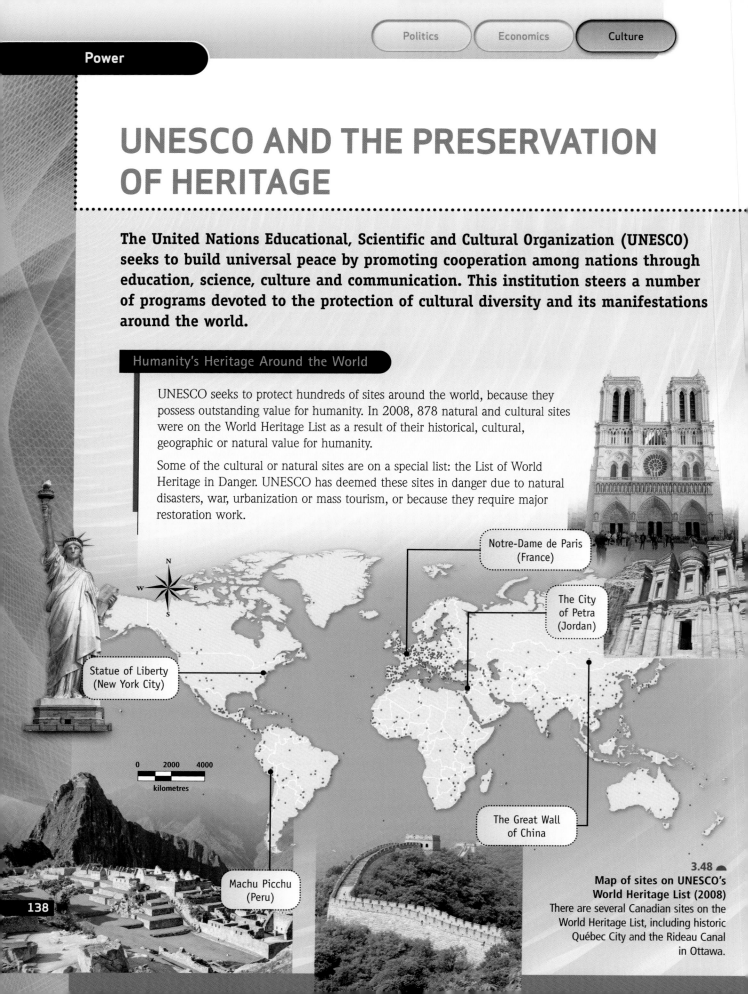

Notre-Dame de Paris (France)

The City of Petra (Jordan)

Statue of Liberty (New York City)

The Great Wall of China

0   2000   4000
kilometres

Machu Picchu (Peru)

3.48
Map of sites on UNESCO's World Heritage List (2008)
There are several Canadian sites on the World Heritage List, including historic Québec City and the Rideau Canal in Ottawa.

SAFEGUARDING THE ABU SIMBEL TEMPLES

From 1960 to 1968, UNESCO began dismantling the Abu Simbel temples in Egypt and rebuilding them 60 metres higher up river. Without this initiative, these majestic temples, built by Pharaoh Ramses II in the 13th and 14th centuries BCE, would have been flooded by the rising waters of the Nile caused by the construction of the Aswan hydroelectric dam. FORTY-SEVEN COUNTRIES AGREED TO FINANCE THIS MASSIVE PROJECT. This was a symbolic event, since it was UNESCO's first safeguarding operation.

3.49 ▶
The Great Temple of Abu Simbel

The Preservation of Intangible Cultural Heritage

Since culture is not only expressed through objects and monuments, UNESCO is also devoted to the preservation and dissemination of intangible heritage. This heritage, including oral traditions, languages, customs, dance, performance arts and traditional craftsmanship, forms the living expression of various cultures. With globalization and the homogenization of culture, this heritage is in danger of extinction, particularly because it is most often handed down orally from generation to generation.

To establish an inventory of intangible heritage around the world and work to safeguard it, UNESCO adopted the Convention for the Safeguarding of the Intangible Cultural Heritage in 2003. The list of intangible heritage already includes 90 masterpieces recognized since 2001, which are covered by a safeguarding plan, such as the Baltic songs and dances of Latvia, Estonia and Lithuania and the Day of the Dead festivities in Mexico. UNESCO is also working to draw up a list of heritage that requires emergency safeguarding, with objectives similar to those for heritage in danger.

◀ **3.50**
Dancers disguised as devils during the Oruro carnival in Bolivia (2001)
During the Oruro carnival parade, sumptuous costumes, magnificent painted masks, folkloric dances and songs reflect the influences of both indigenous and Spanish cultures.

MANAGING THE INTERNET

Since the 1990s, the Internet has revolutionized the world of culture and communications. Every day, cyberspace expands with thousands more new sites that can be viewed from anywhere on the planet. A key actor in globalization, some believe that the Internet should be managed by an organization and subject to international laws.

A Cultural Epicentre

The Internet is an incredible vector of culture. A virtually infinite source of information, it features all forms of expression: written, oral and visual. Millions of books and articles, reproductions of archives and works of art, photographs, video and comic strips can be found there. Internet surfers can also easily express their own ideas and opinions in cyberspace. Moreover, the Internet brings isolated communities into contact with knowledge, ideas and cultures from the rest of the world. It can therefore have a significant impact on populations, which has motivated some governments to try to control its content.

The enemies of the Internet according to Reporters Without Borders (2008)
Reporters Without Borders has denounced censorship of the Internet and the arrest of cyber-dissidents by establishing a list of enemies of the Internet.
▼ 3.51

0   2000   4000
kilometres

THE GREAT WALL OF CHINA

China places more limits on access to the Internet than any other country. The Chinese government hunts down sites that deal with human rights, democracy and freedom of thought. It has banned numerous foreign sites, as well as many Chinese sites, particularly blogs. The government achieves this through a combination of Internet filters (often referred to as the "Great Wall") and direct Internet surveillance of the network by tens of thousands of cyber police. It has not hesitated TO ARREST DOZENS OF INTERNET SURFERS ACCUSED OF PROPAGATING IDEAS THAT CONTRADICT THOSE OF THE COMMUNIST GOVERNMENT IN POWER.

Intellectual Property on the Internet

The rapid development of the Internet has raised serious copyright issues. Many surfers download music, films and photographs without paying royalties to the artists or the cultural industries that produced them. Others copy articles and excerpts of books that are available on the Internet, and then claim the content as their own. For artists and cultural industries, this theft of their works results in declining revenues.

To counter this phenomenon, the World Intellectual Property Organization (WIPO), a specialized UN organization, developed two international treaties in 1996. Adopted at a time when the Internet was only in its infant stages, these treaties are no longer able to respond to the current realities of the Internet. They are nonetheless a first step toward modernizing copyright law in light of these new technologies. Updating these treaties and ensuring their effective application would, however, require the creation of an international agency solely devoted to issues related to managing the Internet.

3.52 ◢

Brazilian journalists working in the main media centre of the Beijing Olympic Games
During the 2008 Olympic Games, foreign journalists covering the event had only limited access to the Internet.

Internet Corporation for Assigned Names and Numbers (ICANN)

Who? ▪ ICANN is one of the only international authorities that regulates the Internet. The organization was founded following a directive from the American Department of Commerce, but it brings together staff and administrators from around the world.

When? ▪ The organization was created in 1998 following negotiations between U.S. Vice-President Al Gore and telecommunications industries, equipment manufacturers and Internet content providers.

Why? ▪ This non-profit organization contributes to the operational stability of the Internet by ensuring that each site has a unique name.

How? ▪ ICANN manages the technical elements of the Internet: the organization is responsible for allocating space for Internet Protocol addresses (IP addresses), managing the Domain Name System (DNS) and so on. For example, ICANN attributes a national code to the Internet sites of each country.

Criticisms ▪ Many countries would like to see ICANN's functions taken over by a UN agency, because they feel that the organization is too closely linked to the U.S. administration.

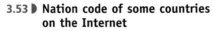

3.53 ▶ Nation code of some countries on the Internet

Country	National code
Germany	.de
Belgium	.be
Canada	.ca
France	.fr
Japan	.jp
Lebanon	.lb
United Kingdom	.uk
Senegal	.sn

CONCEPTS

Topic to Be Interpreted
The disparity in the distribution of wealth

Disparity (p. 153)
Concentration (p. 161)
Economic Development (p. 149)
Flows (p. 151)
Social Justice (p. 171)
Resource (p. 161)

Taking a Position (TAP)
TAP 1   Balancing social justice and economic development
OR
TAP 2   The control of resources

Despite the **sustained growth of the world economy** in the second half of the 20th century, **the distribution of wealth remains unequal.** What are the **causes** of this disparity and what **solutions** could be adopted to mitigate it?

WEALTH

4.1 ▶
More than a thousand women and children line up to get food at a humanitarian distribution centre in Niger (2005)

Knowledge Related to the Theme

- Debts and obligations of states (p. 154-155)
- Emerging economies (p. 152-153)
- Influence of colonization, decolonization and neocolonialism (p. 164-165)
- International organizations (p. 166-167)
- International trade (p. 150-151)
- North-South relations (p. 152 to 155, 162-163)
- Power of multinational firms (p. 162-163)
- Social gaps (p. 152-153, 156-157)
- Wealth creation (p. 148 to 151)

Cultural References

- Oxfam (1942) (p. 174)
- *We Are the World* (1985) (p. 175)
- Fair Trade/TransFair Canada (1997) (p. 173)
- Muhammad Yunus (1940-) (p. 170)

ECONOMIC CONCEPTS AND INDICATORS

To measure the wealth of a country and its population at a specific point in time, economists developed economic concepts and indicators that help them to understand the disparities in the world's wealth.

What Is Wealth?

Wealth is the result of a community's economic activity, of the **production**, **distribution** and **consumption** of goods and services.

Production consists of creating goods and services for trade on the market. It excludes work done for oneself.

Distribution includes all the operations that follow production and precede the purchase of the good by the consumer: transportation, marketing, inventory management, etc.

Consumption is the use of a good or service by a customer, a person or a company.

Comparison Tools

Economic indicators make it possible to compare the wealth of countries, regions or cities and to measure their economic development. The results are generally presented in U.S. dollars.

- **Purchasing-Power Parity (PPP):** Using a common currency is not sufficient when comparing countries' economies. Economists use purchasing-power parity to take into account the fact that the cost of living differs from one country to the next. This method measures the quantity of goods and services that can be purchased with a given currency in each of the countries or regions being compared.

- **Constant dollar:** The constant dollar is a theoretical currency whose purchasing power does not change over time. In other words, it eliminates variations due to inflation (rising prices) and deflation (falling prices). The constant dollar is useful when studying the development of the economy over time.

4.2 ▶ The Big Mac Index for several countries, in US$ (2008)

Country	Index
Norway	7.88
Switzerland	6.37
United Kingdom	4.57
Canada	4.09
United States	3.57
Russia	2.54
South Africa	2.24
Sri Lanka	1.95
China	1.83
Malaysia	1.70

Source: *The Economist, Big Mac Index*, [On-line], 2008.

The price of a Big Mac is a good way of comparing the cost of living in different countries.

100-TRILLION DOLLAR BILLS

Since 2000, the African country of Zimbabwe has seen unprecedented inflation. In July 2008, the inflation rate was estimated at 230 million percent a year. This hyperinflation forced the Bank of Zimbabwe to issue bills in denominations of 10, 20, 50 and 100 trillion Zimbabwean dollars to counteract the cash shortage. WHEN THEY WERE ISSUED IN JANUARY 2009, EACH ZIMBABWEAN 100 000 000 000 000-DOLLAR BILL WAS WORTH ONLY US$30.

4.3 ▶ A Zimbabwean 10-trillion dollar bill (2009)

4.4 ▶ **Main economic indicators (2007)**

	Canada	Brazil
Population	32 876 000	191 791 000
Total GDP (PPP)	US$1.266 trillion	US$1.836 trillion
GDP (PPP) per capita	US$38,435	US$9,695
GNI (PPP) per capita	US$35,310	US$9,370
Annual growth	2.7%	5.4%
Inflation rate	2.1%	3.6%
Importation of goods and services	US$469.46 billion	US$157.87 billion
Exportation of goods and services	US$497.72 billion	US$184.54 billion

Sources: L'État du monde, *Encyclopédie de l'État du monde*, [On-line], 2008, and World Bank, [On-line], 2008.

Gross domestic product (GDP)
The gross domestic product (GDP) measures the wealth created in a given year, i.e. a country's production of goods and services.

Annual growth
This refers to the annual growth of the GDP. To avoid variations due to price increases, the growth rate is calculated in constant dollars.

Gross domestic product per capita
The GDP per capita measures the standard of living and attributes a value to the population's purchasing power. It is obtained by dividing the total GDP by the number of inhabitants.

Inflation rate
The inflation rate measures the overall increase in the price of goods and services for a given period, usually one year.

Gross national income (GNI) per capita
The GNI per capita is the average income (salaries and investment income) earned by a country's population. It includes net income from investments and property held outside of the country.

Imports and exports
Imports are goods and services entering a country from another country. Exports are goods and services a country sells to other countries.

HUMAN DEVELOPMENT INDEX (HDI)

Since 1990, the United Nations Development Programme (UNDP) has been using the Human Development Index (HDI), an indicator based on a vision of development that goes beyond income and the economy. In addition to assessing the economic production of the individuals who make up a society, the HDI takes into account aspects related to individual well-being and ability.

What Is the Human Development Index?

The HDI is a composite index, which means that it integrates several series of data to take into account the income, health and level of education of a State's population. Below is how the data used to calculate the HDI are weighted:

1/3

Gross domestic product at purchasing-power parity (PPP) per capita in US$

This measure indicates the average standard of living.

1/3

Life expectancy at birth

This measure gives an indication of the population's health.

2/9

Adult literacy rate
Percentage of the population over the age of 15 that can write.

1/9

Enrollment rate
Proportion of young people of a given age who are educated.

These data make it possible to measure the population's level of education.

The result

The calculation gives a result between 0 (deplorable) and 1 (excellent). Generally speaking, the least developed countries have an HDI under 0.5, while the HDI of developed countries is over 0.8.

Advantages of the HDI

The HDI revolutionized the analysis of inequalities in the world because it is more complete than the previous indicator, the GDP (PPP) per capita. In addition to measuring economic production, it illustrates the ability of different States to invest public funds in health and education.

A country can have a higher HDI than another country and still have a lower GDP per capita. This is the case of Poland, for example, which ranks 37th in terms of the HDI with a GDP of US$13,847 per capita (2006), and the United Arab Emirates, which ranks 39th with a GDP of US$25,514 per capita (2006).

Young Indian students
In India, only two out of every five girls can read and write.
◆ 4.5

◀ 4.6
**Civil war in Sierra Leone
(1999)**

Changes in the HDI

Generally speaking, the Human Development Index has grown worldwide since 1990, particularly in countries with emerging economies, such as Brazil, China and India. These countries' demographic weight has an impact on overall changes in the HDI.

The HDI in Canada has also grown in recent years. It has increased by more than 10% since 1975, rising from 0.897 to 0.961.

However, the situation has not improved in Sub-Saharan Africa, where most of the least developed countries are located. In fact, the HDI has even declined in several countries, including Côte d'Ivoire, the Democratic Republic of the Congo and Zambia.

4.7 ▶ Human Development Index (2005)

	Indice
World	**0.743**
Developed countries	0.897
Developing countries	0.691
Least developed countries	0.488
The five highest-ranking countries	
❶ Iceland	0.968
❷ Norway	0.968
❸ Australia	0.962
❹ Canada	0.961
❺ Ireland	0.959
The five lowest-ranking countries	
173 Mali	0.380
174 Niger	0.374
175 Guinea-Bissau	0.374
176 Burkina Faso	0.370
177 Sierra Leone	0.336

Human Development Index (2006)
➥ 4.8

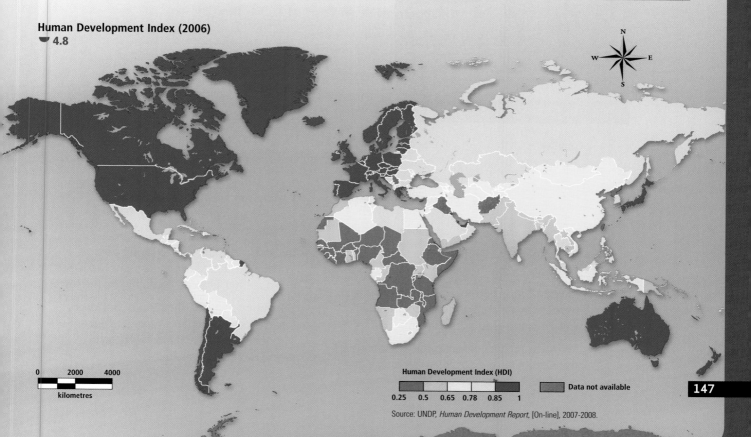

Human Development Index (HDI)

| 0.25 | 0.5 | 0.65 | 0.78 | 0.85 | 1 | Data not available |

Source: UNDP, *Human Development Report*, [On-line], 2007-2008.

ECONOMIC GROWTH

Since the Second World War, the international economy has experienced sustained growth. Despite a few slowdowns, production has increased worldwide. Between 1950 and 2000, the gross domestic product (GDP) per capita tripled, an unprecedented level of growth.

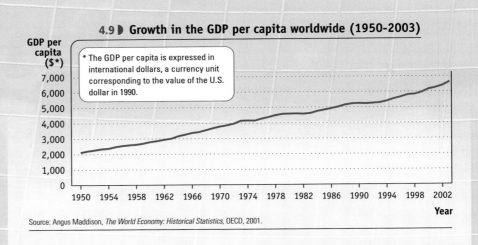

4.9 ▶ Growth in the GDP per capita worldwide (1950-2003)

GDP per capita ($*)

* The GDP per capita is expressed in international dollars, a currency unit corresponding to the value of the U.S. dollar in 1990.

Source: Angus Maddison, *The World Economy: Historical Statistics,* OECD, 2001.

Factors of Economic Growth

Economic growth, or an increase in production volume, is the result of a combination of interrelated factors. Below are a few of the most important ones:

- Companies' increased **productivity**: This is the driving force of economic growth since companies are the main producers.

- **Investment** growth: Investments are essential for company start-ups and expansions.

- Increased **international trade**: International trade increases employment opportunities and promotes greater investment.

- Improved production **techniques**: Improved techniques make it possible both to increase quantities produced and to reduce production costs and time.

- **Population** growth: Population growth provides additional labour and increases consumer demand.

- Increased consumer **purchasing power**: When individuals have more money to spend on goods and services, consumption increases.

- **Education** and **qualification** of the labour force: A competent labour force increases corporate productivity and contributes to technical development.

148

4.10 ▷ **Asia**

Uneven Growth

Economic growth is not the same in every region of the world.

1 After the Second World War, the Triad countries (North America, Western Europe and Japan) experienced the strongest growth.

2 In the late 1960s, the Asian Dragons, then the Tigers, began an important phase of economic expansion.

3 Since the 1990s, China, Russia, Brazil, India and Mexico have been gaining influence in the world economy. They will play a major role in the coming decade.

Asian Dragons and Tigers

The Asian Dragons refer to four Asian countries that have experienced extremely rapid economic expansion and modernization since the late 1960s. They are South Korea, Singapore, Taiwan and Hong Kong (returned to China in 1997). Economic growth in these countries has a few things in common:

▪ Opening up their economies was facilitated by their coastal location.

▪ They benefited from the proximity of Japan, which provided both a model and the necessary expertise and investments.

▪ They had access to cheap labour from the outset.

▪ During the Cold War, they benefited from their alliance with the United States.

Like Japan, the Asian Dragons invested in and relocated some factories to neighbouring countries. Thus, they contributed to the rapid economic growth in the 1980s of Thailand, Indonesia, Malaysia and the Philippines, which are today called the Asian Tigers. However, these countries were gravely affected by the Asian economic crisis of 1997-1998.

4.11 ▷ **Share of world GDP (2004-2050)**

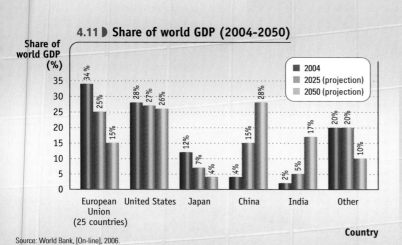

Share of world GDP (%)

Legend:
- 2004
- 2025 (projection)
- 2050 (projection)

Country	2004	2025 (projection)	2050 (projection)
European Union (25 countries)	34%	25%	15%
United States	28%	27%	26%
Japan	12%	7%	4%
China	4%	15%	28%
India	2%	5%	17%
Other	20%	20%	10%

Source: World Bank, [On-line], 2006.

SNAPSHOT OF TODAY

a After reading these pages, define the concept of economic development.

b How is this concept dealt with in the news?

149

THE GROWTH OF INTERNATIONAL TRADE

In the second half of the 20th century, international trade experienced spectacular growth. The phenomenon, first seen in developed countries, gradually extended to the entire planet and transformed the dynamics of world trade.

Tremendous Growth

Globalization transformed international trade, which took a giant leap forward. Farm products, which represented more than half of all merchandise traded in 1950, accounted for less than 10% in 2005. At the same time, the share of manufactured products grew from less than 40% to 75%.

4.12 ▶ Growth of world merchandise trade

Merchandise trade (billions US$)
- Exports
- Imports

25,000 / 20,000 / 15,000 / 10,000 / 5,000 / 0

1948 1953 1963 1973 1983 1993 2003 2005

Year

Source: WTO, *International Trade Statistics*, [On-line], 2007.

The Globalization of Trade

Economic globalization is the growth in the movement of goods, services, funds, technologies and labour on a worldwide scale.

Causes

- The development of communications technologies and means of transportation
- Government efforts to liberalize international trade through measures, such as GATT, the WTO and the creation of free-trade zones
- The multiplication and rapid development of multinationals

Advantages

- The diversification of products and services available on the market
- Lower prices
- An international division of labour

Disadvantages

- The increased interdependence of trading nations
- Increased inequality between developed and developing countries
- The relocation of certain industries to places where labour is cheaper
- Increased competition between industries

A cargo ship carrying containers (2001)
In the 1950s, the invention of the container revolutionized trade by facilitating loading and unloading operations. These standardized boxes can be carried by truck or train or can be stacked on cargo ships.
▼ 4.13

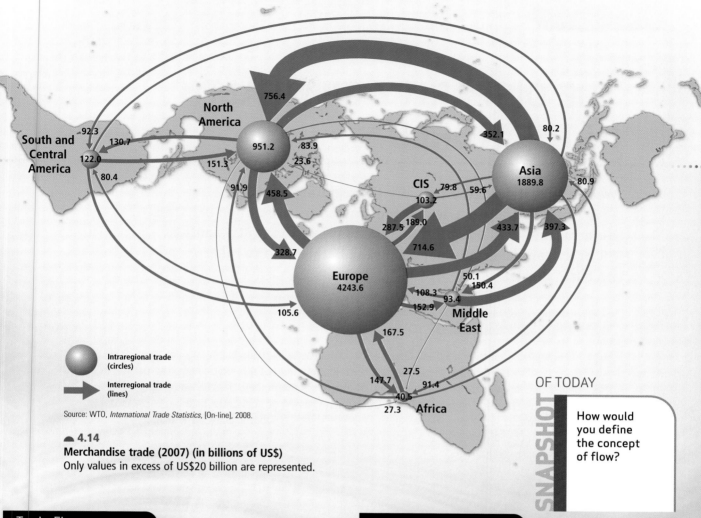

SNAPSHOT OF TODAY

How would you define the concept of flow?

Intraregional trade (circles)

Interregional trade (lines)

Source: WTO, *International Trade Statistics*, [On-line], 2008.

4.14
Merchandise trade (2007) (in billions of US$)
Only values in excess of US$20 billion are represented.

Trade Flows

After the Second World War, trade took place mainly between the countries in the North, which were experiencing a period of economic expansion (the "Glorious Thirty"). In 1973, more than 75% of merchandise trade took place between developed countries, particularly between members of the Triad (United States, Western Europe and Japan).

In the 1980s, developing countries, in particular countries with emerging economies, began participating in international trade. In 2005, almost 35% of world merchandise exports were from developing countries, a 15% increase over 1973. China is a particularly eloquent example. Its weight in international trade has grown by 15% a year since 1980, making it the second largest commercial force in the world today.

Balance of Trade

Value of exports
– Value of imports
—————————
Balance of trade

When the value of a country's imports exceeds that of its exports, it is said to have a trade deficit. Conversely, if the value of its exports is greater than the value of its imports, it is said to have a surplus, or positive, balance of trade.

States prefer to have a surplus balance of trade, since this allows them to increase their foreign exchange reserves and keep tighter control over their monetary policies. However, this is not always easy. For example, developing countries generally have a trade deficit (20% to 25%), since they primarily export raw materials and import manufactured products, which are more expensive.

THE DISPARITY OF WEALTH IN THE WORLD

Wealth is distributed unequally throughout the world. It is concentrated in a few dozen countries, which benefit from high income and a comfortable standard of living. In another 50 or so countries, the population is barely able to meet its basic needs.

Classification of Countries

The world's countries are often classified according to level of development. For years, the classification criterion was the gross domestic product (GDP), which served to define levels of economic development. Today, countries are more often classified according to the Human Development Index (HDI), which is based on individual income, education and well-being. However, there is not always a consensus as to the exact definition of each category and definitions may vary depending on the institution or specialist using them.

Developed Countries

These are the wealthiest countries, with a GDP (PPP) per capita of over US$8,000. In these countries, people earn enough to meet their basic needs, get an education and enjoy a certain level of comfort.

This category includes countries whose Human Development Index (HDI) is at least 0.8. In 2006, 70 countries (seven more than the previous year), located for the most part in Europe, North America, East Asia and Oceania, were classified in this category.

Because of their geographic location, developed countries are sometimes called Northern countries. They are also known as industrialized countries because their economies are based mainly on industrial activities.

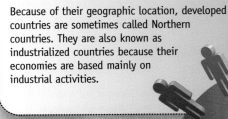

Least Developed Countries (LDCs)

Created in 1971 by the United Nations, this category includes the poorest and least developed countries in the world, which, as a result, require special attention from the international community. They have a GDP (PPP) per capita of under US$900 and a Human Development Index of less than 0.5. From 25 in 1970, the number of least developed countries has risen to 49, most of them in Sub-Saharan Africa.

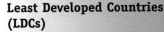

ⓐ After reading these pages, how would you define the concept of disparity?

ⓑ Is there anything in the news about this concept?

OECD ORGANISATION FOR ECONOMIC CO-OPERATION AND DEVELOPMENT

Founded in 1961, the OECD is an international organization for economic study. Its aims are to support economic and trade growth, develop employment and maintain stability; it shares its expertise with other countries. The organization is made up of 30 mostly developed countries (Turkey is the exception), all of which adhere to the principles of democracy and of market economy. OECD member States are the wealthiest in the world, producing 78% of the world's gross national income (2008). For this reason, the term "OECD country" is sometimes confused with "developed country."

Developing Countries (DC)

This category is made up of countries whose Human Development Index is greater than 0.5 but less than 0.8, which is to say that they are neither part of the developed nor the least developed categories. These countries, somewhere between the two, form a heterogeneous group. Generally located in the Southern hemisphere, they are sometimes called Southern countries, as opposed to the developed Northern countries.

Countries in this category can sometimes make the transition to another category. Many of them are experiencing impressive growth and human development, approaching those of developed countries. For example, South Korea, which was long a developing country, is now a developed country and has been a member of the OECD since 1996.

Countries With Emerging Economies

These countries are a subcategory of developing countries. Their economic growth is impressive and their standard of living tends to increasingly resemble that of Northern countries. Emerging countries, which include India, China, Brazil, Russia and the Asian Dragons and Tigers, will play a major role in the world's economy in the coming decades. They are rapidly becoming part of the world economy, increasingly exporting to and investing in foreign countries, and acquiring substantial technological expertise. Since the concept of emerging economy is relatively vague, it is difficult to establish an accurate list of the countries in this category.

Classification of countries based on the HDI (2006)
▼ 4.15

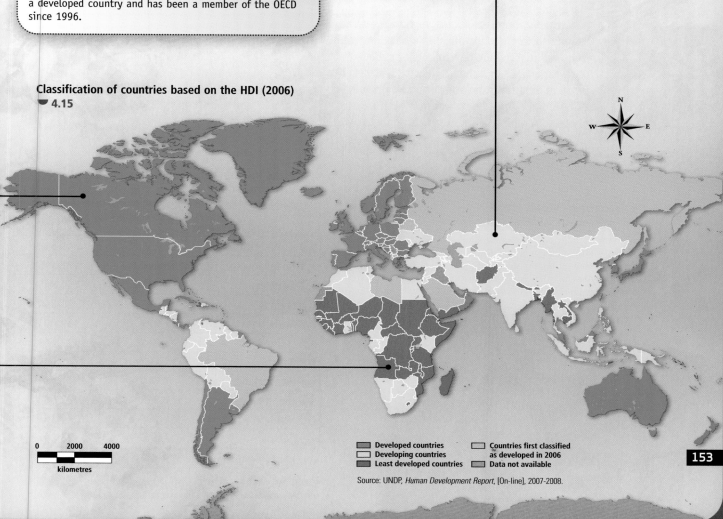

Developed countries	Countries first classified
Developing countries	as developed in 2006
Least developed countries	Data not available

0 2000 4000 kilometres

Source: UNDP, *Human Development Report*, [On-line], 2007-2008.

Wealth

THE DEBT BURDEN

After the Second World War, the economic growth of many States was stimulated by government spending. Governments did not hesitate to go into debt to invest in the economy, education and health. In some cases, the increased debt load had a negative impact on the economy.

Foreign Debt

Foreign debt refers to the money a country owes to foreign creditors. These creditors can be international institutions, such as the International Monetary Fund (IMF) and the World Bank, other States or private creditors.

States might go into debt to finance large infrastructural projects (dams, highways, etc.), to fund social measures (health, education, etc.), to invest in corporate development or the extraction of raw materials or to cover their budget deficits. Being in debt is not necessarily a bad thing for a State, since the money it borrows can be used to create wealth and stimulate economic growth.

Carrying a heavy debt load can be risky for some countries. Generally speaking, a debt is said to be insolvent when its amount exceeds the country's gross domestic product (GDP). Also, if a country's currency suffers a large devaluation and its debt is expressed in a foreign currency (in US$, for example), the interest can quickly become unserviceable.

In the 1980s, inflation and high interest rates led to a serious financial crisis. Many countries, starting with Mexico, found themselves unable to pay the interest and capital on their debts and were forced to declare insolvency.

Outdoor market, Bolivia (2006)
In absolute terms, the foreign debt of developing countries is lower than that of Northern countries. However, developing countries do not have the same ability to pay and cannot support the same level of debt as Northern countries.
🔻 4.16

154

4.17 ▶ The most indebted countries in 2007 (in billions of US$)

Country	Total debt (billions US$)	Debt per capita
❶ United States	12,250	40,614
❷ United Kingdom	10,450	171,215
❸ Germany	4,489	54,565
❹ France	4,396	71,240
❺ Netherlands	2,277	139,001
❻ Ireland	1,841	421,649
❼ Japan	1,492	11,677
❽ Switzerland	1,340	177,481
❾ Belgium	1,313	123,568
❿ Spain	1,084	24,154
⓭ Canada	758.6	23,005

Source: CIA, *World Factbook*, [On-line], 2008.

The States with the highest debt are all among the wealthiest countries in the world.

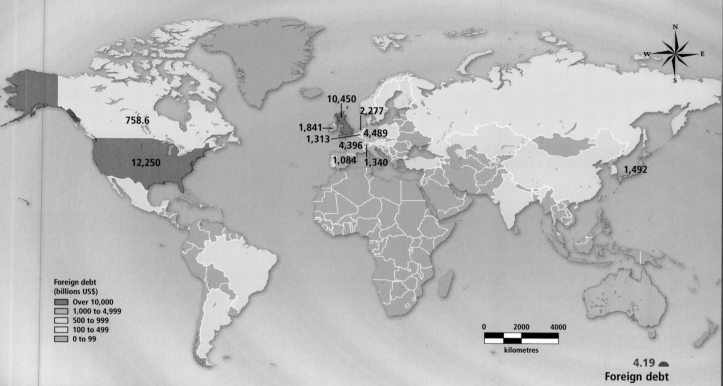

◀ 4.18
Live 8 concert in Philadelphia (2005)
In 2005, as part of the "Live 8" campaign, concerts were held in a number of cities around the world to promote cancelling Third World debt and reducing poverty.

10,450
2,277
1,841
1,313
4,489
4,396
1,084
1,340
758.6
12,250
1,492

Foreign debt (billions US$)
- Over 10,000
- 1,000 to 4,999
- 500 to 999
- 100 to 499
- 0 to 99

0   2000   4000
kilometres

4.19 ●
Foreign debt

Developing Countries and Debt

After decolonization, developing countries contracted sizeable debts with the IMF, the World Bank and other States. This enabled many of them to gain their independence. They then had to construct major infrastructures and invest in industrialization. Dictatorial regimes borrowed large sums of money, sometimes with the support of foreign powers, to finance civil wars and oppressive social structures or to line their pockets.

According to the Committee for the Abolition of Third World Debt, the cumulative debt of developing countries rose from US$8 billion to US$2.6 trillion between 1960 and 2004. Since 1980, these countries have paid back 10 times what they borrowed, but interest has nonetheless increased their debt by a factor of five.

In 1996, the International Monetary Fund and the World Bank launched an initiative to substantially alleviate the debt of heavily indebted poor countries (HIPCs) that were unable to pay back what they owed.

To be eligible, countries must meet several conditions. Their debt must be impossible to sustain and they must commit to major reforms aimed at economic recovery.

In 2007, 41 countries, three quarters of them in Sub-Saharan Africa, were eligible for the program. According to the IMF, the total cost of aid to these countries is more than US$70 billion.

INTERNAL INEQUALITIES

Wealth is unequally distributed among countries as well as among members of any given society. In some countries, both developing and wealthy, there are major social differences between rich and poor and between men and women.

Unequal Income

In all societies, there is a significant income gap between the wealthiest and the poorest. This gap is more marked in Southern countries, especially in Africa and Latin America.

Although inequalities also exist in industrialized countries, they are generally less marked than in developing countries. In many cases, tax policies in developed countries help limit inequalities. The wealthy must pay higher taxes, and the government redistributes some of the money collected to the poor through a variety of social measures.

A widening gap

In recent decades, the gap between rich and poor worldwide has been getting worse, even in developed countries. For example, in three quarters of the OECD countries, the income gap has grown since the mid-1980s, especially in the United States, Canada and Germany. This can be partially explained by the fact that the income of the wealthy has increased substantially in recent years in comparison to that of people with medium or low levels of income.

4.20 ▶ Gini index

Country	Indice
Japan	0.249
Sweden	0.25
France	0.327
Australia	0.352
India	0.368
Russia	0.399
China	0.469
Argentina	0.513
Sierra Leone	0.629
Namibia	0.743

Source: UNDP, *Human Development Report*, [On-line], 2007-2008.

Gini Index

The Gini index is an indicator that measures inequalities in the distribution of income. Its value is between 0 (perfect equality) and 1 (absolute inequality), two extreme situations that cannot exist in real life.

4.21 ▶ Evolution of the Gini index in North America (1975-2005)

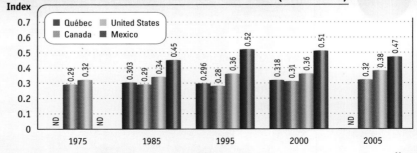

Sources: OECD, [On-line], 2008, and Institut de la statistique du Québec, [On-line], 2007.

4.22 ◢
Woman on a farm, Myanmar
Although people who live in
rural areas generally earn less
than those who live in cities,
at times they are better off.
Though poor, they can often
produce some of what they
consume, which is not the case
for the urban poor.

The Urban-Rural Gap

People in the city generally earn more money than people in rural areas.
This disparity is more or less acute depending on the country in question.
For example, according to a 2005 European study, city dwellers earned on
average about 100 euros (approximately C$150) more a month than
their rural counterparts. However, the gap was much more marked in the
poorer European countries than in the wealthier ones.

In countries with emerging economies, the income disparity between those
who live in cities and those who live in rural areas is growing, since salaries
increase more rapidly in urban areas. For example, in 2007, the income of
Chinese city dwellers was 3.3 times higher than that of their rural counterparts,
the largest gap observed since 1978. In addition to having more money, urban
populations have better access to services, especially in the areas of health
and education.

Gender Inequalities

In today's world, women suffer many forms of discrimination.
Consequently, they are poorer than men and do not have the same
opportunities.

- In 2008, 1.3 billion people, 70% of them women, were living
  in extreme poverty.

- On average, women earn 17% less than men.

- Of all the children in the world without an education, 57% are
  girls. Consequently, the world literacy rate is higher among men
  (83.7%) than among women (71.4%).

- Women workers are often less involved in decision-making
  than their male counterparts.

- Sexual discrimination is not the same everywhere. It is more
  marked in South Asia, Africa and the Middle East than in the
  rest of the world.

4.23 ◢
**Women wearing the burka
in Afghanistan (2001)**
Under the Taliban in Afghanistan (1996-2001),
women's rights were extremely limited.
They were forced to wear the burka and
were not allowed to leave the house unless they
were accompanied by a man. They could not
work or attend school.

EXTREME CASES: NORTH AMERICA AND AFRICA

In terms of economic and human development, North America and Sub-Saharan Africa are two extreme cases. These regions illustrate the disparity in the world's wealth and living conditions, as well as inequalities with respect to future opportunities.

Human Development Index (HDI) in North America (2006)
▼ 4.24

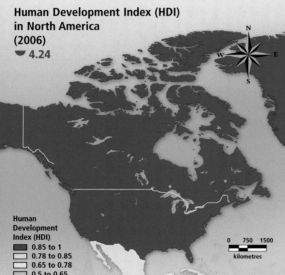

Human Development Index (HDI)
- 0.85 to 1
- 0.78 to 0.85
- 0.65 to 0.78
- 0.5 to 0.65

0   750   1500
kilometres

4.25 ▶ Statistics for North America (2005)

	Canada	USA	Mexico
HDI	0.961	0.951	0.829
Life expectancy at birth (years)	80.3	77.9	75.6
Infant mortality	5‰	6‰	22‰
Literacy rate	99%	99%	91.6%
Enrollment rate	99.2%	93.3%	75.6%
GDP (PPP) per capita in US$	33,375	41,890	10,751
Economic growth (average annual rate 1990-2005)	2.2%	2.1%	1.5%
Electricity consumption (kW/h/inhabitant)	14 408	14 420	2 130

Sources: UNDP, *Human Development Report*, [On-line], 2007-2008, and CIA, World Factbook, [On-line], 2008.

Obesity: A Serious Problem

Since the beginning of the 1980s, the obesity rate in North America has tripled. In the United States and Mexico, 30% of adults are obese while in Canada the rate is 23% (2005-2006). Children are also affected, especially in the United States, where 16% of young people between the ages of 2 and 19 are seriously overweight. A diet high in fat and sugar and a lack of physical activity are to blame. Obesity has become a public health problem, since it significantly increases the risk of developing diabetes and cardiovascular disease.

An Educated Population

In North America (except Mexico) and in Western Europe, the enrollment rate in higher education is on average 70%. In these knowledge-based societies, research and development are a driving force in the economy. With globalization, research is becoming an international affair and universities are competing to attract both the best researchers and foreign students. The United States is the uncontested leader in this area. On a list of the world's 100 best universities compiled by Shanghai University, American universities hold more than 50 positions, including 8 of the top 10. Four Canadian universities are also on the top 100 list.

4.27 ▶
Shantytown in Kibera, Kenya (2000)

Downtown Los Angeles (1990)
▼ **4.26**

4.28 ▶ **Statistics for Sub-Saharan Africa (2005)**

HDI	0.493
Life expectancy at birth (years)	49.1
Infant mortality	144‰
Literacy rate	60.3%
Enrollment rate	50.6%
GDP (PPP) per capita in US$	1,998
Economic growth (average annual rate 1990-2005)	0.5%
Electricity consumption (kW/h/inhabitant)	478

Source: UNDP, *Human Development Report*, [On-line], 2007-2008.

An Undernourished Population

In Sub-Saharan Africa, 236 million people, or approximately one third of the population, suffer from hunger and chronic undernourishment. Some 40% of children are underweight, explaining the low life expectancy and the high infant mortality rate. In 2008, the Food and Agriculture Organization of the United Nations (FAO) estimated that 21 countries were facing a food crisis and required international aid. This situation is due in particular to climate disasters, rising food prices and the conflicts and civil disorder in many African countries.

Generalized Poverty

Sub-Saharan Africa, especially East and Central Africa, is the poorest region in the world. It contains 34 of the 49 least developed countries, where 30% of the world's population lives in absolute poverty (less than $1 a day). Urban poverty is even worse: 62% of city dwellers live in shantytowns in deplorable living and hygiene conditions.

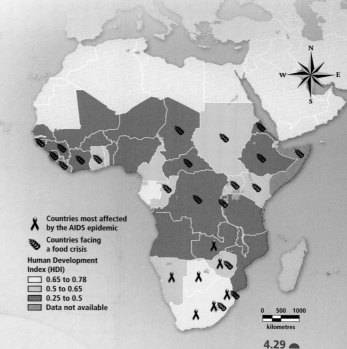

Countries most affected by the AIDS epidemic

Countries facing a food crisis

Human Development Index (HDI)
- ☐ 0.65 to 0.78
- ☐ 0.5 to 0.65
- ☐ 0.25 to 0.5
- ☐ Data not available

0   500   1000
kilometres

4.29 ▲
Human Development Index (HDI) in Sub-Saharan Africa (2006)

The prevalence of AIDS
Sub-Saharan Africa has the highest rate of AIDS in the world. Some 22 million people are infected. Between the ages of 18 and 24, women are three times more likely than men to become infected. Children are also affected: 1.8 million of them have HIV.

General
Information

Disparity

The Causes
of Disparity

Possible
Solutions

Wealth

CONTROL OVER RESOURCES

The unequal distribution of natural resources is one reason for the disparity of wealth in the world. Having resources often contributes to the economic growth of a State, giving it power over importing countries. However, this rule does not always apply, since it is not enough merely to possess resources: the State must control them and be able to develop them.

Control Over Natural Resources

Natural resources, in particular energy resources, are important to a State's development. Many developed and emerging countries get rich from these resources.

However, even though they have large reserves of raw materials, some countries, especially developing countries, do not get rich. A number of factors explain this:

- Developing the natural resources is too costly and the necessary investments are unavailable.

- The natural resources are primarily developed by foreign companies, which take all of the profits.

- The economies of some countries are based too heavily on their natural resources, which places them at the mercy of international market fluctuations.

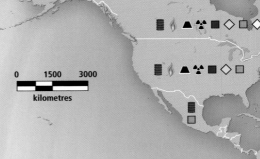

0   1500   3000
kilometres

DIVERTED RICHES

IN BRIEF

The soil in the Democratic Republic of the Congo contains a tantalizing wealth of minerals (cobalt, copper, diamonds, nickel, gold, etc.). In power from 1965 to 1997, the dictator Mobutu nationalized a large portion of mining production and pocketed much of the profits generated. When he was deposed in 1997, his personal fortune was estimated at $8 billion, while the country was $12 billion in debt.

4.30 ▶
Joseph-Désiré Mobutu (1975)

OPEC ORGANIZATION OF THE PETROLEUM EXPORTING COUNTRIES

Created in 1960, OPEC is an intergovernmental organization that negotiates oil production and price fixing with oil companies. It is made up of 12 countries, which produce a little over 40% of the world's oil and own more than three quarters of the planet's known oil reserves. This allows them to influence the price of oil on the international market.

4.31 ▶
OPEC member countries (2009)
Saudi Arabia, Iran, Iraq, Kuwait, Qatar, United Arab Emirates, Libya, Algeria, Nigeria, Angola, Venezuela, Ecuador

0 2000 4000
kilometres

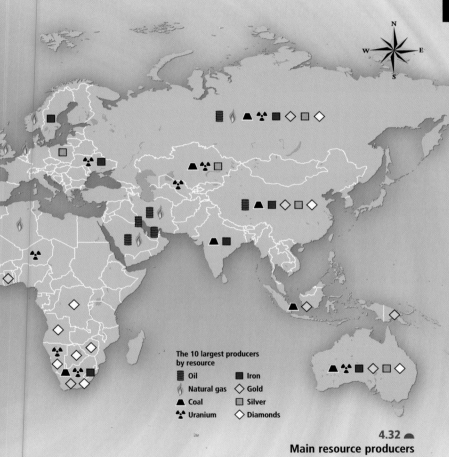

The 10 largest producers by resource

Oil	Iron
Natural gas	Gold
Coal	Silver
Uranium	Diamonds

4.32 ◖
Main resource producers

Energy Resources

Because of the importance of energy resources, many countries are dependent on energy producers.

Major fluctuations in the price of oil have a negative impact on world economic growth. This is what happened in 1973 and 1979, when the OPEC countries decided to limit their oil exports, causing an increase in the price of a barrel of oil. Events such as these encourage countries to develop alternative energy sources (nuclear, electrical, etc.), especially wealthy countries that can afford to invest in research.

Natural gas also creates interdependence between importers and producers. For example, Russia, the world's largest producer, supplies almost half of Europe's natural gas thanks to a network of pipelines in the Ukraine. Many Central European and Balkan nations were hard hit when Russia decided to cut Ukraine's gas supply in 2006 and 2009 because of a tariff dispute.

SNAPSHOT OF TODAY

a How would you define the concepts of concentration and resource?

b Is there a current news item that addresses these two concepts?

THE ADVANTAGES AND DISADVANTAGES OF GLOBALIZATION

Between 1990 and 2000, thanks to China's economic growth, the number of Chinese living in extreme poverty fell from 361 to 204 million. Yet, in Sub-Saharan Africa, the number rose by 82 million during the same period. How can this difference be explained? What role did globalization play, if any?

Globalization: Problem or Solution?

Globalization is not necessarily a source of inequalities. On the contrary, the opening up of economies and societies allows for a better circulation of ideas, knowledge and goods. This can encourage collaboration between countries and contribute to their development.

However, not all States benefit from this situation. Some have assets that enable them to take advantage of globalization, while others simply do not have the means. Worse yet, the wealthiest countries often take advantage of their position to exploit less developed countries. This vicious circle, which is extremely difficult to break, allows wealthy States to become wealthier, while the poorest States remain underdeveloped.

Taking advantage of the poor

Developing countries offer advantages for investors from wealthy States. They usually have an abundance of cheap, unskilled labour. Labour laws are often more lax, which makes it possible to fire employees more easily and to offer fewer benefits. Also, environmental standards are often less strict. All of these factors allow developed countries to earn greater profits and to become wealthier without contributing to the development of the less developed countries.

Child working in a match factory in India (1998)
In 2005, an estimated 210 million children under the age of 15 were working, primarily in developing countries.
▼ 4.33

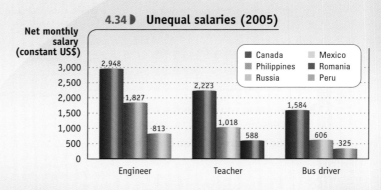

4.34 ▶ Unequal salaries (2005)

Net monthly salary (constant US$)

Legend: Canada, Mexico, Philippines, Romania, Russia, Peru

Engineer: 2,948; 1,827; 813
Teacher: 2,223; 1,018; 588
Bus driver: 1,584; 606; 325

Occupation

Source: World Salaries, *International Average Salary Income Database*, [On-line], 2009.

162

◀ 4.35
Workers in a Chinese electronics factory (2000)
Until now, China has been able to take advantage of globalization thanks to its large, cheap labour force.

Multinationals

Multinationals are in a particularly good position to take advantage of globalization. Because they operate at an international level, they can benefit from the advantages of each country in which they do business. Their presence in developing countries enables them to produce cheap goods and services. These are then sold for profit in industrialized States, where the population can afford to spend more.

This model can be so beneficial that many companies close some of their facilities in industrialized countries and move them to developing countries where operating costs are much lower. This is called relocation. This phenomenon benefits companies, but costs numerous jobs in the countries they leave. Also, relocation does not necessarily contribute to the advancement of less developed countries, since multinationals are not particularly interested in improving working conditions.

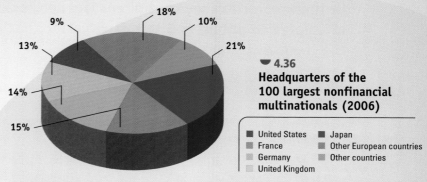

▼ 4.36
Headquarters of the 100 largest nonfinancial multinationals (2006)

- ■ United States
- ■ France
- ■ Germany
- ■ United Kingdom
- ■ Japan
- ■ Other European countries
- ■ Other countries

Source: UNCTAD, *World Investment Report 2008: Transnational Corporations and the Infrastructure Challenge*, [On-line], 2009.

Because of globalization, multinationals are establishing operations in a growing number of countries. Their profits, however, benefit only a small number of already wealthy States, as can be seen by the location of the headquarters of most multinationals.

Elements Required to Benefit From Globalization

☑ A solid economy
A stable economic base is definitely an advantage. Diversified and solidly established industries, capital to be invested in foreign countries and a vast market for consumer development are all assets.

☑ Good governance
Open and democratic countries obtain better economic results than those in which human rights are at issue. Government corruption and poor management of civil servants discourage many investors.

☑ Effective social policies
An educated and healthy population with a reasonable standard of living costs more in salaries, but it is also more productive, creative and capable of adapting to change.

☑ International influence
International trade and finance regulations benefit wealthy and powerful countries, since they are the ones that draw them up. The weaker and poorer States cannot really change the system, since they are unable to make themselves heard.

COLONIZATION

For a long time, colonialism was a major source of inequalities. Colonizing States exploited and profited from the resources and people in the territories they controlled. The decolonization movement attempted to put an end to this situation, but half a century later, the inequalities are still there.

Colonialism

Colonialism is the occupation and economic, political or social exploitation of a territory by a foreign State.

Many factors have been cited to justify colonialism. However, its main benefit is economic, the goal being to generate profits for the mother country, which is usually impossible without acting against the colonies' interests. Colonial powers take advantage of their position to obtain a variety of cheap resources. This exploitation is the cause of considerable disparity between the wealth of the mother country and its colonies, and between the leaders and the local populations within a given colony.

Decolonization

In the mid-20th century, colonial abuse provoked a strong reaction on the part of colonized countries. These countries took action to break their ties with the mother country through negotiation, nonviolent demonstrations and even armed struggle. Between the end of the Second World War and the 1970s, almost all of the African and Asian colonies had won their independence. This decolonization movement allowed many populations to rekindle their pride and their desire to regain control of their country.

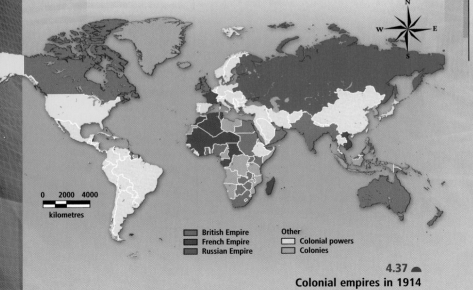

0 2000 4000
kilometres

British Empire
French Empire
Russian Empire

Other
Colonial powers
Colonies

4.37 ◢
Colonial empires in 1914
The colonial system has a long history, from the Portuguese and Spanish colonies in the 16th century to the French and British international empires that existed until the mid-20th century.

Mohandas Karamchand Gandhi

Decolonization often came only at the price of costly wars. However, other means of resistance were also used, such as the nonviolent civil disobedience promoted by Gandhi (1869-1948) during India's struggle for independence. This charismatic leader encouraged Indians to join forces and refuse to obey the British, forcing the latter to negotiate. India won its independence in 1947.

4.38 ◢
Patrice Lumumba, Prime Minister of the former Belgian Congo (1960)
The former colonial leaders also participated in the 1961 assassination of the prime minister of the newly independent Belgian Congo.

Maintaining Influence

To maintain their influence, the former colonial powers did not hesitate to support governments favourable to them, even dictatorships, and to depose uncooperative regimes. To do so, they relied upon financial support, corruption or mercenaries and supported local rebellions.

That is what happened, for example, in the Belgian Congo, now the Democratic Republic of the Congo, after the country gained its independence in 1960. Union minière de Haut Katanga, a Belgian company that controlled most of the country's mining operations, actively encouraged the wealthy province of Katanga to separate, plunging the region into civil war for many years.

Neocolonialism

In theory, colonies that win their independence are free to determine their own policies. In reality, however, the former mother countries often continue to exercise considerable influence. The direct political and military control of the colonial era gives way to more subtle but equally powerful financial and commercial control. Foreign companies in particular continue to play a predominant role in the local economy.

As in the colonial era, this economic domination hinders development and maintains inequalities and disparities in wealth. The relationship of domination between the developed countries and the less advanced countries may have changed form, but it remains in force. This is referred to as neocolonialism or economic imperialism.

Chinese oil worker in Nigeria (2006)
The influence of former colonial powers can be replaced by that of new countries practising a new form of economic imperialism. In the 1990s, trade between African countries and China increased by 700% and, in 2007, it was estimated that more than 750 000 Chinese were working in Africa.
▼ **4.39**

4.40 ▶ **Foreign investment in former colonies (2007)**

	Former mother country	Year of independence	Main investing country in 2007	% of foreign investment from this country
Guinea-Bissau	Portugal	1974	Portugal	22
Uzbekistan	Russia	1991	Russia	30
Philippines	United States	1946	United States	14
Senegal	France	1960	France	22

Source: CIA, *World Factbook*, [On-line], 2008.

With globalization, foreign investment has increased, but it primarily comes from a small number of countries. In 2007, fewer than 10 States, almost all of them former colonial powers, managed 84% of all foreign investment in the world.

INTERNATIONAL AID

Many socioeconomically fragile States receive international aid to support development. This aid can come from another country, an international organization, such as the IMF or the World Bank, or a private organization, such as an NGO or a company.

4.41
Honduran school (1990)

Multi-Faceted Development and Aid

A country's development can take many different forms. The economic aspect obviously plays an important role, but social and human factors must also be taken into account. These are necessary for economic development and, particularly for the population's well-being. Thus, education, health, democracy, human rights and the environment are essential to well-balanced development. Since there are many aspects to development, it is understandable that international aid also takes a variety of forms to better meet diverse needs.

4.42 ▶ Possible forms of international aid

Form	Description	*Example*
Financial support	Money is provided.	Amounts paid directly into the State's budget, financial support for specific projects, etc.
Material support	Supplies needed for development are provided.	Pharmaceutical products and medical equipment for hospitals, food to combat malnutrition, etc.
Sharing of technology	Technology is transferred to less advanced countries.	Implementation of computer networks, construction of nuclear reactors to supply energy, etc.
Training and education	Specialists are provided to share general or specialized expertise.	Literacy programs, police and bomb-disposal training, etc.
Participation in the construction of infrastructures	Resources (human, financial, technical) are provided to help construct or repair various infrastructures.	Specialized personnel, such as engineers, to help construct roads, wells, dams, etc.
Expert advice	Knowledge and experience are shared.	Assistance for holding free and democratic elections, for the development of new economic policies, etc.

CIDA — CANADIAN INTERNATIONAL DEVELOPMENT AGENCY

Since 1968, official development assistance in Canada has been managed by the Canadian International Development Agency (CIDA). This government agency implements projects primarily aimed at reducing poverty and promoting democracy, health and basic education. It is headed by the Minister for International Cooperation.

4.43 ▲
CIDA aids the population of Myanmar in the wake of a cyclone (2008)

4.44 ▲
Food distribution in Uganda (2009)
In 2007, 86.1 million people in 80 different countries received aid from the World Food Programme (WFP).

The Role of International Organizations

Many international organizations have developed aid programs for developing countries. For example, the OECD offers economic advice, while NATO builds security and defence partnerships.

The United Nations System includes many organizations devoted to international development. For example, the United Nations Conference on Trade and Development (UNCTAD) deals with questions related to international trade, while the World Food Programme (WFP) provides food for populations facing famine. The United Nations Development Programme (UNDP) plays an important role in the field by coordinating the efforts of all the United Nations funds, agencies and programs aimed at supporting development.

Official Development Assistance

States are major players in international aid. Most industrialized countries have a variety of programs to assist less developed countries. This official development assistance can take the form of financial donations, debt relief or low-interest loans. The United Nations, the European Union and G8 members believe that the Millennium Development Goals could be achieved if developed countries devoted 0.7% of their gross national income (GNI) to official development assistance.

4.45 ▶ Official development assistance

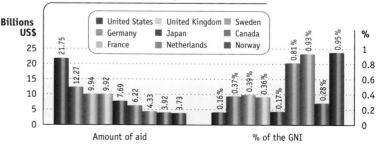

Legend: United States, United Kingdom, Sweden, Germany, Japan, Canada, France, Netherlands, Norway

Billions US$ — Amount of aid: 21.75, 12.27, 9.94, 9.92, 7.69, 6.22, 4.33, 3.92, 3.73

% of the GNI: 0.16%, 0.37%, 0.39%, 0.36%, 0.17%, 0.81%, 0.93%, 0.28%, 0.95%

Source: OECD, *Net Official Development Assistance in 2007*, [On-line], 2009.

In 2007, official development assistance totalled $103.6 billion worldwide. Developed countries devoted on average 0.45% of their GNI to development assistance.

MILLENNIUM DEVELOPMENT GOALS

In 2000, the United Nations held a world conference to coordinate international aid efforts. Eight Millennium Development Goals were established at the summit. These goals were a first attempt at globalizing development and identifying specific and measurable targets.

① Reduce Extreme Poverty and Hunger

Target ▪ Halve, between 1990 and 2015, both the number of people whose income is less than US$1 a day and the number of people suffering from malnutrition.

Results ▪ Although the number of children under the age of five who suffer from malnutrition has decreased since 1990, 10 million people still die from hunger every year (2005). The rate of extreme poverty in the world fell from 42% in 1990 to 26% in 2005, but 1.4 billion people still live on less than US$1.25 a day (2005).

② Achieve Universal Elementary School Education

Target ▪ Ensure that children everywhere, boys and girls alike, are able to complete elementary school.

Results ▪ In 2006, more than 570 million children were enrolled in school, an increase of 30 million over 1999. However, 73 million children, primarily girls, had received no education.

③ Promote Gender Equality and Empower Women

Target ▪ Eliminate gender disparity, particularly in the areas of employment and education, by 2015.

Results ▪ Increasing numbers of women have access to employment, but they still earn on average one third less than men. In 2008, only 17.9% of parliamentary seats worldwide were held by women.

④ Reduce Child Mortality

Target ▪ Reduce by two thirds, between 1990 and 2015, the under-five mortality rate.

Results ▪ Between 1990 and 2006, the world infant mortality rate for children under the age of one dropped from 93 to 72 deaths per 1000 births. However, a child born in a developing country is 13 times more likely to die before the age of five than a child born in an industrialized country.

168

◀ 4.46
A woman with her daughter and granddaughter in India (1995)

Improve Maternal Health

Target ▪ Reduce the maternal mortality rate by three quarters between 1990 and 2015.

Results ▪ In 2005, it was estimated that one woman died from pregnancy- or childbirth-related complications every minute. Of these approximately 500 000 deaths, 99% occurred in developing countries.

Combat HIV/AIDS, Malaria and Other Diseases

Target ▪ Halt and begin to reverse the spread of pandemics, such as HIV and malaria, and other major diseases, such as tuberculosis.

Results ▪ In 2007, 33.2 million people were suffering from HIV/AIDS, with the situation being particularly grave in Sub-Saharan Africa. Despite a slight decline in the number of deaths, malaria still kills one child every 30 seconds, or almost one million children a year.

Ensure Environmental Sustainability

Target ▪ Encourage the principles of sustainable development, halve the proportion of the population without access to safe drinking water and achieve a significant improvement in the lives of at least 100 million slum dwellers, by 2020.

Results ▪ Since 1990, there has been an increase of 1.6 billion people with regular access to safe drinking water. However, 1 billion people still lack this access, 1.6 billion have no access to electricity and 2.4 billion are without heating or modern cooking equipment.

▲ 4.47
Digging a well in Niger

Develop a Global Partnership for Development

Target ▪ Develop more open and equitable trade and financial systems, reschedule poor countries' debt repayment, provide access to essential pharmaceutical products at reasonable prices and make information and communications technologies available.

Results ▪ Between 1990 and 2006, the number of telephone users (land lines and cellphones) worldwide skyrocketed from 530 million to more than 4 billion. However, in 2007, barely 11% of people living in developing countries had access to the Internet.

Progress Report

Although some goals are in the process of being achieved, others appear to be out of reach for now. There have even been significant setbacks in some cases. Progress is very uneven, depending on the region. In general, Asia has experienced rapid and significant progress, while Sub-Saharan Africa has fallen into woeful stagnation.

169

SOCIAL MEASURES

To be truly effective, the battle to reduce inequalities must be fought on both the national and the international levels. Governments are in the best position to implement the social measures essential for development in their country.

Different Degrees of Involvement

The level of government social involvement varies considerably from one country to the next. While some have taken little action, most have at least adopted measures to stimulate their economies and redistribute social wealth. Countries whose public administration favours the development of social policies, adopting measures aimed at reducing inequalities between citizens, are referred to as welfare States.

Social policies address various areas, such as health, education, family, employment and the fight against poverty. Their scope and application vary considerably from one country to the next, but they generally aim at being accessible to as many citizens as possible and at contributing to the development of social justice.

4.48 ◢
Adult literacy program in Brazil (1985)

Muhammad Yunus and Microcredit

Social measures and economic measures are not necessarily incompatible. That is what Bangladeshi economist Muhammad Yunus demonstrated by developing the microcredit system. While traditional banks refuse to lend to the poor for fear of being unable to recover their investment, microcredit institutions agree to loan these people small amounts. These amounts are generally sufficient to start small businesses, such as chicken farms or craft shops. Microcredit enables many families to climb out of extreme poverty and promotes initiative and entrepreneurship.

◢ 4.49
Muhammad Yunus and microcredit users in Bangladesh (1998)
Known as the "banker to the poor," Muhammad Yunus received the Nobel Peace Prize in 2006.

(a) Define the concept of social justice.

(b) Is there a news item that would illustrate your definition of the above concept?

SEEN AND HEARD

" Sustainable peace cannot be possible for large numbers of people unless they have been given the opportunity to get out of poverty. "

Ole Danbolt Mjoes, Nobel Committee Chairman

Social Policies

The social policies developed by States are aimed at achieving social balance and development. They are a testimony to the solidarity among citizens in a given country.

Redistribution

The measures taken to reduce disparity in the distribution of wealth between individuals reflect the desire to achieve greater social justice. Income tax is the most familiar form of redistribution of wealth, but the nationalization of certain resources or industries also allows States to distribute income among all citizens.

Regulation

To defend the weak and to prevent abuse, States can control various activities through appropriate regulations, usually in the form of laws. Depending on the country, labour laws can ensure fairer working conditions and authorize the unionization of employees.

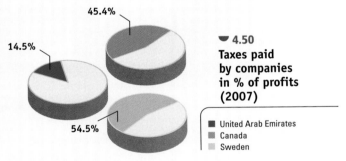

45.4%

14.5%

54.5%

▼ **4.50**
Taxes paid by companies in % of profits (2007)

■ United Arab Emirates
■ Canada
▨ Sweden

Source: World Bank Group, *Paying Taxes 2009 – The Global Picture*, [On-line], 2009.

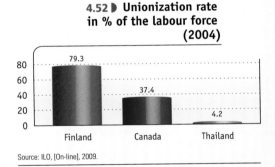

4.52 ▶ Unionization rate in % of the labour force (2004)

79.3

37.4

4.2

Finland   Canada   Thailand

Source: ILO, [On-line], 2009.

Capacity building

Certain State actions aim at creating more equal opportunities for individuals in an effort to make each one capable of taking charge of their own life. The development of effective and accessible health and education systems is a good example of this type of State measure.

Protection of human dignity

States are also in a position to protect the dignity of their citizens by taking action to defend and promote human rights. For example, they can adopt a charter of rights and freedoms or organize public awareness campaigns on certain issues, such as gender equality.

4.51 ▶ Government spending in % of the GDP

Country	Health (2004)	Education (2002-2005)
Iceland	8.3	8.1
Canada	6.8	5.2
Indonesia	1.0	0.9

Source: UNDP, *Human Development Report 2007-2008*, [On-line], 2009.

4.53 ▶ When women obtained the right to vote

Country	Year
New Zealand	1893
Canada (federal)	1917
Saudi Arabia	–

Source: UNDP, *Human Development Report 2007-2008*, [On-line], 2009.

FAIRER AND MORE EQUITABLE TRADE

International trade can be both a source of great wealth and the cause of serious social injustice resulting from the exploitation of the poor. Many solutions have been proposed to make trade fairer and more equitable for everyone involved.

Fair Trade

The model based on free trade and the abolition of trade barriers, which is currently in vogue, is not everyone's preferred option. A number of groups believe that less developed countries should have the right to protect their markets, allowing them to more effectively compete with industrialized countries. This protection is especially important for essential products, such as food, to which everyone should have access.

Others who do not go so far as to reject free trade nonetheless denounce the hypocrisy of developed countries forcing poorer States to open their borders to trade, while they themselves continue to subsidize production in their own countries.

THE TOBIN TAX

IN BRIEF

In 1972, American economist James Tobin suggested TAXING ALL INTERNATIONAL MONETARY AND FINANCIAL TRANSACTIONS. This small tax (between 0.05% and 1%) would slightly reduce the number of monetary transactions, thereby stabilizing the financial system. Also, although this was not Tobin's objective, the profits obtained could be handed over to an international organization for redistribution to developing countries. The "Tobin tax" has yet to be implemented, but a large anti-globalization group, the Association for the Taxation of Financial Transactions for the Aid of Citizens (ATTAC), continues to promote the idea.

◀ 4.54
Sari factory in India (1995)
The WTO allows some States to adopt temporary protectionist measures to protect local industries threatened by foreign competition.

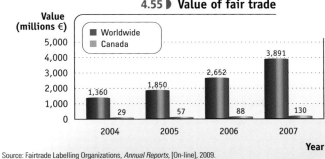
Fair trade represents only a small portion of international trade, but it is a rapidly expanding market. In 2007, approximately 1.5 million producers and workers benefited from fair trade in 58 countries in Africa, Asia and Latin America. Add their friends and families, and this type of trade meets the needs of an estimated 7.5 million people worldwide, approximately equivalent to the population of Québec.

Source: Fairtrade Labelling Organizations, *Annual Reports*, [On-line], 2009.

Fair Trade

Protagonists of fair trade hope to transform international trade. They would like to see fairer trade and are fighting for the rights of producers and workers, in particular the poor and those living in Southern countries.

The principles of fair trade
🔻 **4.56**

People who participate in fair trade set standards they are prepared to respect and promote. These standards include payment of a fair price for products, transparency, good working conditions, the use of environmentally responsible methods and trade relations based on mutual trust and respect.

Fair trade allows producers to set their own objectives, taking into account both production costs and social and environmental costs. These trade practices are therefore compatible with the principles of sustainable development.

Various national and international organizations make sure that fair trade products meet the established standards.
They offer certification that guarantees the integrity of consumer products. The largest of these organizations in Canada is TransFair Canada, a member of Fair Trade Labelling Organizations International (FLO).

Coffee is the main fair trade product, but it is far from the only one. Fair trade flowers, chocolate, sugar, tea, wine, rice, sport balls, cotton garments, quinoa, spices and fruit are also sold in Canada.

173

THE ROLE OF NON-GOVERNMENTAL ORGANIZATIONS

States and intergovernmental organizations are not the only groups to provide developing countries with international aid. Many citizens are also concerned about the planet's problems and make an effort to do what they can to solve them. To be more effective, they often form non-governmental organizations (NGOs).

A Broad Scope of Action

Many NGOs devote their efforts to international development, working to reduce the disparity in the distribution of the world's wealth and to promote greater social justice.

Their actions can take different forms.

- **Information, protest and mobilization campaigns** that inform the public about the situation in developing countries. Advertising campaigns, petitions, boycotts, forums and the production of annual reports widely published in newspapers or on the Internet are all means that can be used.

- **Informing the public authorities** and pressuring governments or international organizations (lobbying) to get them involved in the causes defended by NGOs.

- **Fundraising** allows NGOs to acquire financing, to provide humanitarian aid in emergency situations and to implement different development projects.

- **Projects** provide direct aid to needy populations. The nature of these projects varies on the basis of the expertise developed by each NGO and the specific needs of the countries in question.

4.57 ▶
Water distribution system provided by Oxfam in Cambodia (1992)
Oxfam International is one of the largest of the humanitarian NGOs. Founded in 1942 to meet the needs of a population facing famine, its scope of action has considerably expanded and now includes most aspects of development.

SOCIALLY CONSCIOUS ENTERTAINERS

Socially conscious public figures, such as stars from the world of sports or music, often lend their support to humanitarian aid campaigns. In the mid-1980s, A NUMBER OF POP ARTISTS JOINED FORCES TO PRODUCE SONGS WHOSE PROFITS WERE HANDED OVER TO ORGANIZATIONS TO HELP FIGHT THE FAMINE IN ETHIOPIA. One example is the song "We Are the World," which was a hit in 1985.

▲ 4.58
United Nations Secretary-General Kofi Annan and singer Bono at the G8 Summit (2005)
Singer Bono of U2 fame regularly attends international summits to raise awareness among world leaders of problems in developing countries.

Development Professionals

Volunteers play an essential role in NGOs that promote international development, providing financial support, raising public awareness or devoting time to developing new projects. However, in the field, NGOs primarily need motivated specialists with experience and skills that can be put to use immediately.

4.59 ▲
Doctor treating Rwandan refugees in Burundi (1994)

Health

Doctors and nurses play a major role in emergency humanitarian efforts. Other health care specialists, such as dentists, nutritionists, midwives and psychologists, also contribute significantly in countries where health professionals are often few and far between.

Construction and Engineering

Roads, bridges, hospitals, schools, water-supply systems and new infrastructures require the expertise of construction specialists. Architects, engineers and building technicians are in demand for development projects.

Communication

Raising awareness of problems in developing countries makes it possible to raise funds and encourages governments to support NGO programs. Public relations and marketing professionals, as well as journalists, can help raise awareness of NGO efforts and their special needs.

4.60 ▲
Photojournalists covering the humanitarian crisis in Somalia (1992)

Distribution of seeds in Cambodia (1992)
4.61 ▼

Agriculture

Agricultural specialists, such as agronomists, veterinarians and land-use planning technicians, can help local populations get more out of their fields and livestock, attacking malnutrition and fostering economic independence in the process.

Management

To be efficient, any organization requires management and supervisory specialists, such as accountants, human resources professionals and other administrators. In the field, project managers, coordinators and logistics specialists manage teams and make sure they have everything they need.

THE RESULTS OF INTERNATIONAL AID

It is often difficult to determine whether international aid truly has a positive effect on the development of poor countries or whether, on the contrary, it actually hinders development. The situation is different in each country and must be carefully analyzed before we can accurately assess the usefulness of international aid.

General and Specific Advantages

International aid, such as the vaccination campaigns to fight certain diseases that have reduced the infant mortality rate in Africa and Southeast Asia, can address specific problems. Aid can also contribute more generally to a country's development by fostering an appropriate environment.

Short- or long-term results?

The assessment of the results of international aid differs depending on whether the aid goes toward an emergency situation or general development.

- **Emergency aid,** or humanitarian aid, is a temporary action aimed at providing immediate help for populations facing specific problems, such as famine or a natural disaster.

- **Development aid** is intended to solve problems in a sustainable fashion by dealing with their basic and sometimes highly complex causes. Generally speaking, this type of aid has gradual results, the impact of which may only be recognized in the long run.

4.62 ▲
Makeshift hospital in a school to treat victims of the Rwandan civil war (1994)

CIDA **CANADIAN INTERNATIONAL DEVELOPMENT AGENCY**

A few results

Education • Between 2000 and 2006, the enrollment rate in elementary school in Tanzania rose from 59% to 96%.

Health • In 11 West African countries, a joint project with UNICEF helped reduce the infant mortality rate by 20%.

Access to safe drinking water • In Honduras, 61 000 people now have access to running water thanks to the development of a new supply system.

Reduction of poverty • Between 1991 and 2006, the poverty rate in Ghana fell from 51.7% to 28.5%.

4.63 ▲
School in Tanzania (2001)

CONDITIONAL AID

Conditional aid is money offered to a developing country on the condition that it is used to procure goods and services from the donor country. THIS FORM OF CONTROL, WHICH MOST OFTEN SERVES THE INTERESTS OF THE DONOR COUNTRY RATHER THAN THOSE OF THE RECEIVING COUNTRY, HAS BEEN WIDELY CRITICIZED.

4.64 ▶ Conditional aid (2007)

Country	% of conditional aid
Greece	47
Italy	32
United States	32
Canada	25
France	7
Japan	5
United Kingdom	0

Source: OECD, *Development Co-operation Report 2008*, [On-line], 2009.

A Few Examples of Problems With International Aid

Corruption

Some unscrupulous local leaders may attempt to use international funds to line their own pockets, for example, by reselling material donations on the black market.

Hidden agenda

The motives behind international aid are rarely purely altruistic. Developed countries commonly use donations to increase their influence over developing countries, to open new markets for their products or to defend ideological causes.

Poorly adapted aid

Some organizations provide aid that comes with preconditions, such as economic reforms that are of no benefit to the beneficiary countries. In other cases, the problems are logistical in nature, for example, when there are many donations, but no means of transportation to get them to where they are needed.

Aid that comes . . . and goes

Much of the aid allocated to developing countries is short-lived. In fact, the money received from wealthy countries is often used to pay debts . . . to wealthy countries or to buy products from these same countries.

Competition and dependence

Goods offered free of charge to poor countries can compete with those produced by the local economy. Small craftsworkers therefore face a decline in the demand for their products, which can be deadly for their businesses. In some cases, this can even reduce the populations in question to a certain dependence on international aid.

4.65 ▲
Humanitarian aid for the victims of the earthquake in Bam, Iran (2003)
Some of the pharmaceutical products sent to aid victims of this natural disaster could not be used. The labels were written only in foreign languages and the locals could not read them.

EXTERNAL INTERVENTION IN A SOVEREIGN TERRITORY

CONCEPTS

Topic to Be Interpreted

The legitimacy of external intervention in areas of tension and conflict

Intervention (p. 199)
Diplomacy (p. 193)
Human Rights (p. 189)
Ideology (p. 187)
Interference (p. 205)
Demand (p. 191)

Taking a Position (TAP)

TAP 1 Application of the principle of humanitarian assistance

OR

TAP 2 The interests of intervening parties versus those of populations

The **causes of tension** and conflict have a variety of causes and can take many forms. To **resolve** them, in some cases, international organizations and third States intervene in various ways in areas experiencing conflict and tension. The **legitimacy of external intervention** is the subject of debate, regardless of the **form** it takes.

TENSIONS AND CONFLICTS

5.1 ▶
Downtown Beirut, Lebanon, before and after the war (1985)

TERRITORY AND RESOURCES

The origin of tensions and conflicts between States or populations is usually complex. There is rarely a single cause. Most often, there is an interplay of several factors: territory, control over resources, issues of identity (religion, ethnicity), the quest for political autonomy, etc.

Territory

To exist, a State must have a territory. Throughout history, defending territory and conquering new lands have been at the heart of many international conflicts.

- Certain territories have major **geostrategic importance**, because they provide access to the sea or to an important trade route, for example. Control over the Suez Canal, which links the Mediterranean to the Red Sea, caused an armed conflict in 1956.

- Certain territories are prized for their **natural resources**. For example, from 1966 to 1989, France and Canada disputed the sovereignty of the fishing waters around the French islands of Saint-Pierre-et-Miquelon, located 25 kilometres from Newfoundland.

- Certain **overpopulated** States covet neighbouring territories for land that could be used to settle and feed their populations.

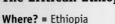

The Eritrean-Ethiopian War

Where? ▪ Ethiopia

When? ▪ May 1998 to June 2000

Who? ▪ The governments of Eritrea and Ethiopia.

Why? ▪ Because Eritrea was demanding land along the border in the areas of Tsorona and Badme.

How? ▪ In May 1998, Eritrea invaded the Badme region of Ethiopia. This invasion provoked a series of armed conflicts along the border between the two countries, involving exchanges of artillery and tank fire, aerial attacks, etc.

Outcome ▪ A peace agreement was signed in December 2000. A border commission, created in collaboration with the Permanent Court of Arbitration in The Hague, drew new borders, yielding the Badme region to Eritrea.

Victims ▪ 70 000 to 100 000 dead

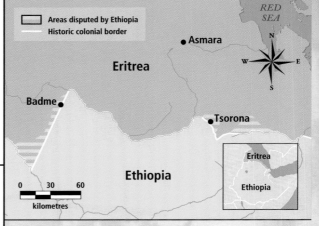

Areas disputed by Ethiopia
Historic colonial border

5.2
Disputed areas (2008)

▲ 5.3
An oil well on fire (1991)
To reduce the aerial visibility for the coalition forces and to spark a decline in the global economy, the Iraqi army set fire to hundreds of oil wells in Kuwait, causing a major environmental disaster.

The Gulf War

Where? ▪ Iraq and Kuwait

When? ▪ August 2, 1990 to February 28, 1991

Who? ▪ Iraq and a coalition of 34 countries led by the United States and supported by the UN.

Why? ▪ On August 2, 1990, Iraq, heavily indebted after eight years of war with Iran, invaded the oil-rich territory of Kuwait to gain the resources necessary to relieve its debt.

How? ▪ The coalition launched an aerial attack to destroy Iraq's military and industrial installations. The military operations ended with a massive land offensive by the coalition forces, which lasted 100 days.

Outcome ▪ Kuwait was liberated and Iraq announced a ceasefire on February 28, 1991.

Victims ▪ 20 000 to 35 000 dead on the Iraqi side; fewer than 400 dead on the coalition side.

Control of Resources

Essential to a State's economic and demographic development, natural resources are a major source of tension and conflict. Since resources are unequally distributed around the world, certain countries are coveted by others, leading to disputes. Struggles break out over the control of resources such as fossil fuels, water and minerals.

Water in the Middle East

In many countries, such as Syria, Iraq, Jordan, Lebanon and Israel, fresh water is scarce and unevenly distributed. To make matters worse, population growth is causing an increase in water needs (consumption, agriculture). This has created ongoing tension between countries hoping to control the major watercourses in the region. During the Six-Day War in 1967, Israel captured the Golan Heights to gain control of one of the sources of the Jordan River. Syria continues to demand the return of this territory.

The resources of the Democratic Republic of the Congo

Since 1994, the Democratic Republic of the Congo has been the theatre of numerous armed conflicts. As a result of the political instability that followed the fall of the dictator Mobutu, fighting broke out between various Congolese factions organized into militias. In addition, the armies of neighbouring countries (Rwanda, Uganda, Burundi, Zimbabwe) invaded the country. With the complicity of a large number of multinationals, the militias and armies pillaged the Congo's wealth, particularly its mineral (diamonds, gold, cobalt) and forestry resources.

5.4 ▶
The Ataturk Dam in Turkey (1992)
Using dams, Turkey controls the flow of the Euphrates, the main source of drinking water in Syria and Iraq. When the Ataturk Dam was filled in 1990, the flow of the Euphrates was virtually cut off for almost a month.

ISSUES OF IDENTITY

Societies are not homogenous. Each population is composed of a multitude of cultures that coexist within a single country or region. However, this coexistence is not always peaceful. Differences in identity, whether religious, ethnic or linguistic, can be sources of tension.

The Proliferation of States

Since the First World War, with the dismantlement of empires (Austro-Hungarian, Ottoman, colonial) and the collapse of communism, nearly 150 new States have been created. However, the borders of these new States do not always take into account the existence of ethnic, linguistic or religious minorities. This sometimes forces different peoples, each with their own strong identity, to live together in a young State that consequently has a weak sense of nationhood.

In some regions of the world, this situation has created tensions and persistent violence, particularly in the Balkans (Southeastern Europe), the Caucasus (former USSR), Central Asia and Africa. For example, from 1991 to 2001, after the fall of communism and the breakup of Yugoslavia, the Balkan region was torn apart by a series of bloody ethnic conflicts.

⌒ 5.5
House destroyed during the siege of Sarajevo (1993)
From April 5, 1992 to February 29, 1996, Serbian forces besieged Sarajevo, a mostly Muslim city. The siege, the longest in the 20th century, caused 10 000 deaths and destroyed the city.

The War in Bosnia-Herzegovina

Where? ▪ Bosnia-Herzegovina, in the Balkans

When? ▪ April 5, 1992 to December 21, 1995

Who? ▪ The ethnic groups of Bosnia-Herzegovina: the Bosnian Muslims (44% of the population), the Orthodox Serbs (31%) and the Catholic Croats (17%).

Why? ▪ In April 1992, Bosnia-Herzegovina declared independence from Yugoslavia, however, the Serb minority refused the secession, preferring to remain within the Federal Republic of Yugoslavia (present-day Serbia).

How? ▪ The Serb minority formed a militia to attack Bosnian Muslims and Croats. It took control of the Serb majority territories and adopted a policy of ethnic cleansing to create a homogenous territory.

Outcome ▪ The Dayton Agreement turned Bosnia-Herzegovina into a confederation of two territories: The Federation of Bosnia and Herzegovina and the Bosnian Serb Republic.

Victims ▪ Over 100 000 dead, including 55 000 civilians

5.6 ▶
A London bus destroyed by a bomb during a terrorist attack (2005)
Members of Al Qaeda claimed responsibility for the attacks that killed 50 and injured 700 in London in July 2005.

The Issue of Religion

Religion and conflict

Religious differences have fed many conflicts throughout history. There are religious dimensions in the Israeli-Palestinian conflict, as there were in the war in Bosnia-Herzegovina. However, religion is rarely the main cause of conflict. It is generally an added element to other pre-existing rivalries (political, economic, social, ethnic), further exacerbating tensions, particularly in internal conflicts between inhabitants of a single State.

A fear of Muslim fundamentalism

The growing number of terrorist attacks by Muslim fundamentalist groups has fed a fear of Islam in the West, particularly following the attacks on September 11, 2001. These fundamentalists are engaged in a holy war against those they see as opponents of Islam. They also believe that the United States and their allies are interfering in the internal affairs of Muslim countries to serve Western interests. That has been the source of their commitment to extreme violence since the Gulf War.

Al Qaeda and Terrorism

Where? ▪ Al Qaeda is not politically linked to any State. It perpetrates terrorist attacks all over the world.

When? ▪ Since the early 1990s

Who? ▪ Founded by the Saudi, Osama bin Laden, and the Egyptian, Ayman al-Zawahiri, Al Qaeda is a terrorist movement organized into a transnational network.

Why? ▪ It adheres to Muslim fundamentalism, a radical reading of the Qu'ran. Its followers seek to convert the world to Islam, attacking those who oppose this goal.

How? ▪ Al Qaeda almost systematically uses suicide attacks. Fundamentalists consider the authors of these attacks to be martyrs who sacrifice their lives for the holy war and are rewarded with eternal salvation.

Outcome ▪ Since September 11, 2001, the United States has made the fight against terrorism a priority. Despite this, Al Qaeda's attacks have continued; for example, in Bali (2002), Istanbul (2003), Madrid (2004), London (2005), Algiers (2007), etc.

◀ 5.7
Attack on the World Trade Center
On September 11, 2001, members of Al Qaeda hijacked planes and flew them into the World Trade Center towers, a symbol of American financial power. The towers collapsed, causing close to 3 000 deaths.

Tensions and Conflicts

THE QUEST FOR POLITICAL AUTONOMY

In the name of self-determination, colonized peoples and minorities demand greater political power so that they can become the masters of their own destinies. Some wish to create their own State or to gain independence for their country, using force if necessary.

One Nation, One Country

A nation is made up of individuals with a shared culture, language and history. For many nationalists, the members of a single nation must be permitted to govern themselves, based on the principle of the self-determination of peoples.

There are also many ethnic, linguistic or religious minorities demanding greater political autonomy that would allow them to participate in making decisions that affect them. Some even demand the creation of their own country, a goal that is not always well received.

These situations can cause tension and conflict. From 1945 to 2005, more than 70 armed conflicts were waged for the right to self-determination.

The Right to Self-Determination of Peoples

The right to self-determination of peoples is the principle according to which all peoples have the right to rule themselves and to make decisions that concern them. This principle was advocated by American President Woodrow Wilson in the aftermath of the First World War and was enshrined in the UN Charter in 1945.

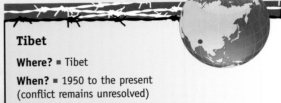

Tibet

Where? ▪ Tibet

When? ▪ 1950 to the present (conflict remains unresolved)

Who? ▪ The Chinese communist government and the Tibetan government-in-exile (in India since 1959), led by the Dalai Lama.

Why? ▪ In 1950, China invaded Tibet and made it a Chinese province. Tibetans first demanded a return to independence. Since 1979, the Dalai Lama has demanded Tibet's autonomy within China and the recognition of the region's cultural identity.

How? ▪ The Chinese government severely represses Tibetan revolts. It has transferred large numbers of Chinese to Tibet in an effort to make Tibetans a minority in their homeland, and thereby assimilate them.

Outcome ▪ Despite numerous meetings between the Chinese and Tibetan governments, no solution has been found (1990).

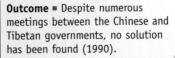

5.8 ▶

A Buddhist monastery in Tibet
During the Cultural Revolution (1966–1976), the Chinese government destroyed close to 6 000 Buddhist monasteries in Tibet, pillaged temples and burned down libraries.

5.9
Indian soldiers stationed on the border of Kashmir (2002)
Since the departure of the British from India and the creation of Pakistan in 1947, there have been tensions between the two States, particularly in the Kashmir region. These tensions have led to three open wars (1947, 1965 and 1971) and many crises.

Decolonization

From the end of the Second World War to the collapse of the USSR, dozens of colonized countries in Asia, Africa and Eastern Europe gained their political independence. They freed themselves from their colonizers according to the principle of the self-determination of peoples. While the process of decolonization can be peaceful, it has often caused tension and conflict.

- In some instances, colonized countries had to use force to gain their independence because their colonial rulers, who wanted to safeguard their economic interests, repressed nationalist movements. This inflamed the situation, causing it to degenerate into violence and, in some cases, full-scale armed conflict. This was the case during both the Algerian struggle for independence from France and the Angolan struggle to free itself from Portugal.

- In other cases, the transition to independence was accompanied by internal ethnic or religious conflict. The colonizing powers, which had favoured certain ethnic or religious groups over others, fed the tensions between minorities. For example, when the British left India in 1947, violence broke out between Hindus and Muslims, leading to the partition of the territory into two States, India and Pakistan, and to massive population relocation.

Barricades Week in Algiers (1960)
In January 1960, part of the French population of Algeria, who felt abandoned, demonstrated against the French government because it was contemplating granting Algerians the right to self-determination.
5.10 ▼

The Algerian War

Where? ■ Algeria

When? ■ 1954 to 1962

Who? ■ France and the Front de libération national (FLN – National Liberation Front), an Algerian nationalist movement.

Why? ■ The Algerians, colonized by France since the 19th century, wanted to win their independence and to take power away from the *"pieds noirs,"* French settlers who had lived in Algeria for generations.

How? ■ The FLN organized guerrilla warfare and terrorist attacks that targeted public buildings, the army and communication networks. France sent a large armed force and severely repressed the movement, torturing dozens of suspects.

Outcome ■ Algeria gained independence in July 1962 and 1.5 million *"pieds noirs"* had to relocate to France.

Victims ■ Close to one million dead

IDEOLOGICAL CONFLICTS

Beyond ethnic or religious differences, there are also ideological differences that can be the source of tension and conflict. These divergences pertain to the type of government, the distribution of wealth, economic development, etc.

5.11 ▲
The Khmer Rouge's agrarian society (1978)
The Khmer Rouge perceived city dwellers as corrupt and forced them to work in agricultural communes, thereby purifying themselves through manual labour. Many died of hunger or treatable disease, since the leaders did not believe in the benefits of Western medicine.

Ideologies

The confrontation of differing ideologies can lead to tension and conflict. In the 1960s, the communist Khmer Rouge led a civil war against the government of Cambodia, in Asia. From 1975 to 1979, the organization ruled the country, managing to destroy the foundations of the society, causing the deaths of two million fellow citizens in the process.

The Cold War

Example of an ideological conflict

From the end of the Second World War to the collapse of the Soviet Bloc (1945–1991), international relations were dominated by the tensions and the ideological conflict between the two superpowers – the capitalist United States and the communist USSR – and their respective allies.

The two superpowers made threats but avoided direct confrontation, preferring to wage war through their allies. They never pushed the conflict to the extreme, fearing the outbreak of a nuclear war. Instead, they waged a war of influence, as well as an arms race (involving conventional and nuclear weapons) and a technological rivalry.

Aerial photograph of Soviet missiles in Cuba (1962)
In October 1962, the Americans discovered nuclear installations built by the Russians in Cuba, less than 200 kilometres from their territory. This episode, which brought the world to the brink of a nuclear war for a few days, marked a turning point in the Cold War.
5.12 ▼

Created in the context of the Cold War, the North Atlantic Treaty Organization (NATO) lost its natural adversary when the Warsaw Pact was dissolved. The organization, which today includes 19 States, has integrated several former members of the Warsaw Pact, including the Czech Republic, Poland and Hungary. NATO CONTINUES TO ENSURE SECURITY AND STABILITY and to defend democracy and human rights within the territory of the alliance.

IN BRIEF

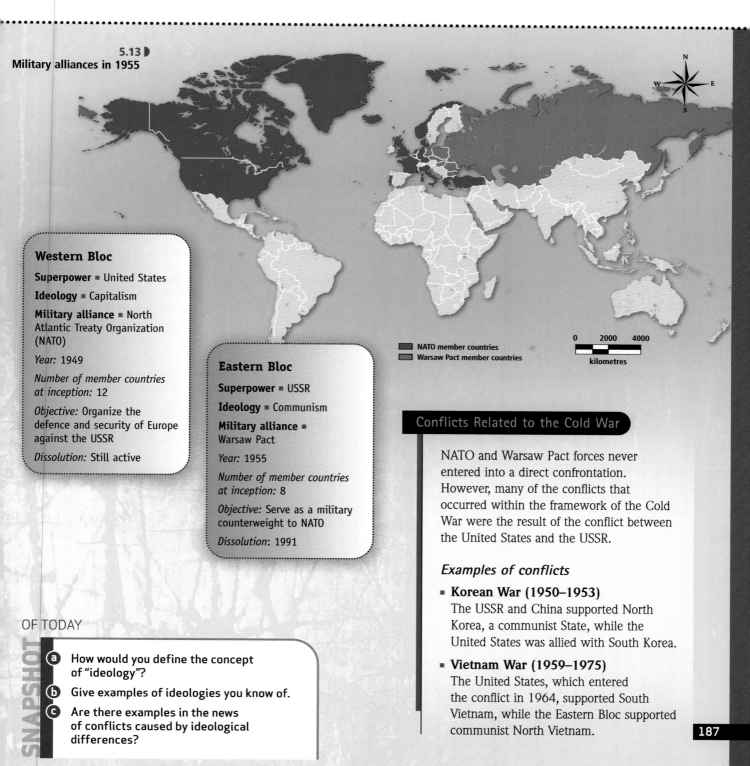

5.13 ▶
Military alliances in 1955

NATO member countries
Warsaw Pact member countries

0   2000   4000
kilometres

Western Bloc

Superpower ▪ United States

Ideology ▪ Capitalism

Military alliance ▪ North Atlantic Treaty Organization (NATO)

Year: 1949

Number of member countries at inception: 12

Objective: Organize the defence and security of Europe against the USSR

Dissolution: Still active

Eastern Bloc

Superpower ▪ USSR

Ideology ▪ Communism

Military alliance ▪ Warsaw Pact

Year: 1955

Number of member countries at inception: 8

Objective: Serve as a military counterweight to NATO

Dissolution: 1991

Conflicts Related to the Cold War

NATO and Warsaw Pact forces never entered into a direct confrontation. However, many of the conflicts that occurred within the framework of the Cold War were the result of the conflict between the United States and the USSR.

Examples of conflicts

- **Korean War (1950–1953)**
  The USSR and China supported North Korea, a communist State, while the United States was allied with South Korea.

- **Vietnam War (1959–1975)**
  The United States, which entered the conflict in 1964, supported South Vietnam, while the Eastern Bloc supported communist North Vietnam.

SNAPSHOT OF TODAY

ⓐ How would you define the concept of "ideology"?

ⓑ Give examples of ideologies you know of.

ⓒ Are there examples in the news of conflicts caused by ideological differences?

EXERCISING RIGHTS AND FREEDOMS

In the aftermath of the Second World War, the United Nations adopted the first international declaration of human rights. Sixty years later, in spite of the apparent progress with respect to rights and freedoms, many abuses still exist, fueling tension and conflict.

The UN's Universal Declaration of Human Rights

Adopted on December 10, 1948, by the UN General Assembly, the Universal Declaration of Human Rights explicitly sets out the rights and freedoms of every human being, establishing them as universal values.

This highly symbolic text is not a tool of international law. It cannot be used to penalize human rights violations. There are other instruments for this purpose, such as the International Covenant on Civil and Political Rights and the International Covenant on Economic, Social and Cultural Rights, as well as institutions like the International Criminal Court.

Principal Human Rights

- The right to life, liberty and security
- Freedom of thought, expression, religion and association
- Equality before the law
- The right to paid work and social security
- The right to education
- The right to privacy
- The free circulation of citizens

SEEN AND HEARD

" **Article 1**
All human beings are born free and equal in dignity and rights. They are endowed with reason and conscience and should act toward one another in a spirit of brotherhood.

Article 2
Everyone is entitled to the rights and freedoms set forth in this Declaration, without distinction of any kind, such as race, colour, sex, language, religion, political or other opinion, national or social origin, property, birth or other status. "

Universal Declaration of Human Rights, 1948

◀ 5.14
Shirin Ebadi
A lawyer by training, Iranian Shirin Ebadi became the first Muslim woman to win the Nobel Peace Prize, in 2003.

SNAPSHOT

ⓐ After reading the list of the principle human rights, identify three of their defining characteristics.

ⓑ Give an example drawn from the news of human rights violations.

A FEW FIGURES (2007)

- In 81 COUNTRIES, men and women were tortured.
- In 77 COUNTRIES, freedom of expression was denied.
- In 54 COUNTRIES, men and women were denied a fair trial.
- In 24 countries, 1252 PEOPLE were executed by the State.

Source: Amnesty International.

Violations of Rights and Freedoms

Despite the international community's efforts to safeguard rights and freedoms, many abuses, including torture, slavery, censorship, arbitrary arrest and the recruitment of child soldiers, still occur around the world. These violations of rights and freedoms are more frequent under authoritarian regimes that hold onto power by controlling information, making arbitrary arrests, inflicting degrading or cruel treatment, etc. These methods are also used in certain democracies.

A cause of conflict

The violation of rights and freedoms is a source of tension and conflict. Populations or minorities subject to these violations use various means (demonstrations, petitions, strikes, etc.) to demand respect for their rights. Their demands sometimes lead to violence, degenerating into riots or armed insurrections. In some cases, demonstrations are repressed by force, as was the case in Tiananmen Square, in China. Human rights violations can also legitimize armed intervention by the international community in a country, as occurred in Somalia in 1992.

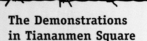

The Demonstrations in Tiananmen Square

Where? ▪ Beijing, China

When? ▪ April 15 to June 4, 1989

Who? ▪ A movement of students and intellectuals and the Chinese communist government.

Why? ▪ The demonstrators denounced the corruption of the communist regime and demanded political and democratic reforms, particularly a multi-party system and freedom of expression.

How? ▪ Through hunger strikes and numerous demonstrations in Tiananmen Square, which brought together hundreds of thousands of people.

Outcome ▪ On May 20, 1989, the Chinese government declared martial law, suspending citizens' rights. On June 4, it sent the army into Beijing to crush the movement.

Victims ▪ 700 to 3000 dead

5.15 ▶
Soldiers and demonstrators in Tiananmen Square (1989)
In 2009, the Chinese government has yet to acknowledge the scope of the events in 1989 and refuses to talk about them.

THE COMPLEXITY OF CONFLICTS:
The Israeli-Arab Conflict

The Israeli-Arab conflicts have endured for over 60 yeas, illustrating the multiple causes than can lead to tensions and the complexity of a conflictual situation. These conflicts are also a case study of how the international community intervenes in a conflict area.

The Causes of the Conflicts

Territory ▪ On May 15, 1948, Zionist Jews created the State of Israel in Palestine, despite the presence of Arab Palestinians living in this territory. The Palestinians consider their territory occupied and resist this foreign presence.

Resources ▪ While the Middle East is suffering from hydric stress, Israel controls important sources of drinking water, namely the basin of Lake Tiberias and the main tributaries of the Jordan River (since its occupation of the Golan Heights in 1967).

Religion ▪ The conflict pits Israeli Jews against Palestinians and several Arab States with majority Muslim populations. Control over the city of Jerusalem, a sacred site for Jews, Muslims and Christians, is also a major issue.

Ethnicity ▪ Zionism, the movement behind the creation of Israel, considers Jews not only to be followers of Judaism, but also the members of a nation, the people of Israel. They therefore also form an ethnic and cultural community.

The quest for political autonomy ▪ As a nation, Jews wish to rule themselves and govern their own State. For their part, Palestinians want to create a Palestinian State recognized by the entire international community, a goal they have yet to attain.

Israel
Majority Palestinian territories occupied since 1967:
• Gaza
• West Bank
Territory occupied since 1967 and annexed in 1981
• Golan Heights

5.16 ▲
Israel (2009)

ZIONISM

Arising at the end of the 19th century, Zionism is an ideology and political movement that advocates the creation of a Jewish State in Palestine that will bring together all of the Jews of the Diaspora. This movement seeks to deliver to Jews the land they possessed in antiquity and sees in the creation of a State a remedy for anti-Semitism.

SNAPSHOT OF TODAY

ⓐ How would you define the concept of "demands"?

ⓑ Various types of demands can be made during a conflict. Cite an example of a current conflict and identify the types of demands advanced by the two parties involved.

First Israeli-Arab War

In May 1948, several Arab States (Egypt, Transjordan, Syria, Iraq, Lebanon) refused to recognize the existence of Israel and joined the Palestinians to attack this new country. Israel won the war, expanding its territory in the process.

The Six-Day War

The rise in Arab nationalism exacerbated tensions with Israel. When Egypt imposed a blockade on the Strait of Tiran, Israel launched lightning attacks. It invaded the Sinai Peninsula in Egypt, the Gaza Strip, the West Bank, East Jerusalem and the Golan Heights in Syria.

The First War in Lebanon

Israel invaded Lebanon to attack bases of the Palestine Liberation Organization (PLO), a resistance movement founded in 1964. The PLO was forced out of Lebanon, and Israel continued to occupy part of southern Lebanon until 2000.

1948 1949   1956   1967 1973   1982   2000 2006

The Suez War

When Egypt announced the nationalization of the Suez Canal, Israel joined France and Great Britain to respond militarily. However, after the victory of these allies, the United States and the USSR forced Israeli and European troops to withdraw from Egypt.

The Yom Kippur War

To recover the territories lost in 1967, Egypt and Syria attacked Israeli troops stationed in the Sinai Peninsula and the Golan Heights. Israel won the war and signed a peace treaty with Egypt that included restoring the Sinai to Egypt.

The Second War in Lebanon

In July 2006, Israel attacked Lebanon in an effort to destroy Hezbollah, a Lebanese Shiite political movement created after the 1982 invasion. In August, the UN Security Council ordered a ceasefire and called on the Israeli troops to withdraw.

5.17 ◖

Signature of the Oslo Accords under the aegis of the President of the United States, Bill Clinton (1993)
In 1993, following secret negotiations held in Oslo, Denmark, the representatives of Israel and Palestine, Yitzhak Rabin and Yasser Arafat, signed accords that provided for the creation of an autonomous Palestinian Authority.

External Interventions

Since the beginning of the conflict, the international community has intervened extensively in the Middle East. In 1947, the UN drew up a plan to divide Palestine, but the Arab States never endorsed it. Since then, the Security Council and the General Assembly have adopted nearly a hundred resolutions dealing with the Israeli-Arab conflict.

Foreign powers, particularly the United States, have also been involved in a peace process that began in 1993, with the goal of finding a lasting solution to the conflict. In 2009, the situation remains unresolved.

DIPLOMACY

Tensions between States or within populations do not always degenerate into armed conflict. In many cases, the parties manage to reach an agreement and negotiate a compromise through diplomacy rather than violence. In cases of armed conflict, diplomatic discussions often help to restore peace.

What Is Diplomacy?

Diplomacy involves the practices and institutions that a State uses to peacefully interact with other countries and implement the foreign policy adopted by its government. Diplomats representing a State are responsible for developing friendly political, economic, social and cultural relations with other countries.

Through negotiation and bargaining, they must find common ground between their sometimes diverging interests. Diplomatic relations can therefore be tense and conflictual.

The steps of international negotiations
▾ 5.18

1 Preliminary Condition
The States must have common or complementary interests to negotiate.

2 Prior to Negotiations
- The States (two or more) identify their common interests.
- Each party presents its maximum demands.
- Each party tries to understand the minimum expectations of the other States (to what extent are they prepared to be flexible), being careful to avoid revealing their own minimum expectations.

3 Negotiations
- Lengthy discussions are often required to reach an acceptable compromise between the minimum and maximum expectations of each of the parties.
- If the negotiations are not successful, the parties can try to bargain.

4 Bargaining
- States bargain to encourage the other parties to accept their demands, simultaneously trying to get them to reduce their own.
- The most commonly used bargaining tools are threats of sanctions (economic sanctions, reduced military aid, etc.) and promises of rewards (investments, liberalized trade, etc.).
- A State's bargaining room is determined by its economic, political and military strength.

5 Results of Negotiations
- If the parties reach a compromise at the end of the negotiations or bargaining, they may sign an agreement.
- If negotiations and bargaining fail, the problem remains and the situation may degenerate into armed conflict.

THE RED PHONE

On August 30, 1963, when the world was brought to the brink of a nuclear disaster during the Cuban missile crisis, THE UNITED STATES AND THE USSR DECIDED TO ESTABLISH A DIRECT LINE OF COMMUNICATION BETWEEN THEIR HEADS OF STATE. They wanted to avoid a similar crisis in the future and to prevent the Cold War from deteriorating into a nuclear war. This communication line, which the media dubbed the "red phone," was in fact a teleprinter circuit.

The Main Diplomatic Actors

Inside the country

Central government ▪ A country's foreign policy orientations are determined by its central government, namely, its head of State and ministers.

Minister of Foreign Affairs ▪ The Minister of Foreign Affairs manages the implementation of a State's foreign policy and the country's diplomatic corps, both domestically and abroad.

Abroad

Embassy ▪ Established in a foreign capital, an embassy is the permanent diplomatic presence of one country in another. It serves to protect the interests of its country, to negotiate agreements on its behalf and to gather information on the host country for its government.

Consulate ▪ It is responsible for protecting and providing administrative services to its nationals in a foreign country. It also promotes the development of trade, economic, scientific and cultural relations with the host country. A State may open several consulates in another country, usually in the major cities.

Other diplomatic missions ▪ States send diplomatic delegations to represent them within international organizations or at international meetings and summits. In certain organizations, such as the UN, these delegations play a role equivalent to embassies.

EMBASSY TERRITORY

By virtue of the principle of extraterritoriality, States enjoy full sovereignty over their embassy's territory and buildings. This means that no search can be conducted and no summons served at the embassy by the host country's authorities without it being perceived as an invasion. That is why people demanding political refugee status often attempt to flee their country by seeking refuge inside a foreign embassy.

▲ 5.19
Seizure of the American embassy in Tehran, Iran (1979)
In 1979, Islamist students attacked the American embassy in Tehran, seizing classified documents and taking some 60 hostages. This was considered an attack on the United States.

SNAPSHOT OF TODAY

ⓐ What do you think diplomacy means?

ⓑ Using an example drawn from the news, explain how diplomacy can be used to resolve a disagreement between two countries.

ARMED CONFLICTS (I)

When tensions between peoples or States are not resolved by diplomatic means, they can descend into violence. This violence can take the form of sporadic incidents (riots, assassinations, terrorist attacks) or armed conflict (conventional war, civil war, genocide, etc.).

Conventional War Between States

Conventional war pits regular State armies (ground, maritime and air) using non-nuclear weapons (guns, tanks, fighter aircraft, bombers, submarines, etc.) against each other. This type of conflict has not completely disappeared, but is in decline. In fact, the most powerful States try to avoid it due to its high cost in terms of weaponry, equipment and human life.

Moreover, the geography of inter-State (between States) conflicts has changed. There are more conflicts in the South than in the North, particularly in Africa and Asia. From 1998–2007, only four inter-State conflicts were recorded: Eritrean-Ethiopia (1998-2000), India-Pakistan (1998-2003), Iraq-United States (2003) and Israel-Lebanon (2006).

Nuclear War

To this day, nuclear war has been more theoretical than real. The atomic bomb has been used twice in the context of war: in 1945, the United States dropped the first atomic bomb on Hiroshima and the second on Nagasaki, two cities in Japan. The Cold War was marked by the nuclear arms race, but fortunately these weapons of mass destruction remained a means of persuasion.

In 1968, to prevent nuclear arms from spreading around the world, many countries signed the Nuclear Non-Proliferation Treaty on the initiative of the United States and the USSR. The International Atomic Energy Agency (IAEA), an organization affiliated with the UN, monitors its application.

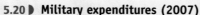

5.20 ▶ **Military expenditures (2007)**

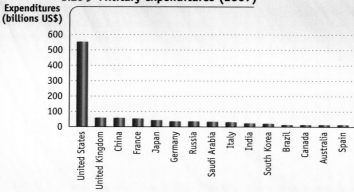

Expenditures (billions US$)

Country

Source: Stockholm International Peace Research Institute, [On-line], 2009.

◀ **5.21**
Nuclear test in the Pacific (1952)

Civil War

A civil war is a conflict that takes place within a State. It pits the government's regular army against groups of armed citizens. An internal conflict can be caused by political, religious, ethnic, economic or other tensions.

Since the end of the Cold War, inter-State conflicts have become rare, while civil wars have multiplied, except in North America and Western Europe. Armed struggles, which go beyond insurrection and last for a certain period of time, often use less costly forms of combat than conventional war, such as guerrilla or militia attacks.

Guerrilla warfare

A combat strategy based on mobility, harassment and the element of surprise, guerrilla warfare allows small armed groups to attack a more powerful army, such as the national army. This tactic is often employed by ad hoc armies with limited military capacity.

Militia war

A war led by private armies whose fighters are recruited on the basis of identity (ethnic, religious, familial) or partisanship (attachment to a politician). They are often composed of mercenaries who are paid to fight.

◢ **5.22**
Child soldiers recruited by the Tamil Tigers (1991)
According to UNICEF, in the last decade, over 300 000 children under 18 years of age have participated in more than 30 armed conflicts around the world.

The Sri Lankan Civil War

Where? ▪ Sri Lanka

When? ▪ 1983 to 2009

Who? ▪ The Sri Lankan government and the Liberation Tigers of Tamil Eelam (LTTE).

Why? ▪ The Tamil minority (18% of the population) is demanding the creation of an independent State in the north and east of the island.

How? ▪ In addition to employing conventional war tactics and guerrilla warfare, the Tamil Tigers used terrorist suicide attacks that targeted civil society. Hundreds of child soldiers are involved in this conflict.

Outcome ▪ Truces were negotiated several times, but they were invariably broken. In 2009, the military launched a major offensive, crushing the LTTE, which admitted defeat on May 17 of that year.

Victims ▪ 70 000 to 100 000 dead and one million displaced persons (2009)

ARMED CONFLICTS (II)

Terrorism

Terrorism is characterized by major acts of violence designed to create as many victims as possible. The goal is not to destroy the enemy, but rather to sow terror in an effort to demoralize the enemy and lead to capitulation. Terrorist acts are generally spectacular: hostage taking, assassination, destruction of buildings, etc. Some attacks only target State representatives: diplomats, members of the military or police, politicians. Others target civilians, striking crowded public areas, such as shopping centres, airports, train stations, places of worship or financial institutions.

A combat strategy

Terrorism is a strategy of the weak against the strong. These acts require limited means, but have a very big impact. Terrorism is used in armed conflicts, particularly in civil wars, but also during periods of peace. It is a strategy to put pressure on a country without resorting to war. In many cases, it is committed by organized groups that belong to transnational networks, many of which, such as Al Qaeda, are based in the Middle East.

Fighting terrorism

After the September 11, 2001 attacks, the United States made the fight against terrorism a top priority. It created an international coalition to fight terrorism. However, the members of terrorist networks are hard to identify and are often mistakenly believed to be agents of their country of origin. Consequently, it is difficult to militarily pursue them, as this usually involves attacks on sovereign territory.

TERRORISM IN NUMBERS

In 2007 there were:

- 14 499 TERROR ATTACKS committed worldwide, 43% of which occurred in Iraq

- 355 ATTACKS resulting in the death of at least 10 people

- 22 685 DEATHS, 44 310 INJURED AND 5 071 KIDNAPPINGS as a result of terrorist attacks

Source: US Department of State, *Country Report on Terrorism*, [On-Line], 2007.

IN BRIEF

5.23 ▶

5.23 On November 15, 2003, car bombs destroyed two synagogues in Istanbul, Turkey, killing 25 and injuring more than 300
The images of terrorist attacks are widely circulated in the media, which contributes to maintaining a climate of fear and insecurity among the population. Terrorist groups use this media coverage to claim responsibility for an attack and to diffuse their message.

" In the present Convention, genocide means any of the following acts committed with intent to destroy, in whole or in part, a national, ethnical, racial or religious group, as such:

a. Killing members of the group

b. Causing serious bodily or mental harm to members of the group

c. Deliberately inflicting on the group conditions of life calculated to bring about its physical destruction in whole or in part

d. Imposing measures intended to prevent births within the group

e. Forcibly transferring children of the group to another group. "

Convention on the Prevention and Punishment of the Crime of Genocide, Article 2

Genocides

The intentional extermination of an ethnic, racial or religious group, genocide is considered a crime against humanity. It was defined in the Convention on the Prevention and Punishment of the Crime of Genocide, which the United Nations adopted unanimously in 1948, in the aftermath of the Jewish Holocaust.

5.24 ▶

Concentration camp survivors (1945)
During the Second World War, the Nazis attempted to systematically eliminate the Jews by sending them to death camps. This genocide killed five to six million Jews.

Roméo Dallaire

The Lieutenant-General of the Canadian Army, Roméo Dallaire, led the UN peacekeeping forces in Rwanda in 1993-1994. Ordered not to directly intervene, he became a powerless witness to the genocide. He relates his version of events in his book *Shake Hands with the Devil*.

The Rwandan Genocide

Where? ■ Rwanda

When? ■ April to July 1994

Who? ■ Two ethnic groups: the Hutus, who held the power, and the Tutsis, who belonged to the Rwandan Patriotic Front (RPF).

Why? ■ The Tutsis, many of whom had been forced out of Rwanda by the Hutus between 1959 and 1963, had been trying since 1990 to return and resume their place in the political life of the country. Tensions between the Hutu majority and the Tutsi minority were re-ignited with the implementation of a peace plan that included a power-sharing agreement between the two ethnic groups.

How? ■ Tens of thousands of Hutu militiamen and a segment of the population systematically murdered Tutsis using light arms, particularly machetes.

Outcome ■ The victory of the RPF troops (Tutsis) in July 1994 brought the genocide to an end.

Victims ■ 800 000 dead (mainly Tutsis), 2 million Hutu refugees and 1.5 million displaced persons inside the country (end of 1994)

THE RIGHT TO INTERVENE

The legitimacy of war is an age-old question. International law recognizes each country's right to defend itself when under attack, but prohibits any encroachment on the sovereignty of other States. Under these conditions, are there any circumstances that would justify military intervention in another country?

5.25 ▲
Representatives of the United States sign the Charter of the United Nations (1945)

Two Major Steps

1928 ▪ Signing of the Kellogg–Briand Pact

The 60 or so countries that signed this international treaty renounced war as a means for resolving their disagreements. While in practice the Pact was a failure – the Second World War broke out a few years later – its principles became an integral part of international law. In fact, they were restated a few years later in the Charter of the United Nations.

1945 ▪ Signing of the Charter of the United Nations

Every member of the United Nations agreed to adhere to the principles set out in the Charter, which includes several provisions on the laws of war.

SEEN AND HEARD

The Charter of the United Nations and the laws of war

" Article 2.4 All Members shall refrain in their international relations from the threat or use of force...

Article 2.7 Nothing contained in the present Charter shall authorize the United Nations to intervene in matters which are essentially within the domestic jurisdiction of any state...

Article 7.42 Should the Security Council consider that measures provided for in Article 41 would be inadequate or have proved to be inadequate, it may take such action by air, sea, or land forces as may be necessary to maintain or restore international peace and security. Such action may include demonstrations, blockade, and other operations by air, sea, or land forces of Members of the United Nations.

Article 7.51 Nothing in the present Charter shall impair the inherent right of individual or collective self-defence if an armed attack occurs against a Member of the United Nations. "

The Charter of the United Nations

OF TODAY

5.26
Kigali, Rwanda (1994)
A major in the Canadian Armed Forces walks with children displaced by the civil war in Rwanda.

SNAPSHOT

(a) The key concept of this theme is "intervention." What do you think this concept means?

(b) Is there a conflict being reported in the news that involves an intervention? Which conflict is it?

(c) Who intervened?

(d) What were the effects of this intervention?

The Laws of War

Today, war is considered acceptable only if it respects certain basic and universally accepted principles.

- **Appropriate authority:** War must be waged by public authorities and never by individuals.

- **Just cause:** Force can only be used to correct very serious public wrongdoings.

- **Good intention:** The intention that justifies war must be sincere. There must not be a hidden agenda.

- **Last resort:** War must only be used when all other possible means, for example, negotiations, have been exhausted.

- **Proportionate means:** The means of intervention must suit the scope of the initial problem.

- **Reasonable perspectives:** The probability of the success of war must be sufficient. In other words, the expected damages must not be greater than the problem that led to the war in the first place.

When Is It Legitimate to Intervene in a Conflict?

The principle of non-interference

The Charter of the United Nations prohibits the use of war between States, except in the case of legitimate defence (articles 2.4 and 7.51).

The Charter defends the principle of the sovereignty of States by declaring that no one, including the United Nations, may intervene in the affairs of a State (article 2.7).

Three possible exceptions to the principle of non-interference

1 A State may intervene in the affairs of another State if the latter expressly requests an intervention. A country may, for example, ask for external assistance to bring an end to a rebellion within its borders.

2 The United Nations Security Council may decide to authorize a military intervention to re-establish peace or international security (article 7.42 of the Charter of the United Nations). This is the only international authority that has this power, which must only be used as a last resort.

3 Some people believe that it is legitimate to intervene in the affairs of a State on humanitarian grounds, for example, in the case of massive human rights violations. However, for greater legitimacy, such an intervention should be approved by the United Nations Security Council and carried out by a multinational force.

5.27
Civilians hiding in the forest to escape the fighting in the Democratic Republic of the Congo (2008)
The protection of civilian populations under threat is one of the reasons invoked by the proponents of the right to intervene on humanitarian grounds.

199

THE UNITED NATIONS SECURITY COUNCIL

The Security Council is the executive organ of the United Nations. Its role is to maintain international peace and security, prevent conflicts whenever possible and encourage cooperation among countries.

How the Security Council Functions

An international problem, such as a conflict between two countries, is brought before the Security Council. The United Nations General Assembly, the Secretary General or any member of the Council can present a conflict to the Security Council.

The Council can try to resolve the problem by making a non-binding **recommendation**.

The Council may adopt a **resolution**, which is a decision that must be implemented. It is the only United Nations organ with this power. Between 1946 and 2008, 1859 resolutions have been adopted.

Resolutions are adopted following a vote among members of the Council, each of whom has one vote. To be adopted, a resolution must receive at least nine votes, including those of all of its permanent members, which in practice gives them **veto power**. This right gives permanent members a great deal of power since a resolution cannot be passed if one of these members opposes it.

5.29 ◢
Meeting of the Security Council (2003)

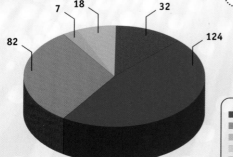

7 18 32

82

124

▼ 5.28
Use of *veto* power by the permanent members

- ■ Russia
- ■ United States
- ■ China
- ■ France
- ■ United Kingdom

Between 1946 and 2008, permanent members exercised their *veto* power 263 times. Russia (then the USSR) used this power often between 1940 and 1950, whereas the United States used it frequently in the 1970s. Today, the *veto* power is exercised more sparingly. During the decade 1998–2008, it was only exercised 16 times.

Composition of the Security Council

- **Five permanent members:** China, United States, France, United Kingdom and Russia.

  These countries are the main victors of the Second World War. Taking into account the British and French colonial empires, they represented the majority of the world's population. These countries also constitute the five nuclear powers.

- **Ten non-permanent members:** elected for two years by the United Nations General Assembly.

  Half of these members are replaced each year. These countries must represent the world's main regions: Africa, Asia, Latin America and the Caribbean, Eastern Europe, Western Europe and others. Between 1946 and 2009, Canada has been chosen for this mandate six times.

◀ **5.30**
Meeting of the Security Council regarding the Korean War (circa 1950)

Functions and powers of the Security Council

- Investigate disagreements and situations that could threaten international peace and security.

- Recommend measures to be taken to reach a peaceful resolution of disagreements.

- Encourage UN Member States to apply economic or diplomatic sanctions to prevent or end aggression.

- As a last resort, take military measures to ensure that its decisions are respected.

Some of the Security Council's Shortcomings

Lack of representativeness

Today, the five permanent members represent less than 30% of the world's population. New powers such as South Africa, Germany, Brazil, India and Japan are demanding that they also receive a permanent seat on the Security Council.

Veto power

The permanent members regularly exercise their *veto* power to prevent the adoption of resolutions that can paralyze the Council. This problem was particularly apparent during the Cold War, with the USSR (now Russia) exercising its *veto* power 106 times between 1946 and 1965. Avoiding this kind of impasse requires long discussions, which delays the adoption of resolutions.

Implementing resolutions

Due to a lack of will or means—the United Nations does not have its own military force—many resolutions are either delayed for extended periods or never implemented. Despite a resolution adopted in 1975 demanding that Indonesia's government withdraw its troops from East Timor, the United Nations only intervened in this region in 1999.

◀ **5.31**
Israel builds a wall around Palestinian territories (2003)
Since 1972, the United States has often used its *veto* power to prevent the Security Council from adopting resolutions regarding Israel, one of its close allies.

201

HUMANITARIAN ASSISTANCE

A request for international intervention in a State's territory does not usually pose a legal problem. However, it is another story in the case of an unsolicited interference that threatens a State's sovereignty. Humanitarian assistance is one of the rare justifications deemed acceptable by the United Nations for departing from the principle of non-interference.

19th Century: Intervention in the Name of Humanity

1 During the 19th century, Western powers invoked the concept of humanitarian intervention to justify colonialism. Many heads of State claimed that it was their duty to intervene in the affairs of African and Asian countries in an effort to defend their own citizens, to fight barbaric practices such as slavery and, generally, to bring civilization. These interventions in the name of humanity were clearly motivated by the interests of colonial States that were eager to reap significant political and economic benefits.

The Biafran War

Where? ▪ Nigeria

When? ▪ 1967 to 1970

Who? ▪ The government of Nigeria and separatist troops in the Biafran region (Igbo people).

Why? ▪ The wealthy region of Biafra was seeking independence.

How? ▪ A number of conventional military operations were employed and the Nigerian government imposed a land and sea blockade on Biafra.

Outcome ▪ The rebellion was quashed, but the blockade led to a terrible famine.

Victims ▪ Over one million dead, primarily civilians due to malnutrition

The 1970s: The Right to Humanitarian Interference

2 The modern idea of humanitarian interference emerged during the Biafran War. Despite broad media coverage of this humanitarian disaster, Western States officially remained neutral, invoking the principle of non-interference in a country's domestic affairs.

Several public figures, such as French doctor Bernard Kouchner, future founder of Doctors Without Borders, denounced this position. They defended the idea that in certain extreme situations, such as massive and repeated human rights violations, external intervention should be allowed on humanitarian grounds, even if it threatens State sovereignty. This is called the "right to interfere."

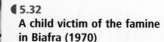

◀ **5.32**
A child victim of the famine in Biafra (1970)

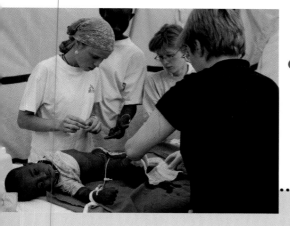

◀ 5.33
A Sudanese refugee camp in Chad run by Doctors Without Borders (2004)
Doctors Without Borders is a non-governmental organization (NGO) created in 1971. The goal of this international association is to facilitate humanitarian medical intervention among populations in crisis situations.

The 1980s: The Obligation to Interfere on Humanitarian Grounds

3 The concept of a right to humanitarian interference gained momentum in the 1980s. In 1988, this principle was officially adopted by the United Nations General Assembly for dealing with victims of natural disasters and other emergency situations. Gradually, people expanded this concept, referring to it as "the obligation to interfere." The proponents of this concept agreed that in the context of a humanitarian crisis, States should not only have the right to intervene, but a moral obligation to act. They rejected what they called the "right to indifference."

United Nations Operation in Somalia (UNOSOM)

Where? ▪ Somalia

When? ▪ 1992 to 1995

Who? ▪ Leaders of the Somali militia and a multinational force led by the United States with UN approval.

Why? ▪ Following the outbreak of civil war in Somalia, the UN decided to intervene to protect humanitarian aid convoys bringing food supplies to the civilian population facing famine.

Outcome ▪ Somali militiamen attacked and killed UN soldiers, leading to a decision on the part of the international community to abandon the country to its fate. The country is still plagued by civil war today (2009).

Particular characteristic ▪ Despite its failure, this operation is one of the first international interventions based on the right to humanitarian interference.

◀ 5.34
A military operation in Somalia (1992)

2001: The Responsibility to Protect

4 In 2000, UN Secretary General Kofi Annan publicly addressed the need for the United Nations to reconcile the basic idea of State sovereignty and the obligation to interfere on humanitarian grounds. The Canadian government created an independent organization mandated to examine this question: the International Commission on Intervention and State Sovereignty (ICISS).

In 2001, the Commission released a report that presented a new concept: the responsibility to protect. According to this principle, protecting civilian populations is an essential condition for State sovereignty. As such, sovereignty is a right that also includes obligations. If a government does not fulfill its obligation to protect its citizens, other States must intervene. This operation of last resort should ideally be authorized by a recognized international organization, such as the United Nations, and should be carried out by a coalition of countries.

Causes of
Tension

Resolving
Tensions

**Legitimacy of
Intervention**

Types of
Intervention

Tensions and Conflicts

INTERESTS OF THE DIFFERENT PARTIES

Few governments are genuinely prepared to take political, financial or human risks with the sole purpose of lending assistance to a foreign population. This is why most international humanitarian interventions are motivated by other interests.

Opposition to Humanitarian Interference

Convened at the Havana Summit in Cuba in 2000, the heads of States of 130 developing countries signed a common declaration denouncing the right of humanitarian interference. In their opinion, this practice is incompatible with the Charter of the United Nations, which defends the sovereignty of every State. The opponents of humanitarian interference base their opposition on four principles:

❶ Uneven intervention

Humanitarian interference always targets poor or weak States, never the richest and most powerful. For example, it would be hard to imagine sending Rwandan troops to protect victims of terrorist attacks in Europe, although the opposite could easily occur.

❷ The risk of non-humanitarian interference

Actors are rarely neutral or impartial. Humanitarian assistance can be used as a pretext to interfere in a country's affairs.

❸ The lack of a systematic approach to intervention

Intervention is carried out on a case-by-case basis: only conflicts that receive broad media coverage are targeted. Chronic humanitarian disasters, such as famines, are rarely taken into consideration.

❹ Insufficient means

Often, those who intervene lack the necessary resources to successfully carry out their mission.

HUMANITARIAN BOMBINGS?

5.35 ▶
A man examines the damage caused by NATO bombings in Serbia (1999)

Some critics feel that humanitarian military interventions do more damage than good for civilian populations. For example, in 1999, NATO bombings during the Kosovo war DESTROYED NOT ONLY MILITARY TARGETS BUT ALSO IMPORTANT CIVILIAN INFRASTRUCTURES, such as roads, bridges, power stations, a television station and even a hospital.

IN BRIEF

SNAPSHOT

(a) How would you define the concept of "interference"?

(b) Give an example of a conflict involving interference.

◀ **5.36**
Food distribution in Cambodia (1992)
The distribution of humanitarian aid provides assistance to populations in need and gives the donor country a good international image.

Many Reasons to Intervene

During the colonial era, the ideals of humanitarian assistance were often used to conceal the political and economic activities of Western powers. Things have not changed much since then. Today, States that engage in international humanitarian interventions usually have a variety of reasons for doing so. Specific State interests often play a role that is just as important, if not more so, than the interests of the local populations they are defending.

5.37 ▶ Some of the reasons for participating in international interventions

Obtaining territorial or economic benefits	Sending troops into another country often provides an opportunity to obtain, directly or indirectly, territorial advantages, such as setting up military bases, or economic benefits, such as privileged access to natural resources.
Defending its citizens and its national interests	Most States have foreign investments and some of their citizens living abroad may require protection during periods of instability.
Defending collective security	Certain extremist regimes can threaten the balance of world peace, by producing weapons of mass destruction, for example.
Improving its international image	Participating in a humanitarian intervention can improve a country's image, contributing to better diplomatic relations with other States.
Increasing its political, military, economic, cultural or other influence	International interventions are a good opportunity to forge privileged ties with certain groups. Generally (but not always), those who have received aid will feel indebted to their benefactors.
Reducing the influence of its rivals	While not providing immediate advantages, interventions can prevent rival States from taking advantage of the situation to increase their own influence.
A sense of identity with the protagonists	Many people are more inclined to support intervention if they share certain characteristics with the victims: ethnicity, religion, political ideology, etc.
Providing assistance to populations in need	Often, humanitarian assistance is but one among many motives, but it may nevertheless be a genuine motive.

Tensions and Conflicts

ECONOMIC AND DIPLOMATIC INTERVENTION

The principles that underpin international relations dictate that the use of armed force must always be a solution of last resort. Before using force, countries must exhaust all other possible forms of pressure, such as economic sanctions or diplomatic intervention.

Economic Intervention

5.38 ▲
Iraqis demonstrate against the United Nations embargo (1993)

Economic sanctions designed to influence State leaders can take various forms. These sanctions may be commercial – involving a ban on the export of certain products, such as arms or military equipment, to the country in question – or they might constitute a complete embargo, terminating all economic relations between two countries. They can also take the form of financial sanctions, such as imposing restrictions on economic aid programs or seizing the assets of the country's leaders.

Economic penalties are used to weaken a State without the direct use of force. Although these measures usually target the leaders of a country, they can inflict considerable suffering on civilians who are deprived of many goods. To avoid this situation, the embargo is often lifted on certain essential goods, such as foodstuffs and pharmaceutical products.

Economic sanctions can be imposed by a single country or by a group of nations. The Charter of the United Nations authorizes the Security Council to adopt a variety of measures of this kind to ensure that its decisions are implemented. From 1990 to 2003, the United Nations imposed an almost total trade embargo on Iraq because the government was suspected of possessing weapons of mass destruction.

Economic Sanctions Adopted by the Canadian Government (2008)

- Ban on the export of all goods: Belarus, Myanmar
- Ban on the export of arms and military equipment: North Korea, Côte d'Ivoire, Iraq, Lebanon, Democratic Republic of the Congo, Rwanda, Sierra Leone, Sudan, Zimbabwe
- Ban on the export of arms and military equipment and the import of diamonds: Liberia
- Ban on the export and import of equipment related to nuclear technology: Iran

CONFLICT DIAMONDS

In 2000, the United Nations General Assembly launched an appeal condemning the trade in diamonds from certain African countries ravaged by civil war. THE SALE OF THESE DIAMONDS IS USED TO FINANCE ARMED GROUPS, PREVENTING THE ESTABLISHMENT OF LASTING PEACE in these regions. A number of countries, including Canada, responded to the General Assembly's appeal by adopting laws that prohibit the purchase of these "conflict diamonds."

Diplomatic Intervention

Sanctions

The state of diplomatic ties between two countries clearly illustrates the quality of their relations: the better these ties, the better their relations in general. Diplomatic sanctions therefore play an important symbolic role in expressing one State's displeasure with another. These sanctions can take various forms, from imposing mandatory visas on visitors from certain countries to the temporary or even permanent withdrawal of ambassadors.

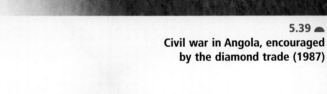

5.39
Civil war in Angola, encouraged by the diamond trade (1987)

Mediation

A country can undertake positive diplomatic intervention by using its influence to calm tensions and help resolve a conflict in another country. Certain respected States can, as a result, play the role of mediator between two adversarial parties. They can organize and supervise meetings between two enemy groups on neutral territory and facilitate negotiations. For example, in 2005, Norwegian diplomats served as mediators in Sudan, Bosnia, Sri Lanka and Colombia.

The U.S. Embargo Against Cuba

Where? ▪ Cuba

When? ▪ Since February 7, 1962

Who? ▪ The United States and Cuba

Why? ▪ To put pressure on Cuba's communist government, which nationalized many American businesses in its territory.

How? ▪ The United States prohibits its citizens from engaging in any trade, economic or financial relations with Cuba.

Outcome ▪ In the early 1960s, the United States was Cuba's main trading partner. The embargo was therefore a severe blow to Cuba's economy, although its effects were mitigated by support from the Soviet Union until the beginning of the 1990s. Since then, the country has diversified its trade relations, but its economic situation remains precarious. Cuba's communist government is still in place today.

5.40
Getting around in Havana (2007)
One of the more visible effects of the embargo is the almost total absence of cars in the capital city of Havana. Many of the cars on the road date back to the 1950s.

Tensions and Conflicts

HIDDEN INFLUENCES

Extremely sensitive in nature, open international intervention generally requires a great deal of diplomacy, money and time. Moreover, it is often difficult to predict the outcome. This is why many States use techniques that are both more direct and more discreet to exercise their international influence.

Intelligence

While James Bond's spectacular spy missions are pure fiction, the intelligence services of each State play a major role in international relations. These services allow governments to gather information vital to both national security and the national economy, to define their diplomatic policy and to conduct military operations in enemy territory. This information is obtained through a wide variety of means, including intercepting communications, using radars, satellites, and covert agents and conducting detailed analyses of public data.

5.41 ▲

Image of a neighbourhood in Baghdad taken by a U.S. satellite (2004)
Spy satellites can observe any location on the planet with very high precision.

▲ 5.42
Fidel Castro (2006)
During his career, Cuban leader Fidel Castro was the target of several hundred assassination attempts – some estimate as many as 638. Various means were used, from a fountain pen filled with poisonous ink to an exploding cigar.

Covert Intervention

Governments can try to intervene in a foreign country by carrying out covert operations using their intelligence services or troops trained for these kinds of activities. Usually illegal under international law, which explains their covert nature, these operations can include kidnappings, attacks, assassinations and targeted military raids. The objectives vary, and may include destabilizing a government, eliminating enemies, supporting a coup d'état, freeing prisoners, etc.

A famous example of this type of operation is the landing in the Bay of Pigs in Cuba, in 1961. The CIA—the U.S. foreign intelligence agency—had recruited, trained and armed a group of Cuban exiles in an effort to overthrow Fidel Castro's communist government. However, Cuban troops decimated these mercenaries, to the great embarrassment of the American government. More sinister and more successful, Operation Condor was a joint campaign of assassinations and political repression carried out by the secret services of several South American dictatorships (Chile, Argentina, Bolivia, Brazil, Paraguay and Uruguay) in the mid-1970s.

◀ **5.43**
An arms merchant in Iraq (1999)

Supporting Foreign Groups

Direct intervention in the affairs of another country always involves significant risks. Intervening governments are obliged to justify their actions or, failing that, to face reprisals in the event of defeat. This is why some States prefer to extend their influence in a more indirect way, by supporting groups whose interests are similar or favourable to their own.

This support can be financial, material or logistical. For example, it can involve the sale of arms and military equipment, training troops or sharing information. It may be recognized publicly, such as in the case of military aid provided by the United States (see the diagram), or it may be secret, such as terrorist training camps in Afghanistan during the Taliban regime.

5.44 ▶ **Military aid from the United States (2006)**

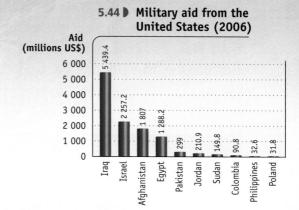

Source: *The U.S. Overseas Loans and Grants (Greenbook)*, [On-line], 2008.

The United States provides military aid to many countries. This results in both better diplomatic relations with these States and increased military capacity for U.S. allies. It also helps less wealthy countries maintain order within their borders.

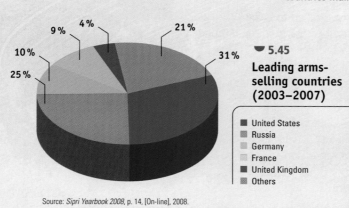

▼ **5.45**
Leading arms-selling countries (2003–2007)

- ■ United States
- ■ Russia
- ■ Germany
- ■ France
- ■ United Kingdom
- ■ Others

Source: *Sipri Yearbook 2008*, p. 14, [On-line], 2008.

The availability of arms plays an important role in fueling tensions and conflicts in the world. In 2007, the total value of the legal trade of arms was estimated at US$60 billion. Another several billion dollars can be added to this amount for illegal arms trafficking.

A DANGEROUS GAME

YESTERDAY'S ALLIES CAN EASILY BECOME TOMORROW'S ENEMIES, as the United States learned the hard way in Afghanistan. During the 1980s, a number of Islamist groups fought against the Soviet invasion of Afghanistan. In the context of the Cold War, the United States invested heavily to support these anti-Soviet combatants, providing them with funding, arms and training. In 1989, once the Soviet invasion had been defeated, these groups, now well equipped and experienced, went on to pursue their own independent objectives. From among their ranks rose the Taliban and the Al Qaeda terrorist network, whose hostility toward the United States triggered a new war in 2001.

IN BRIEF

209

BLUE HELMETS AND PEACEKEEPING MISSIONS

For a long time, the United Nations intervention in world conflicts was limited to sending peacekeeping forces. However, since the end of the Cold War, as recognition of the principle of humanitarian interference has grown, the UN has participated in increasingly ambitious missions.

Different Types of Peace Missions

➊ Prior to the conflict

Conflict prevention ▪ Measures designed to prevent the outbreak of a conflict or to mitigate the effects. This involves being well informed about the cause and the nature of tensions. Various means can then be implemented in an effort to encourage dialogue and build trust between the opposing parties.

➋ During the conflict

Peacemaking ▪ Measures taken to bring conflicting parties closer together in a non-binding manner, with the goal of achieving an agreement. This includes diplomatic negotiations and mediation, as well as preventive deployment of military forces.

Peace enforcement ▪ Coercive measures, including the use of military force, implemented to eliminate threats against peace or to stop acts of aggression.

5.46 ◢
A Spanish Peacekeeper in Bosnia (1993)

➌ After the ceasefire

Peacekeeping and peacebuilding ▪ This is the main form of intervention employed by the United Nations to monitor the application of a ceasefire that has already been reached. It is only possible with the consent of the parties involved. It can include disarming combatants, protecting civilian populations, ensuring public order, supporting humanitarian missions, providing electoral support and encouraging economic and social development. Peacekeeping is part of a larger set of measures that can be implemented to ensure peacebuilding in a conflict-torn region.

BLUE HELMETS IN NUMBERS

Number of peacekeeping missions (2008): 16

Budget (2008–2009): US$7.1 billion

Personnel in uniform (January 2009): 91 382

NUMBER OF COUNTRIES CONTRIBUTING PERSONNEL: 120

Number of deaths (between 1948 and 2008): 2 560

IN BRIEF

5.47
Lester B. Pearson at the United Nations (1957)
The creation of the Blue Helmets earned Lester B. Pearson, Canada's Minister of Foreign Affairs, the Nobel Peace Prize in 1957. The Blue Helmets themselves received the Nobel Prize in 1988.

The Blue Helmets

The first United Nations peace missions were composed entirely of observers. During the Suez Canal Crisis in 1956, Lester B. Pearson, Canada's future prime minister, proposed sending in armed troops under the leadership of the United Nations to maintain peace between the opponents. This marked the beginning of the United Nations Peacekeeping Forces, also known as the Blue Helmets because of the colour of their helmets.

The Peacekeepers are troops contributed by various countries and serving under the United Nations in the context of well-defined missions. Both officers and soldiers remain members of their respective national armed forces and do not constitute a United Nations army. The Peacekeepers can also include police officers and civilian personnel serving peacekeeping functions.

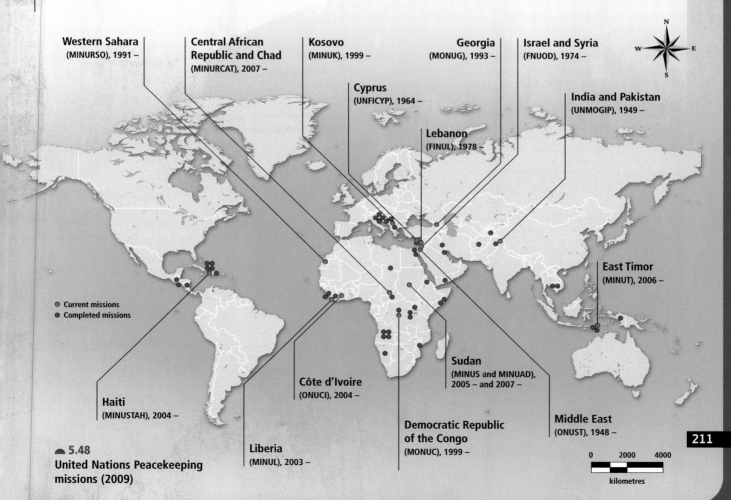

Western Sahara
(MINURSO), 1991 –

Central African Republic and Chad
(MINURCAT), 2007 –

Kosovo
(MINUK), 1999 –

Georgia
(MONUG), 1993 –

Israel and Syria
(FNUOD), 1974 –

Cyprus
(UNFICYP), 1964 –

India and Pakistan
(UNMOGIP), 1949 –

Lebanon
(FINUL), 1978 –

● Current missions
● Completed missions

East Timor
(MINUT), 2006 –

Sudan
(MINUS and MINUAD), 2005 – and 2007 –

Côte d'Ivoire
(ONUCI), 2004 –

Haiti
(MINUSTAH), 2004 –

Middle East
(ONUST), 1948 –

Democratic Republic of the Congo
(MONUC), 1999 –

5.48
United Nations Peacekeeping missions (2009)

Liberia
(MINUL), 2003 –

0   2000   4000
kilometres

Tensions and Conflicts

INTERVENING WITHOUT UNITED NATIONS SUPPORT

To be considered legitimate, peace missions must be carried out with the approval of the international community. The deployment of the United Nations peacekeeping Forces is therefore the favoured solution for resolving international crises. However, some peace missions are carried out outside of the framework of the Untied Nations, with or without its support.

The Limitations of the Blue Helmets

Peace missions are costly and require a lot of personnel. Even if many States provide troops, the distribution of responsibility is often unequal. In fact, many States are no longer interested in sending their soldiers to regions where they have few interests.

Furthermore, some countries, notably the United States, balk at the prospect of submitting their troops to international military command. Instead, it prefers maintaining direct control over its soldiers, even if it means leading its own peace missions. For all of these reasons, sending Blue Helmets into conflict areas is not always possible.

The 2001 War in Afghanistan

Where? ▪ Afghanistan

When? ▪ Since October 7, 2001

Who? ▪ The Taliban, the United States and the International Security Assistance Force (ISAF), a coalition of several dozen countries led by NATO and authorized by the United Nations Security Council.

Why? ▪ The United States is seeking to dismantle the terrorist group Al Qaeda, responsible for the September 11, 2001 attacks and protected by the Taliban regime in Afghanistan.

How? ▪ The United States and the United Kingdom intervened on October 7 and overthrew the Taliban in just a few weeks. On December 20, 2001, the United Nations Security Council authorized the creation of a multinational force to help the new Afghan government establish its authority. However, the Taliban has continued fighting, using guerilla warfare tactics and suicide attacks.

Outcome ▪ A few years after the start of this war, the Taliban is still waging guerilla attacks and the Afghan government, supported by the ISAF, remains fragile due to the many tensions within the country.

Armed Intervention With United Nations Support

5.49 ▲
Canadian soldiers in Afghanistan (2004)

5.50 ▲
A soldier with the Economic Community of West African States (ECOWAS) serving under the United Nations (2004)
Developing countries generally provide more troops for the Blue Helmets.

Country	Blue Helmets
1 Pakistan	10 989
2 Bangladesh	9 424
3 India	8 640
4 Nigeria	6 001
5 Nepal	3 924
6 Rwanda	3 635
7 Ghana	3 283
8 Jordan	3 109
9 Italy	2 565
10 Uruguay	2 538
...	
48 Canada	179

Peace Missions Without United Nations Support

Sometimes a direct United Nations intervention is inadequate or impossible due to insufficient means, a Security Council impasse preventing prompt action or some other obstacle. The United Nations can then choose to authorize international organizations to carry out peace missions. These organizations can be regional, such as the European Union or the African Union, military alliances, such as NATO, or a coalition of volunteer States.

Some States have already conducted peace missions without United Nations authorization. Their actions can be the result of a lack of confidence in the United Nations system, of the urgency of the situation or of an effort to advance particular interests. The legality of these interventions is usually problematic.

Armed Intervention Without the Consent of the United Nations

5.52
Kosovar refugee camp (1999)

The Kosovo War

Where? ▪ Federal Republic of Yugoslavia (today Serbia and Kosovo)

When? ▪ 1999

Who? ▪ The Yugoslav (Serbian) government, the Kosovars (majority Albanian) and NATO.

Why? ▪ The Albanians of Kosovo were seeking independence from Serb-dominated Yugoslavia.

How? ▪ NATO member countries feared that Yugoslav authorities would commit genocide in Kosovo. To react swiftly, knowing that Russia, allied with the Serbs, would likely exercise its *veto* power over the Security Council, they decided to bomb Yugoslavia to force Serbian forces to withdraw from Kosovo.

Outcome ▪ After the withdrawal of Yugoslav troops, Kosovo came under UN administration. In 2008, it proclaimed its independence, which in 2009 was only recognized by some 50 countries, including Canada.

HUMANITARIAN ORGANIZATIONS

States and intergovernmental organizations are not the only international actors that intervene in areas of tension and conflict. Many non-governmental organizations (NGOs) have humanitarian objectives that prompt them to take action in regions affected by war to provide aid to populations in need.

Multiple Forms of Action

The actions of NGOs in areas of tension and conflict can take various forms. Some groups provide immediate and direct assistance in crisis situations in the form of medical care, food distribution or the establishment of refugee camps. Other NGOs engage in long-term development programs with a peacebuilding objective. Finally, some organizations seek to inform the public, raising awareness about the humanitarian situation. Their work draws international attention to cases of abuse with the goal of encouraging appropriate intervention.

Raising Awareness

Amnesty International

Founded in 1961, this organization defends human rights around the world. In particular, it focuses on freeing prisoners of conscience, as well as on abolishing torture and the death penalty. Amnesty International seeks to impartially document human rights violations, releasing an annual report on the human rights situation in each country in the world. The organization received the Nobel Peace Prize in 1977.

Reporters Without Borders (RWB)

Defending freedom of the press and assisting jailed journalists are the main goals of Reporters Without Borders. This organization, founded in 1985, defends the right to free access to information throughout the world, based on the principle that this is an essential condition for the respect of human rights and the establishment of peace.

5.53 ▶ Freedom of the press (2008)

Region	Number of journalists ...		
	killed	arrested	attacked or threatened
Africa	3	263	117
Asia-Pacific	26	60	106
Americas	7	127	414
Europe and countries of the former USSR	8	86	168
Maghreb and Middle East	16	137	124
Total	**60**	**673**	**929**

Source: Reporters Without Borders, *Press Freedom Round-up 2008*, [On-line], 2008.

Demonstration organized by Amnesty International in Italy to demand the creation of an international human rights tribunal (1998)
5.54 ▼

Acting Publicly or Behind the Scenes?

Humanitarian organizations are often torn between two opposing positions.

Exercising Strict Neutrality

- Advantage: NGOs earn the trust of the parties involved, allowing them to act more freely and effectively on the ground.
- Disadvantage: may force NGOs to remain silent about certain crimes against humanity in an attempt to better address these crimes by negotiating with the authorities responsible for perpetrating them.
- Example of an NGO that promotes this principle: Red Cross

VS

Taking a Public Position

- Advantage: NGOs can denounce humanitarian abuses, thereby raising awareness among authorities and the general public, which can use pressure tactics to stop these abuses.
- Disadvantage: the work of NGOs can be used by various parties for their own propaganda purposes.
- Example of an NGO that promotes this principle: Amnesty International

Responding to Emergencies

International Red Cross and Red Crescent Movement

This movement includes both the International Committee of the Red Cross (ICRC) and an international federation that coordinates the activities of over 186 national organizations. Present in almost all States around the world, these organizations carry out numerous humanitarian actions in their country of origin and offer international assistance to populations affected by conflicts and crises, such as natural disasters.

Created in 1863, the International Committee of the Red Cross was responsible for the Geneva Conventions. Elaborated between 1864 and 1949,

these treaties laid the groundwork for international humanitarian law by defining rules to protect the injured, prisoners of war and civilians in the event of an armed conflict. The ICRC's work has earned it the Nobel Peace Prize three times, in 1917, 1944 and 1963.

Doctors Without Borders

In 1971, following the Biafran War, a small group of French doctors came together to found Médecins Sans Frontières (Doctors Without Borders). The organization's objective is to provide emergency medical assistance in the context of armed conflicts or natural disasters, while organizing public awareness campaigns. The organization won the Nobel Peace Prize in 1999.

5.55 ▶
Red Cross workers transporting a wounded Rwandan (1994)
The red cross, the red crescent and, more recently, the red diamond, are emblems of neutrality recognized worldwide.

215

BRINGING WAR CRIMINALS TO JUSTICE

Any war is the cause of great suffering and distress. In the context of war, particularly horrible acts are committed. Once the conflict is over, these acts must not go unpunished. But who should try these cases, which are usually very complex and politically sensitive? International tribunals have been created specifically to handle these cases.

Functioning of the International Criminal Court (ICC)
🔻 5.56

The International Court of Justice (ICJ) is responsible for resolving conflicts between States, while the International Criminal Court tries individuals who have been accused of very serious crimes: genocide, war crimes or crimes against humanity.

Not all States have signed the Rome Statute, the founding treaty of the ICC. Only the accused who are citizens of a State that recognizes the jurisdiction of the ICC or who have perpetrated their crime in such a State can be tried in this Court. In practice, very few cases brought before the Court go to trial.

The prosecutor must investigate the cases retained by the Court and bring specific charges against the individuals in question. Once the decision has been made to prosecute, the case is brought to court. Throughout these trials, the accused are presumed innocent unless proven guilty.

If found guilty, the accused can be fined, have their assets seized and be sentenced to a term of up to 30 years or, in some cases, life. The ICC does not apply the death penalty.

Louise Arbour

Canadian Louise Arbour has made a major contribution to developing the international justice system in recent years. In 1996, she was appointed chief prosecutor of the criminal tribunals for the former Yugoslavia and Rwanda. In this capacity, she determined which individuals should be prosecuted and on what charges. She held this position until 1999, when she was appointed a Supreme Court judge in Canada. Her commitment to defending the oppressed around the world earned her the position of UN High Commissioner for Human Rights, a post she held from 2004 to 2008.

International Criminal Tribunals (ICTs)

In response to particularly violent conflicts, the United Nations decided to create temporary international criminal tribunals (ICTs) to try war criminals based on international law. However, the jurisdiction of these provisional tribunals is limited, since they only handle very specific cases. Moreover, the trials are extremely long.

- International Criminal Tribunal for the Former Yugoslavia (1993)
- International Criminal Tribunal for Rwanda (1994)
- Special Court for Sierra Leone (2002)
- Special Court for Lebanon (2006)

1945 1946 1950 1975 1993 2000 2002

The First International Tribunals

At the end of the Second World War, the Allies instituted two international tribunals to try war criminals from Nazi Germany and Imperial Japan: the Nuremberg International Military Tribunal and the International Military Tribunal for the Far East. These were the first international tribunals to prosecute war crimes.

The International Criminal Court (ICC)

To make up for the shortcomings of ICTs, the International Criminal Court (ICC) was created. Its scope of action was much broader than that of the ICTs, since it encompassed all States that had ratified the Rome Statute, more than 108 countries in 2008. The International Criminal Court is permanent. Its headquarters are in The Hague, Netherlands.

Crimes under the jurisdiction of the ICC

- **Genocide:** intention to destroy, in part or in whole, a national, ethnic, racial or religious group.

- **Crimes against humanity:** serious acts committed against a civilian population, such as murder, torture, rape, slavery, deportation, apartheid crimes, etc.

- **War crimes:** serious infractions of the Geneva Conventions, including the abuse of civilians, war prisoners or the injured.

5.57 ▶
The International Criminal Court (2006)

History Headlines

1 The Domination of Industrial Societies
1880-1914

Construction of the Panama Canal by the Americans in 1913.

■ From One Ocean to Another, Through Panama

Panama, Central America, 1881

Since the 16th century, navigators had dreamed of finding a shortcut between the Atlantic and Pacific oceans. In 1881, the French began construction of a canal through the Isthmus of Panama, a narrow strip of land that lies between the Caribbean Sea and the Pacific Ocean. The goal of this ambitious engineering project, one of the most difficult ever undertaken, was to open a navigable channel between the two oceans. Completed by the Americans in 1914, the Panama Canal became a hub of international trade.

■ Brutal Colonialism in the Congo

Democratic Republic of the Congo, Africa, 1885

During the 1885 Berlin Conference, King Leopold II of Belgium took possession of a territory in Central Africa that he named the Congo Free State. Wishing to profit from the country's natural resources, Leopold II forced the local population to collect rubber. The king also established a militia called the Force publique, which was mandated to physically punish the population if it failed to meet specific rubber quotas. It is estimated that 10 million Congolese died during this period of brutal colonialism.

■ Games to Unite the Countries of the World

Greece, Europe, 1896

The Olympic Games, first held in 776 BCE, were sports competitions in honour of the ancient Greek gods. Abolished with the imposition of Christianity in 393 CE, the games were forgotten for 1500 years. Interest in the Olympic Games was rekindled in the 19th century, thanks in great part to the efforts of French visionary Pierre de Coubertin. He hoped that a renaissance of the Olympic Games would promote international unity by encouraging countries around the world to compete through sports rather than through war. Officially re-established in Athens in 1896, the modern Olympic Games are normally held every four years.

Close to 60 000 spectators crowded into the Panathenaic Stadium to see the first modern Olympic Games in Athens in 1896.

■ The Boers: Victims of British Imperialism

South Africa, Africa, 1899

At the end of the 19th century, the British Empire moved to annex the independent Boer republics that bordered its Cape Colony in South Africa. The Boers, descendents of Dutch and French colonists, rejected the first British push for domination in 1881. However, the discovery of major gold deposits in the Boer republic of Transvaal prompted the British to assert their domination for a second time in 1899. This conflict, known as the Boer or South African War, ended with a British victory in 1902. This conquest was tarnished, however, by a humanitarian crisis and a high death toll among the many Boer families that were displaced and interned in concentration camps by the British.

■ Industrial Progress Celebrated During the Paris World Fair

Paris, France, 1900

Since 1851, nations the world over have used world fairs to present their technological innovations and their major industrial accomplishments. Year after year, major cities around the world have hosted these fairs, which have attracted skilled tradespeople from around the world. The 1900 Paris World Fair was one of the most important, leading to the creation of the first subway line, the projection of films on the big screen by the Lumière brothers and the nighttime use of electricity to light the streets. The Fair also renewed public interest in the Eiffel Tower, built in 1889.

The Eiffel Tower gained in popularity during the 1900 Paris World Fair.

■ Russia on the Cusp of Revolution

Russia, Eurasia, 1905

In 1905, the Russians revolted against the monarchical regime of the czars by demanding major political change, particularly democratic rights. Despite a campaign of repression, Czar Nicholas II was unable to break the population's revolutionary zeal, which had been building over many years, fed by frustration over the lack of progress and the country's economic problems. Ten months later, the Czar granted the Russians a constitution. Their victory was short-lived, however: In the ensuing years, Nicholas II failed to honour his promise of change, unleashing a series of events that would lead to the Bolshevik Revolution in 1917.

■ Mexican Revolutionaries Demand Greater Social Justice

Mexico, North America, 1910

The Mexican Revolution broke out in 1910 when the president, General Porfirio Díaz, was accused of electoral fraud. Socialist, anarchist and nationalist movements profited from the upheaval to denounce Mexico's economic difficulties and to demand better living conditions for the population. In 1917, after several years of violence, the revolution officially ended with the promulgation of a Mexican constitution. This constitution was the first in the world to guarantee the right to collective bargaining, and to provide other social guarantees for the country's workers and farmers.

Mexican rebel in 1914, wearing the typical sombrero of the time.

■ The Empire of Japan Annexes Korea

Korea, Asia, 1910

In 1910, the Korean Peninsula was annexed by the Empire of Japan in its quest to increase its regional domination. The Japanese occupation was extremely cruel: Korea was stripped of its resources and its population was regularly abused and sometimes deported to serve as low-ranking labour in Japanese factories. In 1941, Japan repressed Korean culture by banning the teaching of the Korean language in schools and by forcing citizens to abandon their traditional family names. Despite Japan's withdrawal in 1945, following its defeat in the Second World War, Koreans continued to suffer with the arrival of Soviet and American troops and the beginning of the Cold War.

1899 ▶ The South African (or Boer) War begins

1900 ▶ Paris World Fair

1903 ▶ First motorized flight by the Wright Brothers

1905 ▶ Albert Einstein develops his theory of special relativity
First Russian Revolution

1910 ▶ **Mexican Revolution begins**
Japan annexes Korea

1912 ▶ Alfred Wegener formulates his theory of continental drift

2 The World Wars
1914-1945

■ Russia on the Road to Communism

Russia, Eurasia, 1917

Following the 1905 revolution, Russian discontent continued to grow in the face of Czar Nicholas II's refusal to introduce social and economic reform in the country. In 1917, poverty and corruption reached such proportions that the lower classes demanded major political change and greater social equality. Two figures from the Bolshevik Party, Vladimir Lenin and Leon Trotsky, took advantage of the revolutionary zeal to propose a new socio-economic system based on the egalitarian and socialist ideals of thinker Karl Marx. The Bolshevik regime, which advocated the abolition of capitalism and divisions between social classes, was established in Russia in 1920 following a long and brutal civil war.

■ The Quest for Lasting Peace After the First World War

Switzerland, Europe, 1919

From 1914 to 1918, the First World War ravaged Europe. At the end of this devastating conflict, the Allies and Germany signed a peace treaty that included the creation of an international organization called the League of Nations. This organization, based in Geneva, Switzerland, brought together many major powers and was mandated to prevent wars and resolve conflicts through negotiation. Despite some successes, the League of Nations was unable to prevent the Second World War in 1939. In 1945, the League of Nations was replaced by the United Nations.

■ The USSR: A Superpower Steps Onto the International Stage

Russia, Eurasia, 1922

In 1922, the Bolsheviks established a communist regime in Russia. The revolutionaries also sought to spread their socialist ideals to neighbouring countries. To do so, Russia forcibly annexed Georgia, Armenia and several countries in Central Asia. Other countries, like the Ukraine and Belarus, joined with Russia through treaty agreements. This union led to the creation of the Union of Soviet Socialist Republics (USSR), a federal State which, in 1954, unified 15 republics under a common ideological banner. After the Second World War, the USSR became one of the largest and most powerful States in the world.

◀ Vladimir Lenin addresses the people of Moscow, calling on them to show unity for the glory and prosperity of the Russian nation (circa 1920).

1914 ▶ The First World War begins

1915 ▶ Albert Einstein develops his theory of general relativity (E=mc²)

1916 ▶ First transatlantic radio transmission

1917 ▶ **Bolshevik Revolution in Russia**

1918 ▶ The First World War ends

1919 ▶ **The League of Nations is created**

1920 ▶ Alcohol is prohibited in the United States

Benito Mussolini attends the opening of a university in Rome in 1935.

land, causing massive population displacement and a series of famines. Despite his reign of terror, Stalin resisted Nazi Germany during the Second World War, generating great prestige for the USSR around the world.

Joseph Stalin applauds during the 1936 Soviet Congress.

■ Italy on the Road to Fascism

Italy, Europe, 1922

After the First World War, many Italian nationalists were unhappy with the unfavourable peace treaties their leaders were forced to sign. Taking advantage of this discontent, politician Benito Mussolini founded the National Fascist Party and proposed a national program designed to foster Italian pride. This program, which Mussolini called fascism, also advocated a totalitarian, anti-socialist and anti-union regime. In 1922, Mussolini gained power and remained the leader of the country until 1943. In 1939, Mussolini allied with Nazi Germany during the Second World War.

■ Totalitarianism in the USSR

USSR, Eurasia, 1927

An active member of the Communist Party of the Soviet Union, Joseph Stalin became the leader of the USSR in 1927. On taking power, he transformed the Soviet State into a totalitarian regime, characterized by an obligatory personality cult. During his 25-year reign, Stalin pushed forward the industrialization of the USSR and forcibly nationalized agricultural

■ The New York Stock Market Crash Ushers in an Economic Crisis

United States, North America, 1929

On October 24, 1929, the New York stock index fell steeply, marking the beginning of the Great Depression. This crisis, the most serious of the 20th century, was the consequence of strong economic growth in the United States and artificially inflated stock prices on financial markets during the 1920s. In the following months, the collapse of stock prices led to a severe banking and economic crisis, which spread throughout the Western world. In the United States, the unemployment rate climbed to 24.9% in 1933.

1922 ▶ **The USSR is created**
Mussolini takes power in Italy

1923 ▶ Vladimir Zworykin invents the first "fully electronic" television

1925-1935 ▶ First attempts at colour photographs

1927 ▶ **Stalin takes power in the USSR**
Georges Lemaître develops the Big Bang theory
Charles Lindbergh crosses the Atlantic Ocean in an airplane

1929 ▶ **The New York Stock Exchange crashes**
Edwin Hubble formulates his theory of the expansion of the Universe

Roosevelt Tries to End the Great Depression With the New Deal

United States, North America, 1933

In 1932, Franklin D. Roosevelt was elected President of the United States. In an effort to end the Great Depression, Roosevelt implemented an interventionist economic policy called the New Deal. From 1933 to 1938, Roosevelt's national programs helped to limit unemployment and the worst social consequences of the crisis. Some, however, were concerned about Roosevelt's interventionism, which ran counter to the principles of capitalism and the free market. Others believe that State intervention during these difficult times actually helped save capitalism.

Germany on the Road to Nazism

Germany, Europe, 1933

In 1930, the Great Depression hit Germany and unemployment reached disastrous proportions. Adolf Hitler, then leader of the Nazi Party, profited from the crisis to stimulate German nationalist sentiment through inflammatory and propagandistic speeches. Hitler held Jews and communists primarily responsible for the economic crisis, fostering a sense of paranoia and suspicion that destabilized German society. Through political manoeuvrings and the electoral victory of his party, Hitler was appointed Chancellor of Germany in 1933. In the following months, Hitler suspended civil liberties guaranteed under the German constitution and eliminated his political opponents, paving the way to a totalitarian regime.

Japanese soldiers scale the Great Wall of China at the beginning of the Sino-Japanese War in 1937.

Japan's Invasion of China Takes the World to the Brink of the Second World War

China, Asia, 1937

Following the annexation of Korea in 1910, the Empire of Japan continued to grow as a military power in Asia. After the occupation of Manchuria in 1931, Japan pursued its expansionist policy in 1937 by invading eastern China with the goal of taking control of its natural and industrial resources. The Japanese invasion was brutal: Chinese cities were relentlessly bombed, chemical weapons were used and millions of civilians were massacred. This invasion preceded by a few months Germany's invasion of Poland, which signalled the beginning of the Second World War. The Sino-Japanese conflict ended in 1945 with the surrender of Japan to the United States.

Adolf Hitler inspects Nazi troops in Berlin after his victory in Austria in 1938.

1931 ▸ The Empire State Building in New York becomes the tallest building in the world

1933 ▸ Roosevelt's New Deal is adopted in the United States

Hitler takes power in Germany

1937 ▸ Japan invades China

John Steinbeck publishes his novel *Of Mice and Men*

■ Nazis Trigger the War in Europe by Invading Poland

Poland, Europe, 1939

Adolf Hitler's expansionist ambitions, which had been a cause for concern among European leaders for years, were confirmed when Germany invaded Poland in 1939. Hitler had already annexed Austria, Bohemia and Moravia, claiming that the populations were Germanophone (German-speaking). On the pretext that it was important to create space for Germans living in Poland, Hitler ordered the invasion of this country on all fronts. This aggression was intolerable for France and England, which had been allies of Poland since 1921. The two countries declared war on Germany, triggering the Second World War.

Nazi soldiers triumphantly enter Warsaw, Poland, in 1939.

■ France Under Nazi Domination

France, Europe, 1940

After declaring war on Hitler in 1939, France and England tried to isolate Germany and deprive it of the primary resources needed for its military operations. However, their tactics failed and German forces successively invaded Denmark, Norway, the Netherlands, Luxemburg and Belgium. In 1940, the French army was unable to slow Germany's advance and France itself was invaded. The Germans occupied the north of the country, while the south remained free, administered by the collaborationist Vichy government. Despite the occupation, a clandestine resistance movement emerged.

■ The Nazis Attack the USSR

USSR, Eurasia, 1941

In 1941, Hitler violated the non-aggression pact that established the borders between Germany and the USSR in Eastern Europe. Wishing to overpower the Russians and end the communist influence in Europe, German forces attempted a massive invasion of the USSR. Despite major German advances that reached Stalingrad (today's Volgograd) in 1942, the Soviets managed to start repelling the invaders in 1943. The conflicts, by far the most ferocious and bloody of the Second World War, caused massive destruction and a huge death toll, estimated at 30 million lives. The Soviet victory was decisive in the war against the Germans, paving the way for the victories of the Allies in Western Europe.

■ The United States Enters the Second World War

Hawaii, Pacific, 1941

On December 7, 1941, the Empire of Japan launched a surprise aerial attack against the American naval base Pearl Harbour, located in the Hawaiian archipelago. The Japanese, allies of the Germans since 1936, confirmed their policy of imperial expansion in the Pacific with this attack. The United States suffered significant losses: Many ships and planes were destroyed and close to 2500 soldiers were killed. This event prompted the Americans, who up until that point had refused to get involved in the Second World War, to break with their isolationism and declare war on Japan and Germany. From 1942 to 1945, the United States and Japan engaged in intense fighting in the Pacific.

1938 ▶ Làszló Biró invents the ballpoint pen

1939 ▶ **Germany invades Poland**
The film *Gone With the Wind* is released

1940 ▶ **France falls under Nazi domination**

1941 ▶ **Germany invades the USSR**
Japan attacks the American base at Pearl Harbour
The film *Citizen Kane* is released

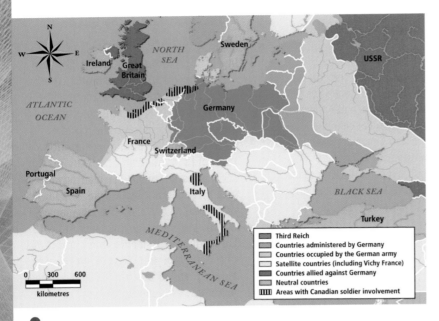

Europe in 1942

The Allies Free France

France, Europe, 1944

After the United States entered the Second World War, it joined the Allies to free the European countries occupied by the Germans. On June 6, 1944, a major offensive was launched on the beaches of Normandy, France. During the operation, three million American, British and Canadian soldiers landed on French soil and engaged in fierce fighting with Nazi troops. The Normandy landing, also referred to as D-Day, marked a decisive turning point in the Second World War, leading to the liberation of France and contributing to the ultimate defeat of Germany.

The UN's Quest for Lasting Peace

United States, North America, 1945

In 1942, 26 allied nations opposed the forces of Germany, Italy and Japan. To cement their alliance, the Allies signed the Declaration by United Nations, which laid the groundwork for a new international policy to end war. In 1943, the USSR, Great Britain and the United States went further, proposing the creation of an organization mandated to resolve international conflicts and oversee greater cooperation among countries. This project led to the creation of the United Nations in 1945. Today, the UN has 192 member States.

Atomic Bombs Dropped on Hiroshima and Nagasaki Signal the End of the Second World War

Japan, Asia, 1945

After years of fighting, American naval forces finally gained the upper hand against Japanese forces in the Pacific. Japan refused to capitulate unconditionally, while the United States wanted to avoid an invasion of the country, which would cost the lives of thousands of American soldiers. Determined to end the war, President Harry Truman ordered the atomic bomb to be dropped on the Japanese cities of Hiroshima and Nagasaki on August 6 and 9, 1945. Profoundly shaken by these attacks, Japan officially ended its hostilities on August 15, 1945, marking the end of the Second World War.

Hiroshima one month after the explosion of the atomic bomb on August 6, 1945. An estimated 110 000 people instantly perished during the bombing of Hiroshima and Nagasaki.

③ The Cold War and the Emergence of the Third World

1945-1990

The Iron Curtain in Europe (1947–1960)

Legend:
- Western Bloc (NATO countries)
- Eastern Bloc (Warsaw Pact countries)
- Neutral countries
- Iron Curtain

0   300   600
kilometres

■ The Marshall Plan Ushers in the Cold War

United States, North America, 1947

In 1947, the United States created an economic aid program to help reconstruct Europe, which had been devastated by the Second World War. Announced by American Secretary of State George Marshall, the plan earmarked $13 billion (equivalent to $100 billion today) to rebuild 16 European countries. The Marshall Plan, which advocated economic liberalism, was rejected by the USSR, since it was incompatible with the planned economy of the communist system. This disagreement triggered an ideological conflict in which every country in Europe was invited to choose a camp, thereby ushering in the Cold War era.

■ The Creation of the State of Israel

Palestine, Middle East, 1948

After the Second World War, several Western countries declared their support for the establishment in Palestine of a homeland for Jews who had survived Nazi extermination. In 1947, the UN adopted a resolution to divide Palestine into two States, one Jewish and the other Arab. While Jews rejoiced over the return to their promised land after 2000 years of exile, Palestinians and the neighbouring Arab countries fiercely resisted the declaration of independence of the State of Israel in 1948. This dispute is at the source of a series of conflicts that persists to this day.

■ People's Republic of China: Another Major Power Steps Onto the International Stage

China, Asia, 1949

At the end of the Japanese occupation in 1945, China became mired in a civil war between the nationalists and communists fighting to take control of the country. The communists supported the revolutionary Mao Zedong, who promised a popular socialist State based on the USSR model. In 1949, Mao Zedong's People's Liberation Army occupied most of the country, paving the way for the creation of the People's Republic of China. In the ensuing years, the country moved away from the Soviet model in favour of a political and economic approach more adapted to the realities of China.

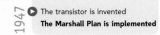

1946 ▶ The microwave oven is invented

1947 ▶ The transistor is invented
The Marshall Plan is implemented

1948 ▶ Israel is founded

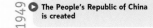

1949 ▶ **The People's Republic of China is created**

■ The Iron Curtain Falls on Europe

Belgium, Europe, 1949

In 1949, the ideological conflict between the United States and the USSR grew deeper. Fearing the rise in power of the Soviet Union, which threatened the security of Europe, several Western countries united to form the North Atlantic Treaty Organization (NATO). This treaty, signed by the United States, France, the United Kingdom and Canada, among others, sought a political and military alliance against the USSR. NATO's creation, however, accelerated the development of an ideological border, referred to as the Iron Curtain, between the countries of the Western Bloc (allies of the United States) and the Eastern Bloc (allies of the USSR) in Europe.

Mao Zedong proclaims the People's Republic of China on October 1, 1949.

■ The Korean War Erupts in the Context of the Cold War

Korea, Asia, 1950

When the allies liberated Korea from Japanese occupation at the end of the Second World War, the USSR took control of the northern Korean peninsula, while the United States occupied the south. In the context of the ideological conflict that marked the beginning of the Cold War, the partition of Korea, which was meant to be temporary, became permanent. In 1950, North Korean communists tried to invade the southern peninsula, triggering the Korean War. North Koreans and South Koreans became embroiled in a vicious conflict, respectively supported by the USSR and the United States for ideological reasons. Despite the signing of a ceasefire in 1953, North Korea and South Korea remain two distinct countries today.

American soldiers rest on a hillside after pushing back a communist contingent during the Korean War (1951).

■ The End of the Stalinist Era in the USSR

USSR, Eurasia, 1953

While the policies and military victories of Joseph Stalin turned the USSR into a global superpower, his long reign was marked, above all, by terror and excesses related to his personality cult. After Stalin's death in 1953, the new leader, Nikita Khrushchev, moved to "destalinize" the USSR. Khrushchev ended the deportations, forced labour and political imprisonments of the Stalinist era. The end of the repression allowed the USSR to open up more to the outside world, but did not end the Cold War.

The Third World Steps Onto the International Stage

Indonesia, Southeast Asia, 1955

After 1945, several African and Asian colonies demanded their independence from Western powers. In 1955, the representatives of 29 newly independent former colonies held a conference in Bandung, Indonesia, to take their place on the international stage. The participants proclaimed their support for the decolonization of all countries and the peaceful coexistence of nations. The signatory countries also expressed their intention to remain neutral in the context of the Cold War, signalling the creation of a third power, or "Third World."

President John F. Kennedy addresses the American people during the 1962 Cuban Missile Crisis.

Nuclear Threat in Cuba

Cuba, Caribbean, 1962

In 1959, revolutionary Fidel Castro took power in Cuba, establishing a communist State. The United States was concerned about the change in regime, since Cuba was located only 180 kilometres from Florida. In 1961, President John F. Kennedy engaged in a failed attempt to invade Cuba to overthrow Castro's government. The Cubans then allied themselves with the Soviet Union in an effort to defend themselves from a future American attack. In 1962, the USSR deployed 36 nuclear missiles in Cuba, making the United States vulnerable to a Soviet attack. This action, which threatened the Cold War principle of peaceful coexistence, sparked a crisis that risked a nuclear confrontation. Through negotiations, the USSR finally agreed to dismantle its nuclear installations in Cuba in exchange for the withdrawal of American nuclear missiles from Turkey.

The Cold War Plays Itself Out in Vietnam

Vietnam, Southeast Asia, 1964

In 1954, after several years of war, Vietnam was divided into two ideologically opposed States: a communist regime in the North, supported by the USSR and China, and a nationalist regime in the South, supported by the United States. When war broke out between the North Vietnamese and South Vietnamese in 1959, the Cold War powers lent their material or military support to their respective allies. In 1965, the United States intervened directly in the war when communist insurgents threatened to overthrow the nationalist government in the South. The war was to be long and difficult for the American forces, which sustained major losses. In 1975, the United States withdrew from the war and South Vietnam was invaded by the communist forces.

A mother and her children escape the American bombing of their village during the Vietnam War.

1955 ◗ **Bandung Conference**

1957 ◗ The Soviets put the first artificial satellite, *Sputnik*, into orbit

1960 ◗ Theodore Maiman demonstrates the first laser

Gregory Pincus invents the contraceptive pill

1962 ◗ **Cuban missile crisis**

1964 ◗ George Heilmeier invents the first liquid crystal screen

The American intervention in Vietnam begins

■ China on the Road to Reform and Totalitarianism

People's Republic of China, Asia, 1966

From 1958 to 1961, Mao Zedong implemented a series of economic reforms that he called the "Great Leap Forward." These reforms, which sought to transform China into an industrial power, were unrealistic and ended in disaster. In just a few years, 30 million Chinese died in one of the worst famines the country had ever known. In 1966, Mao decided to launch a "Cultural Revolution" to regain the confidence of the people. This revolution, which offered greater freedom of expression to the young, slipped out of Mao's control, leading him to bring it to an end in a wave of violent military repression. Much of China's cultural patrimony was destroyed during this revolution.

■ The Death of Salvador Allende Leads to the Pinochet Dictatorship in Chile

Chile, South America, 1973

Salvador Allende, President of Chile from 1970 to 1973, was the first democratically elected socialist leader. During his mandate, Allende made many enemies, however, including the United States, which feared the spread of communism in South America. When an economic crisis hit Chile, former supporters of Allende turned against him. On September 11, 1973, Allende was killed in a *coup d'état* organized by General Augusto Pinochet, who went on to impose a military dictatorship in Chile.

Chilean President Salvador Allende during a press conference in 1973.

■ 1973: First Oil Shock

Kuwait, Middle East, 1973

In 1973, conflicts between Israelis and Palestinians gave rise to a serious oil shock. The crisis erupted when Arab member countries of OPEC (Organization of the Petroleum Exporting Countries) met in Kuwait and announced an embargo on oil exports to countries that supported Israel. The shortage quickly led to the quadrupling of the price of a barrel of oil. The United States, which was hit hard due to its energy dependence on oil, negotiated the end of the crisis by reducing its support for Israel.

■ Afghanistan: The Theatre of the Last Great Cold War Crisis

Afghanistan, Central Asia, 1979

During the Cold War, the USSR supported Afghanistan against the growing influence of the United States in Pakistan. After 1973, a series of *coups d'état* in Afghanistan threatened Soviet control of the country. In 1979, the USSR intervened militarily to support the government of its choice. Many Afghans rejected the Soviet occupation, which imposed socialist ideals that contradicted their traditional values. The resistance led to a guerrilla war between the USSR and Afghan rebel groups supported by the United States. In the wake of a long conflict, in which they were unable to defeat the rebels who were hidden throughout Afghanistan's mountainous regions, the Soviet Union withdrew from the country in 1989.

1965 ● First long-distance computer connection is established between Massachusetts and California

1966 ● Mao's Cultural Revolution begins in China

1973 ● Chile's Salvador Allende is assassinated
First oil shock
Painter Pablo Picasso dies

1979 ● The Soviet Union intervenes in Afghanistan

A pleasant exchange between Mikhail Gorbachev (right) and U.S. President Ronald Reagan (left) during a summit meeting in Geneva in 1985.

■ The USSR Opens Up to the World With the Arrival of Mikhail Gorbachev

USSR, Eurasia, 1985

At the end of the 1970s, the USSR showed the first signs of economic decline in the face of its capitalist rivals. Seeking a solution, the Soviets brought Mikhail Gorbachev to power in 1985. Gorbachev, who represented a new generation of communists, proposed major economic reforms and encouraged a detente with the West. Starting in 1986, the Soviet leader opened up a dialogue with the United States by proposing a nuclear disarmament plan. This initiative by Gorbachev, which helped to thaw Cold War relations, did not, however, slow down the decline of the USSR.

■ Poland Frees Itself From Soviet Control

Poland, Europe, 1989

Since 1952, Poland had been a communist republic under Soviet control. During the 1980s, economic crises weakened the Polish regime and led to the creation of an anti-communist union movement called Solidarity. With the decline of the USSR, Solidarity gained in political importance to the detriment of the communist party, managing to win a surprising victory during parliamentary elections in 1989. The defeat of the communist government inspired regime changes in other Eastern European countries, signalling the dismantling of the Soviet Bloc and the fall of the Iron Curtain.

■ The Fall of the Berlin Wall Marks the End of the Cold War

Germany, Europe, 1989

After the Second World War, Western countries and the USSR divided Germany into two States: the Federal Republic of Germany (western) and the German Democratic Republic (communist). The capital, Berlin, was also divided by a long wall, which became the symbol of the Iron Curtain that divided Europe. In 1989, the disintegration of the Soviet Bloc in Eastern Europe prompted Germans to demolish the Berlin Wall and reunite their country. This highly symbolic event, which made headlines around the world, officially marked the end of the Cold War.

Thousands of Germans celebrate the fall of the Berlin Wall a few days after its demolition on November 9, 1989.

1981 ▶ IBM introduces the first personal computer (PC)
France's TGV (high-speed train) between Paris and Lyon is launched

1985 ▶ Mikhail Gorbachev comes to power in the USSR

1989 ▶ The Solidarity movement comes to power in Poland
The Berlin Wall falls
Painter Salvador Dalí dies

④ The Global Village
1990-2008

Flag of the USSR

Flag of Russia

■ The End of the Cold War Heralds the Collapse of a World Superpower

USSR, Eurasia, 1990

As soon as he came to power in 1985, Soviet leader Mikhail Gorbachev introduced major reforms in an effort to curb the USSR's political and economic decline. Without renouncing communist principles, Gorbachev proposed a more dynamic economic model, adopting private ownership, democratizing the political system and reducing spending on nuclear weapons. However, Gorbachev's reforms were not enough to remedy the situation. The break up of the Communist Bloc in Eastern Europe and the fall of the Berlin Wall in 1989 furthered the destabilization of the USSR. After a few months, the Soviet Union was no longer able to maintain its territorial and political cohesion.

■ 15 new States Emerge From the Ashes of the USSR

USSR, Eurasia, 1991

In 1989, reformist and nationalist movements formed in the Soviet Union's 15 republics. In 1990, reformer Boris Yeltsin issued a declaration of sovereignty for the Republic of Russia, which occupied 76% of the USSR's territory and represented 52% of its population. Over the next few months, other Soviet republics followed suit. These secessions led to the birth of 15 new countries in Europe and Central Asia. Despite their separation, some of these former republics maintained an economic association, creating the Community of Independent States (CIS). Defeated and without a country to lead, Soviet President Mikhail Gorbachev stepped down and the USSR was officially dissolved on December 26, 1991.

■ Toward a New Russia

Russia, Eurasia, 1991

On June 12, 1991, Boris Yeltsin won the presidential elections in the new Russian Federation. A democracy from that day on, Russia still had to overcome major obstacles in its transition from a communist economy to a market economy. Economic liberalization led to steep inflation, corruption and the severe impoverishment of the population. Once seen as a saviour, Yeltsin's popularity plummeted during his two mandates. In 1999, he ceded power to Vladimir Putin, who put Russia on the road to greater economic prosperity and international visibility.

Boris Yeltsin makes a victory signal during the events leading up to the dismantling of the USSR (1991).

▶ End of the Cold War

January 31: The first MacDonald's in the USSR opens its doors in Moscow

March 11: Lithuania declares independence from the USSR

March 18: East Germany holds its first free elections

May 4: Latvia declares independence from the USSR

August 2: Iraq invades Kuwait

August 6: The UN imposes an embargo on Iraq following its invasion of Kuwait

September 11: George H.W. Bush threatens to attack Iraq if it does not withdraw from Kuwait

October 3: Reunification of West Germany and East Germany

Iraq Triggers Gulf War With Its Invasion of Kuwait

Kuwait, Middle East, 1990

In the context of major upheavals around the world following the collapse of the USSR, Iraqi President Saddam Hussein asserted his presence in the Middle East by boldly invading Kuwait in 1990. By annexing Kuwait, Saddam Hussein planned to take control of the country's resources and large oil reserves, with the goal of paying off large debts accrued during previous wars. His plan was to impose Iraq's presence on the regional scene while increasing its access to the Persian Gulf, which, up until then, had been limited by Kuwait. Expecting a timid reaction from the international community, he ordered the invasion of Kuwait on August 2, 1990. Several countries nonetheless denounced the offensive, fearing that the Iraqi President would also invade Saudi Arabia and seize its large oil reserves. On August 7, an international coalition joined forces to liberate Kuwait and put an end to Saddam Hussein's expansionist ambitions.

Iraqi President Saddam Hussein in 1987.

The United States Wins the Gulf War Against Saddam Hussein

Iraq, Middle East, 1991

In January 1991, a UN-led coalition of 34 countries launched a military offensive to free Kuwait from Iraqi occupation. The conflict, which mobilized a number of countries around the Persian Gulf, soon came to be known as the Gulf War. With its might as a world superpower, the United States dominated the war, carrying out air strikes on Iraq's industrial and military infrastructure. Land operations also pushed back Iraqi forces that were waging war in Kuwait. In just a few weeks, the allied forces defeated Iraq's army, but hesitated to invade Iraq out of fear of a high death toll. This compromise allowed Saddam Hussein to remain in power, although Iraq was subjected to major political and economic sanctions.

Oil wells set ablaze during the Gulf War. During the withdrawal from Kuwait in 1991, the Iraqi army set fire to several oil fields in an attempt to disrupt the American offensive.

A New World Order

The dismantling of the USSR created a new world order in which the United States became the sole world superpower. The surviving communist States in China, Cuba, North Korea, Vietnam and Laos chose not to perpetuate the ideological conflict that had fuelled the Cold War. The disengagement of the USSR led to new international power relations and the appeasement of regional conflicts. Some countries, like China, reaffirmed their military and economic might. Others, like Iraq, took advantage of this new world order to achieve their own regional ambitions.

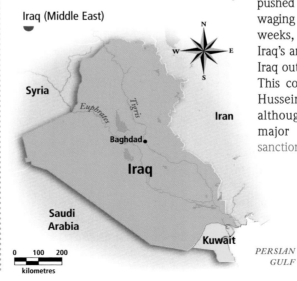

Iraq (Middle East)

Syria

Euphrates

Tigris

Iran

Baghdad

Iraq

Saudi Arabia

Kuwait

PERSIAN GULF

0   100   200
kilometres

October 15: Mikhail Gorbachev receives the Nobel Peace Prize
November 29: A UN resolution authorizes the use of force against Iraq if it fails to withdraw from Kuwait before January 15, 1991

1991

January 16: **Beginning of Gulf War military operations**

February 28: **United States is victorious in the Gulf War**

June 12: **Boris Yeltsin is elected President of the Russian Federation**

December 26: **The USSR is officially dissolved**

South African President Frederik De Klerk (left) in discussion with Nelson Mandela (right) in 1990.

■ South Africa Ends Racial Segregation

South Africa, Africa, 1991

In 1948, South Africa adopted a racial segregation policy known as apartheid (which means separateness in Afrikaans). Apartheid was designed to separate different races and ethnicities within the country along political, social and geographic lines, while conferring more rights to white South Africans. Black South Africans who opposed this system or violated the laws of segregation were mistreated or imprisoned. It was in this context that activist Nelson Mandela was arrested in 1962. Twenty-seven years later, in 1990, Mandela was finally released under a reconciliation policy introduced by South African President Frederik De Klerk. In 1991, the efforts of these two men led to the abolition of apartheid once and for all. The two men shared the Nobel Peace Prize in 1993.

■ A United Europe

Netherlands, Europe, 1992

In 1948, a handful of European countries came up with the idea of an economic, social and cultural union, with the goal of consolidating the peace achieved at such great cost during the Second World War. During the following years, various treaties were adopted in an effort to create an economic community in Europe. These efforts toward unity culminated in 1992 with the Treaty on European Union, signed in Maastricht, Netherlands. The treaty established an intergovernmental and supranational union between 12 European countries: Germany, Belgium, Denmark, Spain, France, Greece, Ireland, Italy, Luxemburg, Netherlands, Portugal and the United Kingdom. The opening of borders between these countries to allow the free circulation of goods and people transformed the European Union into an economic giant able to rival the world's other economic powers. Constantly evolving, the European Union now has 27 member States and represents just over 30% of the world's GDP.

■ Genocide in Rwanda

Rwanda, Africa, 1994

In 1962, the East African country of Rwanda gained its independence from Belgium. However, the colonial period had created tensions between the country's two main ethnic groups, the Hutus and the Tutsis, which were competing for power and post-independence privileges. In 1994, violence erupted when Tutsis exiled in the neighbouring country of Uganda tried to forcibly return to Rwanda, hoping to take power from the Hutus. Hutu nationalists, seeking revenge for perceived past injustices, proceeded to systematically exterminate Tutsis still living in the country. Leaving some 800 000 victims in 100 days, the genocide was the shortest-lived in history, but had the highest daily death toll. The international community intervened too late to prevent the massacres and was strongly criticized in the wake of the genocide.

Refugees flee during the Rwandan genocide in 1994.

▶ **February 11:** Nelson Mandela is released after 27 years in detention in South Africa

▶ **June 17: Apartheid ends in South Africa**

▶ **February 7: The Treaty on the European Union is signed in Maastricht**
April 6: The Bosnia-Herzegovina War begins

▶ *January 1:* The European Single Market enters into force
January 20: Bill Clinton becomes President of the United States
November 1: The Treaty of Maastricht enters into force; the European Union is born

▶ **April 6: The Rwandan genocide begins**

The WTO Ushers in More Liberalized International Trade

Switzerland, Europe, 1995

On January 1, 1995, the world's big economic powers created the World Trade Organization (WTO), headquartered in Geneva, Switzerland. This initiative was part of a trend toward greater globalization and the increased trade of goods, services and capital on a global level. In keeping with this trend, the WTO's mandate is to promote the liberalization of international trade by reducing barriers to free trade and stimulating exports and imports between countries. The WTO also establishes trade regulations and arbitrates disputes arising between member countries. However, anti-globalization groups have accused the WTO of promoting trade at the expense of international human rights standards, the struggle to end poverty and environmental protection.

The Kyoto Protocol Tackles Climate Change

Japan, Asia, 1997

During the 1990s, scientists became increasingly concerned about climate change attributable to human activities and appealed to governments to take action. In 1992, several countries signed the UN Framework Convention on Climate Change in an effort to reduce greenhouse gas emissions, the major cause of global warming. In 1997, the signatories of the Framework Convention took another step by adopting the Kyoto Protocol in Japan. The agreement set out binding measures that obliged industrialized States to reduce their polluting emissions to 1990 levels by the year 2010. The Kyoto Protocol, ratified by a majority of countries, officially came into effect at a conference held in Montréal in 2005. However, some countries, including the United States, refused to ratify the agreement, claiming that major polluters, such as China and India, were not being subjected to the same obligations due to their developing economies.

Genocide in Europe During the Kosovo War

Federal Republic of Yugoslavia, Europe, 1999

After 1992, Yugoslavia was the theatre of a conflict between Serbs and Albanians who were fighting for control of the province of Kosovo. Albanians, the majority in Kosovo, were seeking sovereignty for the region, which the Serbs rejected, claiming that Kosovo was part of their historical territory. When Albanian dissidents took up arms in 1998, Serbian President Slobodan Milošević used counter-terrorism as a justification for attacking the Albanian civilian population in Kosovo. The offensive against the Albanians quickly became a genocidal ethnic cleansing campaign. NATO member countries responsible for security in Europe launched air strikes against Yugoslavia in 1999 to end the massacres perpetrated by the Serbs. After being placed under UN trusteeship, Kosovo declared its independence in 2008, although its status has still not been recognized by all members of the international community.

A melting glacier in Greenland. A great many climatologists believe that the accelerated rate at which glaciers around the world are melting can be attributed to global warming caused by human activity.

Refugee camp during the Kosovo War in 1999. An estimated one million Albanians fled to escape the genocide.

233

1995 ▶ **January 1: The WTO is created**

1997 ▶ *February 22:* The Roslin Institute announces the first animal clone
July 4: The American Pathfinder mission to Mars is successful
***December 1:* The Kyoto Protocol negotiations begin**

1999 ▶ *March 24:* **The Kosovo War begins**
December 2: First breakthrough in cracking the genetic code of a human chromosome

Attacks against the World Trade Center in New York on September 11, 2001.
The terrorist attacks in New York, Washington and Pennsylvania claimed 2974 lives.

■ Attacks on the World Trade Center in New York

United States, North America, 2001

On September 11, 2001, the United States was the target of a series of terrorist attacks that were attributed to the Muslim fundamentalist group Al Qaeda. In just a few hours, four passenger airliners were hijacked by 19 terrorists and steered toward symbols of American financial and military power. Two planes crashed into the twin towers of the World Trade Center in New York, another one struck the Pentagon in Washington, while the last one crashed into a field in Pennsylvania. A few hours after the attacks, the two WTC towers collapsed. The live images broadcast around the world sparked a very strong international reaction. The alleged mastermind behind the attacks, Osama Bin Laden, rejoiced over the attacks, explaining that they were designed to punish the United States for injustices against Islam.

■ The War Against Terrorism Begins

United States, North America, 2001

The conflict in Afghanistan is part of the "war against terrorism" introduced by George W. Bush in the wake of the September 11 attacks. This unconventional war was designed to destabilize terrorist recruitment and training camps around the world using political, financial and military means. At the same time, the United Sates denounced countries suspected of supporting terrorism, specifically identifying Iraq, Iran and North Korea as a new "Axis of Evil." Without excluding the possibility of preventive wars against any perceived threat, the United States also heightened

surveillance of its borders and airports and adopted electronic surveillance programs to thwart terrorist plots on American soil. The United States also organized detention centres to interrogate suspected terrorists and enemy combatants, such as the U.S. military base in Guantanamo, Cuba. Although these measures are part of a worldwide fight against terrorism, many international observers are concerned about potential violations of human rights and international conventions.

Osama Bin Laden in 1988, a few years before he launched his fight against the United States.

■ The United States Invades Afghanistan

Afghanistan, Central Asia, 2001

After the attacks of September 11, 2001, American President George W. Bush demanded the extradition of Osama Bin Laden, who was receiving protection from the Taliban government in Afghanistan.

January 20: George W. Bush becomes President of the United States
***September 11:** Attacks against the World Trade Center in New York*
***September 20:** The war against terrorism begins*

October 4: Incident involving anthrax-contaminated envelopes
***October 7:** The U.S. invasion of Afghanistan begins*

The Taliban, which shared Bin Laden's fundamentalist ideals, refused to comply with the United States' request. With the support of an international coalition composed primarily of troops from the United Kingdom, France and Canada, the United States declared war on the Taliban and invaded Afghanistan from October to November 2001. After the fall of the Taliban regime, NATO made a commitment to rebuild Afghanistan and fight Taliban rebels hiding in the mountains. Military operations against the Taliban are still underway today with the active participation of the Canadian armed forces. Osama Bin Laden is still at large.

■ Europe Introduces a New Currency

Belgium, Europe, 2002

The European Union, created in 1992, took another important step on January 1, 2002, by issuing a new common currency known as the "euro." This currency, officially adopted by 15 European Union member States, had existed since 1999, but its use had been limited to electronic transactions on financial markets. In 2002, the euro was issued in the form of bills and coins, which allowed the population in some parts of Europe to travel freely from one country to another using the same currency. The opening of the "euro zone" also indicated the European Union's economic strength. By 2006, the euro was already the world's leading currency in terms of the number of bills in circulation and the second most common transaction currency, after the U.S. dollar.

■ The Third Earth Summit Looks at the Planet's Bill of Health

South Africa, Africa, 2002

In 2002, the world's leading heads of State met in Johannesburg, South Africa to discuss the environment and the state of the planet. These meetings, known as Earth Summits, are held every 10 years and give the international community a chance to examine the advances and setbacks in environmental protection, sustainable development and social justice in developing countries.

Today, the euro (€) represents the European Union's unity and economic strength.

The meetings also address problems and solutions in the management of natural resources, renewable energies, agricultural productivity and global health. So far, three summits have been held, in Stockholm, Sweden, in Rio de Janeiro, Brazil, and in Johannesburg, South Africa. The Johannesburg Summit was particularly important, because it highlighted the fact that the need to protect the environment is as important as the war against terrorism.

■ Genocide in Darfur

Sudan, Africa, 2003

Since 2003, Darfur, in Africa's western Sudan region, has been the theatre of a civil war that some countries and organizations have described as a genocide. The conflict pits two Sudanese ethnic groups against each other: Arabs and Zaghawas (a black ethnic group originally from Chad), who have long competed for the resources in Darfur.

In recent years, the discovery of oil deposits, combined with drought and a population explosion that has limited the availability of agricultural land, has

Sudanese refugees wait for food distribution at a humanitarian camp in northern Darfur (2005).

exacerbated this rivalry. The war erupted in 2003 when Zaghawa rebels opposed Sudanese President Omar al-Bashir. The government responded by allowing Arab militias, called Janjaweeds, to retaliate by eliminating or displacing Zaghawas and other ethic groups in Darfur. Despite many international sanctions against the Sudanese government, the war in Darfur rages on today, leaving more than 400 000 dead and two million refugees.

■ The U.S. Invades Iraq

Iraq, Middle East, 2003

Following the Gulf War in 1991, American grievances against Saddam Hussein mounted, with the United States accusing him of building weapons of mass destruction. Under the guise of fighting terrorism, President George W. Bush launched a pre-emptive war against Iraq, with the objective of toppling Saddam Hussein's regime. The United States received the support of a number of countries, but others, including France, Russia and Canada, questioned the legitimacy of this war. On March 20, 2003, American and allied forces launched a swift and decisive invasion of Iraq, capturing the capital city of Baghdad on April 9. This marked the end of Saddam Hussein's brutal regime, but no weapons of mass destruction were ever found.

■ Iraq Sinks Into Civil War

Iraq, Middle East, 2003

The success of the American invasion did not end the war in Iraq. The instability caused by the fall of the Iraqi regime and lack of planning by the occupying forces led to a civil war involving the country's main religious and ethnic groups, the Shiites, the Sunnis and the Kurds. American and allied forces clashed with resistance groups and terrorist cells that destabilized the country with suicide bombings, pillaging and the settling of accounts. Hoping to remedy the situation, the United States set up a provisional government and held elections in December 2005. Nonetheless, the United States was obliged to extend its occupation. To date, some 100 000 Iraqi civilians have been killed and over 250 000 have been injured in the daily violence in Iraq.

U.S. soldiers prepare to topple a statue of Saddam Hussein after the capturing of Baghdad on April 9, 2003.

American tanks drive past a ▶ commemorative monument during the invasion of Iraq in 2003.

February 26: Outbreak of the SARS epidemic
March 12: WHO issues a worldwide alert regarding the SARS epidemic
March 20: The American invasion of Iraq begins
April 9: Baghdad is seized, putting an end to Saddam Hussein's regime

April 14: Complete DNA sequencing of the human genome is completed
July 5: WHO announces that the SARS epidemic has been contained
July 22: Saddam Hussein's sons, Uday and Qusay Hussein, are killed
December 13: **Saddam Hussein is captured**

Saddam Hussein Is Captured

Iraq, Middle East, 2003

When Baghdad fell in April 2003, Saddam Hussein fled and went into hiding. For several months, the dictator avoided capture by disguising himself and frequently changing location with the help of his collaborators. His arrest soon became a priority due to fear that he would become a source of inspiration for the Iraqi resistance. On the night of December 13 to 14, 2003, American forces received information about the whereabouts of the deposed dictator that led them to a secret underground bunker. After his arrest, Saddam Hussein was accused of war crimes, crimes against humanity and genocide for abuses committed against the Kurds in 1982. He was found guilty by an Iraqi special tribunal and sentenced to death by hanging on December 30, 2006.

Threat of a World Pandemic

Hong Kong, Asia, 2003

In November 2002, a new disease known as SARS (severe acute respiratory syndrome) appeared for the first time in a hotel in Hong Kong. The disease, which causes high fever and respiratory problems that can lead to death, is highly contagious and treatments are often ineffective. The hotel in Hong Kong, a busy hub for travellers, provided an ideal environment for the disease to spread quickly. Soon, outbreaks were reported in China, Singapore, Vietnam and Toronto, Canada. In March 2003, the World Health Organization (WHO) issued a warning about the risk of a global pandemic. As panic swept over the world, many people refused to travel or wore breathing masks to avoid infection. Medical officials implemented strict quarantine measures and succeeded in containing the disease in 2004. Among the 8445 people infected, 916 died from the disease.

Ukraine's Orange Revolution

Ukraine, Europe, 2004

In November 2004, presidential elections in Ukraine were greeted with peaceful popular protests referred to as the Orange Revolution. Two candidates with very different political agendas faced off in the elections: Viktor Yanukovych, who supported strong ties with Russia, against Viktor Yushchenko, who supported much closer ties with Europe and the West. The Orange Revolution was a response to accusations of electoral fraud made against Yanukovych by international observers. Yushchenko's pro-Western supporters refused to recognize the results of the election and organized mass gatherings and general strikes across the country. On November 23, 500 000 protestors carrying orange flags demanded a new vote. Due to international pressure, Yanukovych was forced to accept and Yushchenko won the election on December 26. This victory was not well received by Russia, whose influence over the former Soviet republics had been eroding since the dismantling of the USSR in 1991.

Thousands of Ukrainians celebrate the first anniversary of the Orange Revolution in 2005.

2004

▶ *March 11:* Terrorist attacks in Madrid, Spain
November 21: Viktor Yanukovych wins the presidential election in Ukraine

November 23: The Orange Revolution in Ukraine begins
December 26: The elections in Ukraine are repeated; Viktor Yushchenko wins

2005

▶ *January 23:* The Orange Revolution ends
October 19: Saddam Hussein's trial begins
November 5: Saddam Hussein is found guilty

2006

▶ *December 30:* Saddam Hussein is executed by the Iraqis

■ Tsunami in Asia

Thailand, Asia, 2004

On December 26, 2004, one of the most violent earthquakes ever recorded occurred in the Indian Ocean. The earthquake caused a major tidal wave, called a tsunami, which battered the coasts of several countries, including Indonesia, Thailand, Sri Lanka and India. This wall of water destroyed beaches, villages and resorts during peak tourist season. The material and human loss was staggering: some 220 000 people were killed or declared missing. The images and video footage of the tsunami broadcast around the world elicited a strong international response. Humanitarian organizations received close to $5 billion in donations to help survivors and to rebuild the hardest-hit areas. This large-scale show of generosity was a testament to unprecedented global solidarity.

Aerial view of a coastline in Indonesia devastated by the tsunami on December 26, 2004.

■ Floods in New Orleans in the Wake of Hurricane Katrina

United States, North America, 2005

On August 29, 2005, Louisiana was struck by one of the most powerful hurricanes in American history. Violent winds measuring 280 km/h accompanied by 11-metre-high waves destroyed the levees that protect New Orleans and the city was quickly submerged. This natural disaster caused major material damage and led to one of the worst humanitarian crises in the history of the United States. On September 24, another storm, Hurricane Rita, hit Texas and part of Louisiana, once again destroying the New Orleans levees. The hurricane also interrupted production in nearby oil refineries, causing a temporary rise in oil prices. This natural disaster, which some scientists associate with climate change, was a reminder to Americans of the dangers of their oil dependency.

■ Pope Benedict XVI Succeeds the Late-Lamented John Paul II

Vatican, Europe, 2005

In 2005, the death of Pope John Paul II marked the end of one of the longest pontificates in the Catholic Church. Elected Pope in 1978, John Paul II was held in high esteem by his Catholic followers, who admired his piety, his extensive travelling and his message of international peace and reconciliation. John Paul II also encouraged open dialogue with the followers of other religions, including Jews, Muslims and Christians of all denominations. During his 26 years of pontifical duties, Pope John Paul II visited 117 countries, which increased the Catholic Church's visibility and prestige around the world. After his death, several heads of State and more than three million people attended his funeral. One of his faithful advisors, Cardinal Joseph Ratzinger, was then elected Pope, under the name Benedict XVI. The new Pope paid tribute to his predecessor's dignity and promised to carry on his work.

Pope John Paul II signs a document in the presence of German Cardinal Joseph Ratzinger, who was elected Pope in 2005, under the name of Benedict XVI.

2004 ▶ *December 26:* Tsunami in the Indian Ocean

2005 ▶ *January 9:* Mahmoud Abbas is elected President of the Palestinian Authority
February 10: North Korea announces that it possesses nuclear weapons

February 16: The Kyoto Protocol comes into effect
April 2: Pope John Paul II dies

April 19: Pope Benedict XVI is elected
July 7: Terrorist attacks occur in London, United Kingdom

Iranian President Mahmoud Ahmadinejad (left) shakes hands with Russian President Vladimir Putin (right) in 2006.

■ Iran Suspected of Aspiring to Become a Nuclear Power

Iran, Central Asia, 2005

In 1979, Iran became an Islamic republic on the heels of a revolution designed to end the United States' growing influence in the country. This anti-American sentiment forced Iran and the United States to break their diplomatic ties in 1980, resulting in tense relations for many years. In 2005, the situation further deteriorated after Iran's election of President Mahmoud Ahmadinejad. Ahmadinejad expressed open hostility toward the United States, which he described as the "Great Satan," as well as making clear his desire to see the State of Israel destroyed. Meanwhile, the United States and other Western countries suspected Iran of planning to build nuclear arms using enriched uranium. Even though Ahmadinejad provided assurances that uranium enrichment was only being pursued to produce nuclear energy, the UN imposed sanctions on Iran in an effort to force it to end these activities.

■ Lebanon Devastated by Israel

Lebanon, Middle East, 2006

Since the creation of the State of Israel in 1948, Israelis have had tense and sometimes hostile relations with some of their neighbours, including Lebanon and Syria. When the Israeli army invaded southern Lebanon in 1982, the Lebanese armed group Hezbollah launched a guerrilla war to recapture the occupied territories. Israel withdrew from the region in 2000, but did not cease its incursions into Lebanese territory. Fighting broke out again in 2006, when Hezbollah entered Israel and took two Israeli soldiers hostage. In response, Israel launched a large-scale military operation to free the soldiers. For 33 days, Lebanon's civilian and military infrastructures were the target of intense Israeli bombing that left many dead and created thousands of refugees. Despite its operations, the Israeli army was unable to free the two soldiers before it withdrew from Lebanon.

■ First Nuclear Test in North Korea

North Korea, Asia, 2006

At the end of the Korean War in 1953, the Korean peninsula remained divided between the communist north and the democratic south. This situation persisted after the Cold War and the fall of the USSR, as North Korea became more and more isolated from the international community. North Korea's regime, one of the most repressive in the world, has been the target of various international sanctions due to its hostility, its human rights violations and its intention to acquire nuclear weapons. In 2006, North Korea defied the international community by staging a nuclear test in an underground complex. North Korea's leader, Kim Jong-il, emphasized the need to defend his regime against foreign aggression, particularly a possible attack by the United States. Several countries, including China, Russia, Japan and the United States, managed to convince North Korea to end its nuclear program in 2007 in exchange for financial aid and the reduction of international sanctions.

North Korean leader Kim Jong-il withdrew his country from the Nuclear Non-Proliferation Treaty in 2003.

August 3: Mahmoud Ahmadinejad comes to power in Iran
August 29: Floods in New Orleans
August 30: Iran's nuclear crisis begins

2006

▶ *July 12:* **Israel's military operations in Lebanon begin**
August 14: The UN orders a ceasefire in the Israel-Lebanon conflict
October 9: North Korea carries out its first nuclear test

■ Annapolis Conference

United States, North America, 2007

The creation of the State of Israel, which forced Palestinians to take refuge in the Israeli enclaves of the West Bank and Gaza, has resulted in decades of hostilities, armed conflicts and deadly attacks between Jews and Muslims. Demanding the return of land that was taken from them, the Palestinians have been struggling for the right to form an independent State in a part of the State of Israel. However, Israelis have flatly rejected this demand, claiming that these territories belong to them for strategic and religious reasons. After numerous peace talks aimed at resolving this dispute, an important step was taken in 2007 during the Annapolis Conference in the United States. Following this meeting, Israeli Prime Minister Ehud Olmert and Palestinian President Mahmoud Abbas officially agreed on the need to create two independent States, a Palestinian State and an Israeli State, in order to end the Israeli-Palestinian conflict. However, this development is only the first step in what will be a long and difficult reconciliation process.

Israeli Prime Minister Ehud Olmert (left) shakes hands with Palestinian President Mahmoud Abbas (right) in the presence of George W. Bush (centre) following the Annapolis Conference in 2007.

■ Major Political Unrest in Pakistan

Pakistan, Central Asia, 2008

On June 20, 2001, Army General Pervez Musharraf became President of Pakistan. Following the terrorist attacks on September 11, Musharraf sided with the United States in the war against terrorism and supported the invasion of Afghanistan, Pakistan's neighbour. However, the war in Afghanistan and other internal factors made Musharraf unpopular among Pakistanis. In 2007, Musharraf allowed the return of Benazir Bhutto,

Pakistan's opposition leader, Benazir Bhutto, waves to the crowd shortly before her assassination, on December 27, 2007.

who had been exiled for eight years. Bhutto, who had been Prime Minister of Pakistan in 1988–1990 and 1993–1996, announced her plans to run against Musharraf in the 2008 presidential elections. On December 27, 2007, Bhutto was assassinated, most likely by Al Qaeda. After Bhutto's death, her husband, Asif Ali Zardari, decided to run for president. Riding on his wife's popularity, Zardari won the 2008 election, taking the reins of power from Musharraf. However, this victory marked the beginning of a period of uncertainty for Pakistan, particularly in terms of its role on the international scene.

■ Fidel Castro Steps Down From Power

Cuba, Caribbean, 2008

From 1959 onward, Fidel Castro led the island of Cuba at the head of a single-party State that did not tolerate any political opposition. In terms of foreign policy, the Cuban dictator also resisted

2007

▶ *November 27:* Annapolis Conference
December 27: Benazir Bhutto is assassinated

2008

▶ *February 17:* Kosovo officially declares independence from Serbia
February 18: General elections in Pakistan; victory of Benazir Bhutto's party

February 19: **Fidel Castro officially resigns from power**

the enemies of his regime and the adversaries of his communist ideals. The United States, among others, was unable to topple Castro's regime, despite a strict embargo that began in 1962. In 2006, due to poor health, the leader, who had successfully resisted tremendous pressure from 10 American presidents, was forced to temporarily cede power to his half-brother, Raúl Castro. Following surgery and several months of convalescence, the dictator's health remained uncertain. No longer in a condition to exercise power, Fidel Castro finally announced his resignation on February 19, 2008. Raúl officially took over the presidency, maintaining most of the ideological foundation of Fidel's regime. However, his more moderate policies have opened up the possibility of improved relations between Cuba and the international community, with the objective of ending a 45-year-old diplomatic impasse.

■ Food Crisis in the Third World
Burkino Faso, Africa, 2008

At the end of 2006, the price of basic food commodities began to increase on world markets. This was the result of a worldwide drop in grain production caused by successive droughts in several producing countries and by a global rise in the price of oil, which increased food transportation costs. Between February 2007 and February 2008, the situation became so bad that the price of wheat doubled on the world market. In some countries, the price of milk and bread doubled as well. Developing countries were the hardest hit. Many populations that could barely eek out a daily living could no longer afford to buy basic food commodities. The crisis culminated between February and April 2008, when protests and riots erupted in the hardest-hit countries, Burkina Faso, Indonesia, Cameroon and Haiti. In April, the World Bank and the IMF (International Monetary Fund) announced various measures to ease the crisis, but their long-term impact is still uncertain.

■ Cold War Tensions Resurface in South Ossetia
Georgia, Eurasia, 2008

The former Soviet republic of Georgia is situated east of the Black Sea in the Caucasus. Although independent since 1991, relations between Georgia and Russia have been strained for many years. Fearing the waning of its influence in the region following the end of the Cold War, Russia opposes Georgia's efforts to become a NATO member. The two countries, which share a common border, are also disputing control of the region of South Ossetia, located in Georgia. This region, which is seeking independence, enjoys support from Russia, but is still being claimed by Georgia. On August 7, 2008, when Georgia tried to take South Ossetia by force, Russia launched a strong military offensive. After expelling Georgian forces from South Ossetia,

Tea producers in Kenya are among the hardest hit by the world food crisis.

January 21: Fear of a recession in the Untied States causes the first stock market plunge
February 22: Riots in Burkina Faso due to the food crisis
February 24: Raúl Castro becomes President of Cuba

***August 7:* The war in South Ossetia begins**
August 8: The Olympic Games open in Beijing, China
September 6: Asif Ali Zardari, widower of Benazir Bhutto, is elected President of Pakistan

the Russian army invaded part of Georgia, remaining for a few days. Despite the signing of a ceasefire on August 16, 2008, the dispute over South Ossetia remains unresolved and the showdown between Russia and Georgia still looms large.

■ Global Financial Crisis

United States, North America, 2008

In February 2007, the early tremors of a financial crisis were felt on world markets. The crisis was due in part to mortgage loans and high-risk investments made by some banks in the United States, which overheated the U.S. economy and created a real estate bubble. In 2008, banks that had not performed as well as expected due to a slowing real estate market were shaken by a shortage of liquid assets and were driven to the brink of bankruptcy. On September 15, 2008, world stock markets, crippled by the worst banking crisis since 1929, experienced major losses due to lack of investor confidence. The financial crisis quickly spread around the globe, causing stock prices to plummet on world markets. Several countries responded swiftly to alleviate the crisis, including the United States,

which introduced an economic recovery plan that injected $700 billion into the U.S. financial markets in an effort to boost the economy. However, the long-term effects of this economic crisis are still uncertain.

Barack Obama after winning the U.S. presidential elections on November 4, 2008.

The New York Stock Exchange on Wall Street.

■ Historic Presidential Elections in the United States

United States, North America, 2008

On November 4, 2008, Americans went to the polls to elect the 44th President of the United States. After many months of competition in the primary elections, two candidates were nominated by the country's two main parties to run in the presidential elections: Senator John McCain of the Republican Party and Senator Barack Obama of the Democratic Party. In many respects, this presidential election promised to be historic. Barack Obama stood to become the first African-American president, while 72-year-old Vietnam War veteran John McCain stood to become the oldest president at the beginning of his first term. It was a tight race, but in the end, the American people chose to elect Obama. Given the wars in Iraq and Afghanistan and the global financial crisis, George W. Bush's successor faces many challenges. Barack Obama was officially sworn in as the President of the United States on January 20, 2009.

▶ *September 15:* Financial markets take a major plunge following the bankruptcy of several U.S. banks

October 3: The United States government invests $700 billion in the American financial markets to alleviate the financial crisis

November 4: Barack Obama is elected President of the United States

The Israeli Military Intervenes in the Gaza Strip

Israel, Middle East, 2008–2009

On December 27, 2008, the Israeli army began bombing the Gaza Strip, launching a land invasion a few days later. The main objective of this military offensive was to crush Hamas, the radical Islamist party in power in Gaza. To justify its actions, the Israeli government invoked its right to defend itself against rocket attacks carried out by Hamas in southern Israel. However, the number of civilian victims caused by this military offensive elicited the censure of the international community. On January 18, 2009, the Israeli government announced a ceasefire, with Hamas quickly following suit. At the end of February 2009, negotiations between the two parties to establish a lasting truce were still underway.

Bolivia Adopts a New Constitution

Bolivia, South America, 2009

On January 25, 2009, close to 60% of Bolivians voted in a referendum to adopt a new constitution. A democratically elected constituent assembly under the leadership of President Evo Morales had been working on this crucial text since 2006. For the first time, Bolivia's indigenous peoples saw their right to self-determination recognized in terms of their identity, values, territories and resources. Moreover, indigenous languages were granted the same official language status as Spanish. The wealthiest regions of La Paz and Eastern Bolivia, primarily populated by people of mixed European and indigenous descent, adamantly opposed the adoption of this constitution.

Sri Lankan Army Moves Toward Victory

Sri Lanka, Asia, 2009

The civil war that had pitted the Sri Lankan government against the Liberation Tigers of Tamil Eelam (LTTE), a minority that had been fighting for an independent State in northern Sri Lanka, came to an end on May 17, 2009, when the LTTE conceded defeat. The Sri Lankan army had by that point recaptured all of the cities that were formerly controlled by the separatists and had isolated the LTTE and tens of thousands of civilians in a small jungle region in north-eastern Sri Lanka.

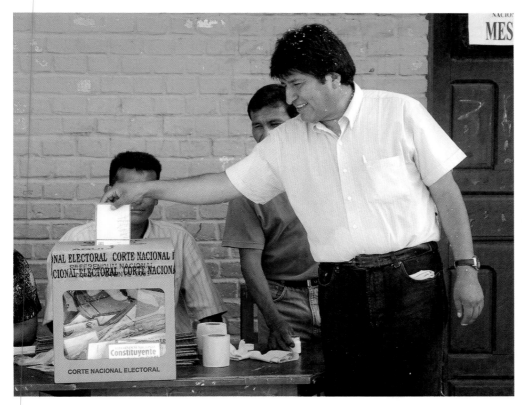

Evo Morales casts his ballot during the constitutional referendum in January 2009. Elected in December 2005, socialist politician Evo Morales became Bolivia's first indigenous president. Indigenous peoples represent close to 70% of the country's population.

December 27: Israeli army begins bombing the Gaza Strip

January 20: Inauguration of Barack Obama as the President of the United States

January 25: A constitutional referendum is held in Bolivia

May 17: The Tamil Tigers acknowledge defeat, ending their war of independence against the Sri Lankan government.

Techniques

In the Contemporary World program, the investigative research procedure is at the heart of the learning process. It allows you to take a more in-depth look at today's world in order to interpret the main problems and take a position on different issues. After your investigation, developing answers and searching for explanations or justifications will help you to acquire knowledge and methodological competencies and to hone your technical skills. To encourage you to use these techniques, we are providing the following methodological sheets.

Have fun!

TABLE OF CONTENTS

Developing an Investigative Research Procedure

1 Choose the situational problem

The situational problem is the problem to be solved. It is essential that you fully understand it. Analyze the related concepts, as needed. The five Ws (Who?, What?, Where?, When?, Why? and How?) can help you define the context of your investigation. It is also important to apply all of your knowledge about the subject.

This new interpretation will raise new questions that other people will want answered and the process will begin again. You will be able to apply the knowledge you acquired to research other questions in other contexts.

2 Formulate a conjecture or a hypothesis to explain the situation

This is the preliminary explanation formulated at the beginning of the process. Apply your current knowledge and understanding of the problem.

The goal is not to come up with *the* correct answer, but to identify an avenue of exploration.

6 Explain the problem and summarize the information

This final step consists of comparing the conjecture or initial hypothesis with the conclusion you have drawn based on your research. The result is usually communicated in a report. The report must meet specific requirements that will demonstrate the reliability of your work. Ask your teacher about this aspect.

3 Conduct the necessary investigations

This is the part of the process where you look for clues to solve the problem.

You can look for information in the classroom, at the library, on the Internet or in the media.

You can use a variety of documents: texts, images, photographs, videos, articles. It is important to keep a list of the documents consulted (record sheets*). You never know when the information they contain will prove useful.

5 Organize and interpret ideas

In the two previous steps you found and sorted the pieces of the puzzle. Now you have to put them together!

You must establish logical connections among the selected items of information (cause and effect, actors and their positions, relationships between the economy, society, politics and culture). You must also decide which ideas are your main ideas and which ones are secondary. The goal is to construct a valid interpretation of the problem. Using a graphic organizer* might help.

4 Analyze the information and arguments

At this stage of the research procedure, you must do a more in-depth analysis of the documents chosen. Several techniques will come in handy (using reading strategies, analyzing images and maps,* reading tables and graphs,* creating a time line*). You must also critically examine the documents to determine their validity. This will enable you to classify the information you find. You must separate the essential from the superfluous. This is also the time to compare positions, debate their validity and develop arguments.

* A specific methodological sheet is available
for this part of the research procedure.

Formulating a Hypothesis

Goal (Why formulate a hypothesis?)

A hypothesis is the common thread that determines how your research is organized. That is why this step is so important.

Characteristics of a good hypothesis (How to go about it)

- ✓ It proposes an answer to the problem.
- ✓ It is short (one or two sentences) and precise (appropriate choice of vocabulary).
- ✓ It is formulated as a statement, not a question.
- ✓ It can be simple or it can propose an explanation.
- ✓ It can be verified using the investigative research procedure.
- ✓ It does not contain value judgments or biases.
- ✓ It does not convey emotion or feeling.

Validating a Hypothesis

The hypothesis is validated at the end of the investigative procedure, when you obtain the answer or the explanation you are looking for.

- If the hypothesis is supported by the results obtained from the investigative procedure, it is said to be **confirmed**, or true.
- If the hypothesis is supported by the research procedure but is incomplete, it is said to be **partially confirmed**.
- If the hypothesis is entirely or partially contradicted by the results obtained, it is said to be **refuted**, or false.

The validation process is usually described in a report that includes the conclusions of the research. It must be carefully prepared. The attention you pay to it will reflect the quality of your research work.

Below are a few suggestions for writing a good report:

- ✓ Write a proper **introduction**, presenting the problem, your hypothesis and the structure of the report.
- ✓ The **body** of the report should present your historical interpretation. Remember that each paragraph should contain only one idea. Quotations and document references help give your work credibility.
- ✓ The **conclusion** is your assessment of the validity of your hypothesis. Close by proposing a new question raised by your research.

Don't forget the **mediagraphy!**

Watching and Interpreting a Televised Report

Goals (Why watch and interpret a televised report?)

- To learn about current events through interviews, news stories, etc.
- To follow developments in a story over time
- To see video images of news stories
- To find specific information about a topic
- To be able to interpret a contemporary world problem
- To be able to take a position on a contemporary world issue
- To determine an actor's point of view

Method (How to go about it)

1 **Define the purpose of the exercise.** Are you simply keeping up to date with the news or are you looking for information about a specific topic with a view to interpreting a contemporary world problem or issue? If you are watching a televised report to gather information about a contemporary world problem or issue, you should compare the information broadcast on different networks.

2 **Watch the televised report and do a content analysis.** At this stage, it is important to take notes on the information you are interested in. It would also be a good idea to record the news stories that address your topic so that you can watch them again.

A content analysis of a televised news story or an interview should take into account the same elements as the content analysis of a written document. You should distinguish between fact and opinion. For interviews, you should also:

- identify the group to which the interview subject belongs
- identify the arguments supporting your opinions
- make sure you fully understand the context in which the words were spoken and the context in which they are being reported

3 **Do a source analysis.** Place the news story in context:

- Specify the type of source. Is the journalist on-site? Are the images borrowed from a press agency or were they taken by the journalist's team?
- Consider the network broadcasting the report. Who owns it? What is its position or ideology?

4 **Determine whether the televised report helps you fulfill your original purpose.** If it does, note the information and references.

> When a quotation is taken "out of context," that means that its context is not explained. Taken out of context, the quotation no longer has the same meaning.

Preparing Record Sheets

Goals (Why prepare record sheets?)

- To record the works you consulted during your research
- To summarize the information you found
- To note a quotation or significant passage
- To note ideas or comments that arise when consulting documents

Method (How to go about it)

1 Use a **quotation sheet** to create a word-for-word record of a passage you find particularly interesting (an author's opinion, for example).

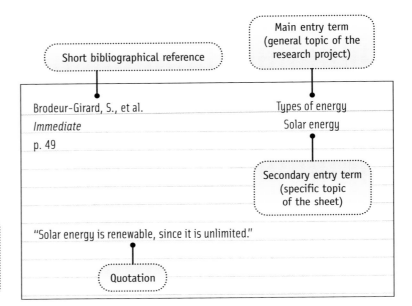

Short bibliographical reference

Main entry term (general topic of the research project)

Brodeur-Girard, S., et al.

Immediate

p. 49

Types of energy

Solar energy

Secondary entry term (specific topic of the sheet)

"Solar energy is renewable, since it is unlimited."

Quotation

Comment: When you remove a non-essential sentence or part of a sentence from a quotation, use ellipsis points ... to indicate the omission.

2 Use a **summary sheet** to reformulate the content of a document in a few words.

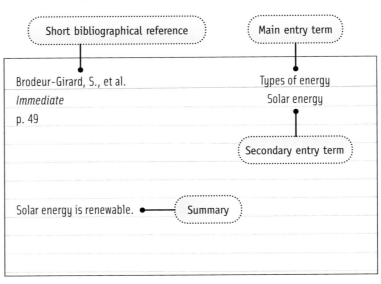

Short bibliographical reference

Main entry term

Brodeur-Girard, S., et al.

Immediate

p. 49

Types of energy

Solar energy

Secondary entry term

Solar energy is renewable.

Summary

Comments:
- The main and secondary entry terms should be no more than two or three words.
- Use a different sheet for each idea.
- In the bibliographical reference, the term *et al.* means "and others."

248

3 Use a **comment sheet** to record a personal comment on part of a document (sentence, passage, chapter) or an idea you would like to develop.

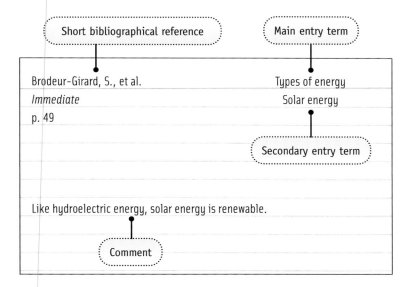

Short bibliographical reference

Main entry term

Brodeur-Girard, S., et al.

Immediate

p. 49

Types of energy

Solar energy

Secondary entry term

Like hydroelectric energy, solar energy is renewable.

Comment

Comment: As with the summary sheet, use a different sheet for each idea.

Preparing a Press Kit

Goal (Why prepare a press kit?)

To organize newspaper and magazine clippings on a given topic

Method (How to go about it)

1 **Determine the subject of the press kit.**
Your press kit can be on any number of subjects, however major or minor. For example, you can prepare a press kit on an international issue that affects several countries on different continents, or on a more local issue that affects several countries in a given region. You can even prepare one for a single country.

2 **Read the newspapers.**
Read newspapers and news magazines on a daily basis. Many of them are available on the Internet.

3 **Record the articles.**
Cut out or print the articles you find interesting or relevant. Note the source (including at least the title of the newspaper or magazine, the publication date and the page number).

4 **Comment on the articles.**
What questions do you have after reading the articles? Do you have any doubts concerning their content? What is your opinion on the subject? etc.

This procedure can also be done in reverse. You could cut out relevant articles before determining a specific subject. Sort the articles according to the program's five themes.

Searching the Internet

Goals (Why search the Internet?)

- To find specific information about a topic
- To find pictures (images, maps, time lines, graphs, etc.)
- To quickly find several sources with a view to verifying a piece of information.

Method (How to go about it)

1 **Define the purpose of your search by specifying the topic.**

2 **Prepare a research strategy.**

- Prepare a list of terms associated with the topic and classify them according to their relevance.
- Prepare a list of the websites and search engines to be used. Start with well-known websites or those that are provided as references. Then, use a general search engine.
- Determine the amount of time you want to spend on the search. This will help you focus on your topic and avoid wasting time.

3 **Search the Internet.**

- Browse the Internet using the lists you prepared. If there is a lot of text on the page consulted, use the key word search function available on most browsers.
- Prepare a list of the Web addresses consulted, especially those you will be using as references. You can cut and paste the addresses into a document you create using a word processing program.
- Establish the credibility of the information. Identify the authors and the type of site (private individual, lobby group, government agency, museum, etc.).

4 **Make sure the information helps you fulfill your original purpose.**
If it does, note the information and references (see Preparing Record Sheets).

> **List of terms associated with "human rights":**
> - Universal Declaration of Human Rights
> - Amnesty International
> - UN
> - International Criminal Court
> - UNESCO

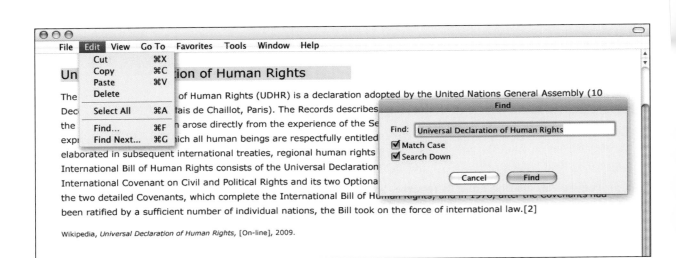

Interpreting a Written Document

Goals (Why interpret a written document?)

- To define the general framework of a theme
- To find specific information
- To establish the point of view of an actor or lobby group

Method (How to go about it)

1 **Define the purpose of the exercise.** If you have a clear idea of what you are looking for, you will find it more quickly.

2 **Scan the document.** This first glance will enable you to assess the relevance of the document. Focus on the headings and subheadings, the conclusion and the paratext (images, tables and graphs accompanying the text).

3 **Read the document and do a content analysis.** At this stage, you are dealing with the information in the document:
- Identify the main idea and the secondary ideas.
- Highlight the information you consider relevant.
- Distinguish between fact and opinion.

4 **Do a source analysis.** Place the document in context:
- Determine the type of document (letter, diary, legal document, etc.).
- Specify the type of source (primary or secondary).
- Identify the date of the document and where it was written.
- Identify the author and the intended audience and establish the relationship between the two.

The source analysis might cause you to reconsider some of the elements identified in the content analysis.

5 **Determine whether the document helps you fulfill your original purpose.** If it does, note the information and references (see Preparing Record Sheets).

Example

1 I want to find the principles that govern relations between States in the area of environmental protection.

2 By scanning the document, I notice that it is an excerpt of a text. The introductory paragraph reveals that the text is related to my search. The document is relevant, so I will continue my analysis.

Good Neighbours

In 1972, delegates at the first major international conference on the environment defined the principles governing relations between States in the area of environmental protection:

"States have, in accordance with the Charter of the United Nations and the principles of international law, the sovereign right to exploit their own resources pursuant to their own environmental policies, and the responsibility to ensure that activities within their jurisdiction or control do not cause damage to the environment of other States or of areas beyond the limits of national jurisdiction."

Source: *Declaration of the United Nations Conference on the Human Environment,* 1972, [On-line].

3 During my content analysis, I observed that, in 1972, the United Nations proclaimed that States have the right to exploit their own resources as they see fit, provided that their activities do not cause damage to the environment of other States.

4 This is an excerpt of a primary document. The Declaration of the United Nations Conference on the Human Environment is a legal document that was written in 1972. It is a credible source.

5 The document helps me fulfill my original purpose because it reveals that there is at least one principle governing relations between States in the area of environmental protection. A State can exploit its own resources as it sees fit only if its practices do not cause damage to a neighbouring State. However, I should find at least one other document to support this information.

Reading and Interpreting a Newspaper Article

Goals (Why read and interpret a newspaper article?)

- To learn about current events
- To follow developments in a story over time
- To find specific information about a topic
- To be able to interpret a contemporary world problem
- To be able to take a position on a contemporary world issue
- To determine an actor's point of view

Method (How to go about it)

1 **Define the purpose of the exercise.** Are you simply keeping up to date with the news or are you looking for information about a specific topic? If you are reading an article to gather information, you should compare the information published in different newspapers.

2 **Scan the article.** This first glance will enable you to assess the relevance of the article. Focus on the headings and subheadings, the bold text at the beginning of the article and the paratext (images, tables and graphs).

3 **Do a content analysis.** You should consider the same elements you would when carrying out a content analysis of a written document, as well as the following:

- Specify the context in which the article is presented. If the context is not clear, try to determine it.
- Identify the actors mentioned in the article, the lobby group to which they belong and their opinions about the topic addressed in the article.
- Make sure you fully understand the context in which the words were spoken and the context in which they are being reported.

4 **Do a source analysis.** Place the article in context:

- Specify the type of article. Does it convey information or an opinion? Was it written by a columnist? Is it a sensationalist article? Is it a news item?
- Specify the type of source. Is the journalist on-site? Is the article from a news agency or was it written by a foreign correspondent?
- Exercise your critical judgment. Consider the newspaper that published the article. Who owns it? What is its position or ideology?

5 **Determine whether the article helps you fulfill your original purpose.** If it does, note the information and references.

Writing a Persuasive Text

Goal (Why write a persuasive text?)

To influence, convince or persuade an audience, using arguments

Method (How to go about it)

1 **Become familiar with the topic.** Start by getting an overview of the topic in question. Then, make sure you understand all of the related concepts and aspects. Take notes: prepare record sheets to help you flesh out your arguments when you write your text.

2 **Establish your position on the issue.** Define your point of view. Your position should be rational, not emotional. Prepare a list of the arguments on which your position is based. These will be your "thesis."

3 **Conduct documentary research to flesh out your thesis.** This will enable you to gain a better understanding of the topic. Find arguments that support your thesis (facts, general statements, values, actors' points of view, etc.). Take this opportunity to examine counter-arguments (counter-thesis) your opponents might raise. Your arguments could be based on:

Reference to an authority: Quote an authority on the issue, a scientific research study, a recognized institution or statistics that support your position.

Reference to a fact: Cite a well-known fact or observation.

An appeal to moral values: Make reference to values your opponent would have difficulty denying.

An appeal to logic: Confront your opponent with implacable logic. Cite proverbs to confirm that your belief is generally accepted and that your opinion is the subject of consensus.

4 **Write the text.** A persuasive text includes an introduction (presentation of the problem, your hypothesis and the structure of the text), a body (three arguments to support your thesis) and a conclusion (reformulation of the thesis and formulation of a desire, a piece of advice, a prediction, etc.). To convince your audience, adopt an argumentative strategy revolving around a dominant argumentative process. Below are a few examples:

Demonstration: Base your thesis on deductive reasoning (you should maintain a certain distance from the topic by using facts, denotation and a neutral tone).

Refutation: Refute the counter-thesis using various techniques, such as declaring the opposing thesis outdated, finding an exception or conceding something in order to gain the advantage.

Text organizers: Well-organized arguments can be convincing. Using words such as "first," "second" and "third" is an effective way of organizing your arguments.

Reported speech: Quoting experts adds weight to your arguments.

Stylistic devices: Use irony (saying the opposite of what you want to say to show the absurdity of the proposition) or repetition to emphasize an idea or an argument.

Interpreting a Picture

Goals (Why interpret a picture?)

- To find information about social organization
- To define the organization of space
- To establish the positions of an actor or lobby group
- To validate the presence of certain elements related to a specific issue

Method (How to go about it)

1 **Define the purpose of the exercise.** Since a picture is worth a thousand words, you should know what you are looking for before interpreting a picture.

2 **Analyze the information.**
- Title: The title often reveals the theme of the image.
- Source: The source reveals the author's name and the date the picture was created or taken. This will help you determine whether the picture is current.
- Explanatory note: Pictures are sometimes accompanied by an explanatory note providing information about their context.

3 **Analyze the content of the picture.**
- First, look at the elements (people, objects, actions) of the picture.
- Second, compare the content of the foreground, the middle ground and the background and establish the relationship between them.

4 **Interpret the picture.** This is where you complete your understanding of the picture. To validate your interpretation, compare it with that of others.

5 **Determine whether the picture helps you fulfill your original purpose.** If it does, note the information and references (see Preparing a Record Sheet).

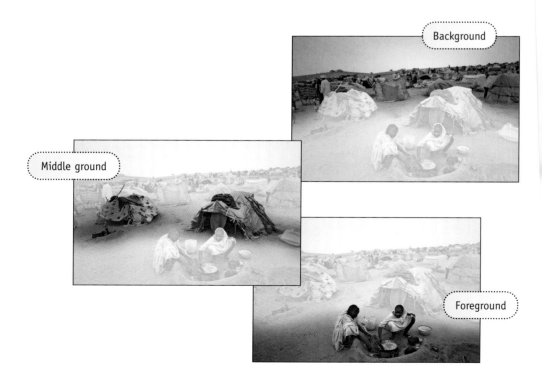

Background

Middle ground

Foreground

Example

1 I want to know what living conditions are like in refugee camps.

3 Analyzing the foreground, the middle ground and the background provides the following information:

Foreground: I see people cooking on the ground over a wood fire. The facility is basic and there are few utensils. The ground appears to be very arid (dry and without vegetation).

Middle ground: I see makeshift shelters made out of tarps and various fabrics. Space is limited and there is no furniture.

Background: I see many more "tents." Some do not even have a roof.

2 The title and explanatory note confirm that this is a picture of a refugee camp, more specifically, a camp in Darfur, a region in Sudan. This photograph was taken on August 17, 2006. It is therefore representative of living conditions in the camp.

● **Sudan – El Fashir – Refugee Camp in Darfur**
A woman prepares a meal in an IDP (internally displaced persons) camp. Seven thousand African Union soldiers are currently deployed in Darfur, where the conflict has so far cost more than 100 000 lives and caused the displacement of millions of people to cramped refugee camps. The soldiers, originally called in to observe a cease-fire, have seen their numbers gradually rise.

4 In light of the information collected, I interpret the picture as follows: Hundreds, even thousands, of people are gathered together on an uninviting (arid) piece of land and are living in very basic conditions. Their tiny shelters are nothing but bits of fabric they brought with them when they abandoned their homes. The camp is disorganized and there are no facilities.

5 The picture partially helps me fulfill my original purpose. Living conditions in a refugee camp are very difficult. However, this is only one example. I need to find other documents to validate the information by comparing this camp with other refugee camps.

Interpreting a Cartoon

Goals (Why interpret a cartoon?)

- For entertainment purposes
- To identify people or events in the news
- To identify an original point of view (comic, ironic or sarcastic)

Method (How to go about it)

1 **Define the purpose of the exercise.** Since a picture is worth a thousand words, you should know what you are looking for before interpreting a cartoon.

2 **Define the period in question.** Since cartoons often appear daily or weekly, it is essential that you have at least some understanding of the time period in question.

3 **Analyze the information.**
- Title: The title reveals the theme of the cartoon and can help contextualize its elements.
- Source: The source reveals the author's name and the date the cartoon was drawn. Don't forget the title of the newspaper or magazine that published the cartoon. The publication's editorial view could help with your interpretation.
- Explanatory note: Cartoons are sometimes accompanied by an explanatory note that can help you interpret them.

4 **Analyze the content of the cartoon.**
- Identify the people represented.
- Describe the actions depicted in the cartoon.
- Determine the social issues addressed (economic, political, social, cultural, territorial, scientific, technical).

5 **Interpret the cartoon.**
- Identify the exaggerated, comic and sarcastic elements.
- Distinguish between fact and fiction.
- Establish connections among the elements and complete your understanding of the cartoon.

6 **Determine whether the cartoon helps you fulfill your original purpose.** If it does, note the information and references on record sheets.

Example

1 I want to discover whether people are making changes to their lifestyle because of rising oil prices.

MORE AND MORE PEOPLE ARE CARPOOLING TO SAVE ON GAS...

2 The title reveals that more and more people are carpooling to save gas. The newspaper *Le Soleil* is intended for a Québec City audience. There is no explanatory note.

3 The cartoon was published on June 11, 2008. It is therefore recent, and appeared during a period marked by soaring oil prices.

André-Philippe Côté,
Le Soleil, June 11, 2008,
[On-line]. [Translation]

4 This cartoon represents a car filled with an exaggerated number of carpoolers.

5 Despite the exaggeration, the idea expressed by the cartoon is that people, concerned about the price of oil, are beginning to make changes to their lifestyle by carpooling.

6 The document partially helps me fulfill my original purpose. It appears that people are making changes to their lifestyle because of rising oil prices. I will validate this conclusion by consulting other documents.

Components of a Time Line

Below are two types of time lines:

One-dimensional time line

All of the information is included on a single line. This type of time line is ideal for presenting dates.

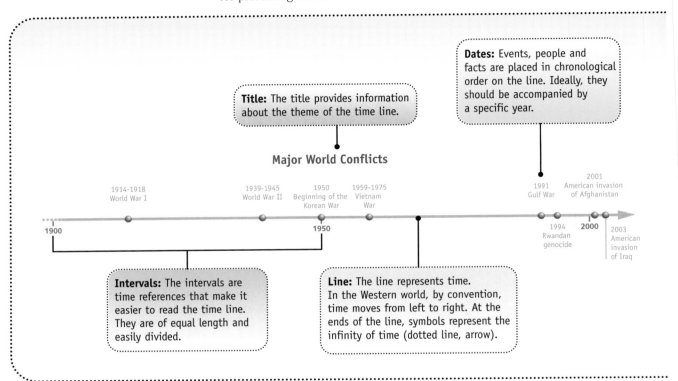

Title: The title provides information about the theme of the time line.

Dates: Events, people and facts are placed in chronological order on the line. Ideally, they should be accompanied by a specific year.

Major World Conflicts

1914-1918
World War I

1939-1945
World War II

1950
Beginning of the
Korean War

1959-1975
Vietnam
War

2001
American invasion
of Afghanistan

1991
Gulf War

1900

1950

1994
Rwandan
genocide

2000

2003
American
invasion
of Iraq

Intervals: The intervals are time references that make it easier to read the time line. They are of equal length and easily divided.

Line: The line represents time. In the Western world, by convention, time moves from left to right. At the ends of the line, symbols represent the infinity of time (dotted line, arrow).

Two-dimensional time line

A two-dimensional time line provides more space for periods and dates.

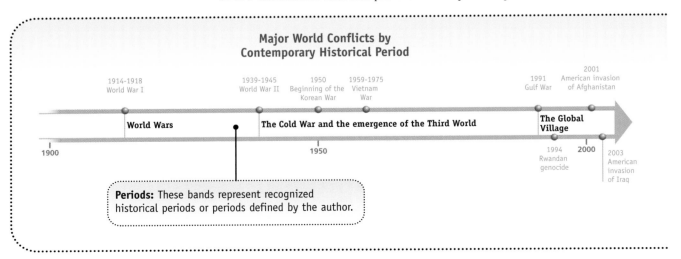

Major World Conflicts by
Contemporary Historical Period

1914-1918
World War I

1939-1945
World War II

1950
Beginning of the
Korean War

1959-1975
Vietnam
War

2001
American invasion
of Afghanistan

1991
Gulf War

World Wars

The Cold War and the emergence of the Third World

The Global
Village

1900

1950

1994
Rwandan
genocide

2000

2003
American
invasion
of Iraq

Periods: These bands represent recognized historical periods or periods defined by the author.

Interpreting a Time Line

Goals (Why interpret a time line?)

- To situate events with respect to one another
- To visualize the chronological sequence of events
- To understand time intervals (between past events or between present and past events)
- To identify causes and effects
- To identify elements of change and elements of continuity
- To compare two societies during the same period or during different periods

Method (How to go about it)

1 **Define the purpose of the exercise.** You should have a clear purpose, since the reason you are consulting the time line determines how you process the information.

2 **Read the title.** The title should reveal the theme of the time line.

3 **Decode the time references.** Verify the dates indicated at the ends of the line and consider the established time scale.

4 **Analyze and interpret the information in order to fulfill your purpose.** Pay attention to dates and time periods.

5 **Determine whether the document helps you fulfill your original purpose.** If it does, note the information and references on record sheets.

Example

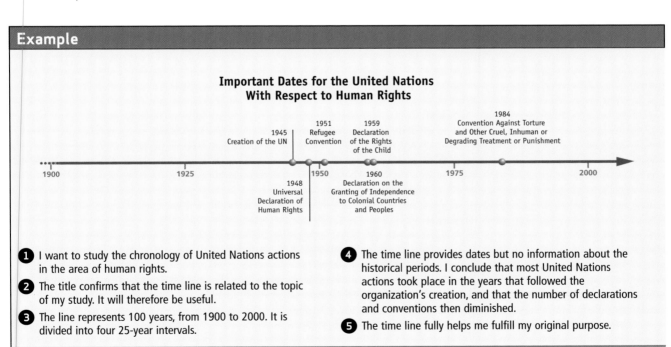

Important Dates for the United Nations With Respect to Human Rights

1 I want to study the chronology of United Nations actions in the area of human rights.

2 The title confirms that the time line is related to the topic of my study. It will therefore be useful.

3 The line represents 100 years, from 1900 to 2000. It is divided into four 25-year intervals.

4 The time line provides dates but no information about the historical periods. I conclude that most United Nations actions took place in the years that followed the organization's creation, and that the number of declarations and conventions then diminished.

5 The time line fully helps me fulfill my original purpose.

Creating a Time Line

Methods (How to go about it)

1 Define the purpose of the exercise (what you want to represent) and the theme and give the time line a provisional title.

2 Prepare a list of information relevant to your theme and purpose. Determine the dates associated with each element and place them in chronological order.

3 Choose the most appropriate type of time line (one- or two-dimensional) depending on the type and quantity of information to be included.

4 Establish the intervals based on the available space and the number of years you need to cover. You should use regular intervals that are easy to divide (rounded numbers).

5 Draw and complete the time line. Give it its final title. You should pay special attention to the accuracy, clarity and neatness of the line, since it must help you fulfill your original purpose.

Example

Periods Proposed for a Historical Perspective of the Program's Five Themes

Beginning of World War I		End of World War II		Demise of the USSR	

The domination of industrial societies | The World Wars | The Cold War and the emergence of the Third World | | The Global Village |

1900 — 1914 — 1945 — 1950 — 1991 — 2000

1 I want to show the contemporary historical periods and the breaking points that marked the changes between the different periods. My provisional title is **Contemporary Historical Periods**.

2 The historical periods are: The domination of industrial societies until 1914, the World Wars until 1945, the Cold War and the emergence of the Third World until 1991, and the Global Village. The breaking points are: 1914 – beginning of World War I; 1945 – end of World War II; and 1991 – demise of the USSR.

3 Two-dimensional time line with dates and historical periods.

4 I am interested in the years 1900 to 2009, an interval of 109 years. I will divide the time line into two 50-year intervals. My time line is 15 cm long. Therefore, each interval will be 7.5 cm long.

5 I will draw the time line and give it a final title: **Periods Proposed for a Historical Perspective of the Program's Five Themes**.

Components of a Map

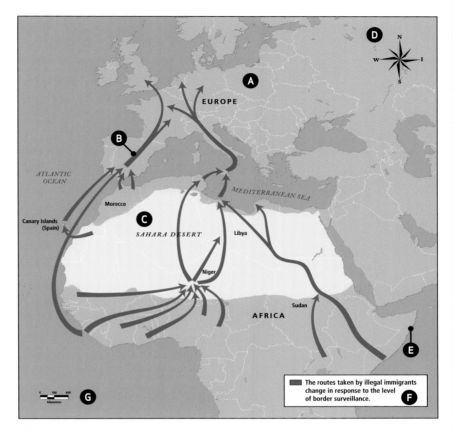

A **Area:** This is information about a particular area.

B **Line:** This is information represented by a line. Quantity can be expressed by making the line thinner or thicker.

C **Point:** This information is indicated at a specific point on the map. Quantity can be expressed by changing the size of the symbol.

D **Compass:** This symbol indicates the points of the compass. It should at least indicate north.

H **Illegal Migrations**

I The routes taken by illegal immigrants change in response to the level of border surveillance.

E **Base map:** This is the background drawing to which all other information is added. It is usually limited to physical boundaries (water-land) and political borders.

F **Legend:** The legend is a box containing the symbols used. It is the key to reading the map.

G **Scale:** The scale is the ratio between the size of the map and the size of the actual area. It is usually represented by a line divided into sections.

H **Title:** The title informs the reader of the theme of the map and indicates the time period in question.

I **Explanatory note:** This is a short text summarizing or explaining certain elements of the map. It is very useful for readers, but is not always included.

Interpreting a Map

Goals (Why interpret a map?)

- To locate a territory or a society
- To find information related to a theme
- To establish the territorial limits of a historical reality
- To visualize a dynamic in a territory

Method (How to go about it)

1 **Define the purpose of the exercise.** If you have a clear idea of what you are looking for, you will find it more quickly.

2 **Read the title.** The title provides information about the theme of the map and the time period in question.

3 **Orient the map and locate a reference point.** Take the time to place the map with north facing up. Then, locate yourself (or a familiar reference point) with respect to the territory on the map. A small box could help you indicate your reference point.

4 **Determine the scale.** The scale will help you determine the limits of the territory you are studying. It will also help you estimate distances more easily.

5 **Analyze the information.** Read the legend carefully. It is essential to understanding the map. Use your observations to establish connections among the elements of information gathered. Use the comments, if applicable.

6 **Interpret the information.** Complete your understanding of the map.

7 **Determine whether the map helps you fulfill your original purpose.** If it does, note the information on record sheets.

Example

Human Development Index (HDI) (2006)

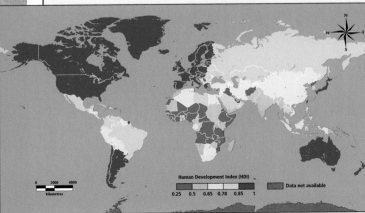

Human Development Index (HDI)
0.25   0.5   0.65   0.78   0.85   1   Data not available

Source: UNDP, Human Development Report, 2007-2008, [On-line].

1 I want to identify the differences in the HDI of various countries.

2 The title is simple, but is directly related to my research.

3 There is a compass and the map is a traditional representation of the world. Therefore, I know that the map is correctly oriented.

4 The scale is indicated, but is unimportant, since I do not want to estimate distances.

5 By consulting the legend, I see that the HDI is represented by different colours, which makes it easier to interpret the map. There are no comments.

6 My interpretation of the map is as follows: the colour of the Western countries indicates that they have the highest HDI, while most of the countries in Africa have a very low HDI.

7 The document helps me fulfill my original purpose, since it clearly presents the differences in the HDI in various countries.

Creating a Map

Method (How to go about it)

1 **Define the purpose of the exercise, the theme and the time period in question.** You could give the map a provisional title.

2 **Prepare a list of information relevant to your theme and purpose.** Take this opportunity to determine the format of each item of information (point, line or area). Be careful! Avoid overloading the map, since that will make it difficult to read.

3 **Determine the symbols and colours you will use.** Carefully choose the symbols and colours so that the map is easy to read.

4 **Find or draw the base map.** It will determine the scale you use. This is the time to think about including a box to indicate a reference point.

5 **Add the information.** Don't forget that clarity and precision are important when drawing a map.

6 **Add the legend, the scale and the compass.** Make sure these components don't hide any information or make the map difficult to read.

7 **Write the final title and the explanatory note, if applicable.**

Example

1 I want to show the African countries most affected by the AIDS epidemic and the food crisis. The title could be: **The African Countries Most Affected by the AIDS Epidemic and the Food Crisis.**

2 This is the information I have: the countries most affected by the AIDS epidemic, the countries most affected by the food crisis and the Human Development Index for Sub-Saharan Africa in 2006.

3 These are the symbols I want to use:
– a ribbon to indicate the countries most affected by AIDS
– a stalk of wheat to identify the countries facing a food crisis
– different shades of orange to indicate the Human Development Index

4 **5** **6** and **7**
I found a base map on the Internet. I will add the information, the legend, the compass, the final title and the explanatory note.

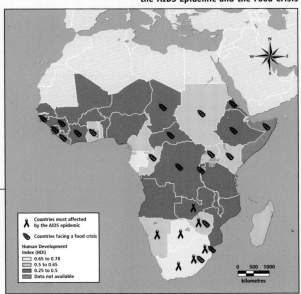

The African Countries Most Affected by the AIDS Epidemic and the Food Crisis

The Prevalence of AIDS

Sub-Saharan Africa is the area of the world most affected by the AIDS virus. Some 22 million people are infected. Women are more at risk than men: Between the ages of 18 and 24, women are three times more likely than men to become infected. Children are also affected: 1.8 million of them have HIV.

Countries most affected by the AIDS epidemic

Countries facing a food crisis

Human Development Index (HDI)
- 0.65 to 0.78
- 0.5 to 0.65
- 0.25 to 0.5
- Data not available

0   500   1000
kilometres

263

Components of a Contingency Table

Units: The units make it easier to define the entries and their quantities. They are usually identified in the title or the headings, indicating how the table is to be read.

Title: The title indicates the subject of the table. It refers to the data used. It often contains a time reference.

Automobile Density by Country (International Comparison), 1990 to 2007

(Number) of cars and utility vehicles per 1000 inhabitants on January 1

	1990	1995	2002	2003	2004	2005	2006	2007
Germany	512	529	580	583	589	592	597	604
Belgium	419	463	520	523	530	537	538	546
Spain	403	430	554	562	577	604	600	609
France	495	520	585	587	594	597	595	598
Italy	507	541	638	656	670	666	673	685
United Kingdom	454	474	536	554	564	572	571	576
Sweden	455	445	502	503	507	513	514	516
Poland	160	229	325	344	353	377	385	415
Turkey	37	65	89	89	93	108	115	122
Canada	617	562	572	584	587	582	585	601
United States	752	759	785	775	803	794	813	824
South Korea	71	177	273	294	306	311	322	331
Japan	456	527	576	580	581	584	593	594
Argentina	180	167	190	183	184	184	181	196
Brazil	87	89	117	118	120	123	124	127
China	5	8	12	14	18	21	23	28
India	5	6	8	8	9	10	12	13

Sources: P.-A. Linteau, R. Durocher and J.-C. Robert, *Histoire du Québec contemporain*, 1989, and Institut de la statistique du Québec.

Headings: The top cell in each column and, sometimes, the first cell in each row.

Rows: Each section defined horizontally.

Columns: Each section defined vertically.

Data: The information in the table, whether words, codes or numbers.

Source and year: The source indicates where the data come from and the year indicates when they were collected. This facilitates the validation of the information.

Interpreting a Contingency Table

Goals (Why interpret a contingency table?)

- To find specific information
- To compare certain data
- To establish connections among certain data
- To identify trends

Method (How to go about it)

1 **Define the purpose of the exercise.** Tables sometimes contain considerable amounts of data. You will save time and work more efficiently if you know what you are looking for.

2 **Read the title.** The title provides information about the theme of the table.

3 **Validate the source and year.** Verifying this information will confirm the credibility of the data.

4 **Read the headings of each column (and each row, if applicable).** This will help you find the rows and columns that are most important to your research.

5 **Analyze the data.** Take the time to fully understand what each piece of information means, especially numerical data.

6 **Interpret the table.** Establish connections among the data selected (similarities and differences, associations, increase/ stability/decrease, etc.).

7 **Determine whether the document helps you fulfill your original purpose.** If it does, note the information and references on record sheets.

Consumption in the United States and China (2007)

	United States	China
Total population	301 621 000	1 319 982 596
Gross national income per inhabitant (adjusted for parity)	US$46,040	US$2,360
Spending on clothes and shoes	US$429.8 billion	US$95.8 billion
Spending on electronic devices (excluding cellphones)	US$162 billion	US$11.8 billion
Spending on alcohol and tobacco	US$205.6 billion	US$31.4 billion
Spending on household goods	US$456.9 billion	US$57.1 billion
Spending on recreation	US$881 billion	US$34.2 billion
Total number of automobiles (per 1000 inhabitants)	824	28
% phone subscribers (landline and mobile)	139%	69%
% Internet users	73%	16%

Sources: World Bank and Euromonitor International, cited in the *New York Times*, [On-line], 2008.

Example

1 I want to compare consumption in the United States and China.

2 The title indicates that the table provides information about consumption in the United States and China in 2007. It can therefore help me find what I am looking for.

3 The source is a serious and trustworthy public organization, which gives the data credibility.

4 The headings of the rows address different categories of consumption, allowing me to compare data by category. In each case, the per capita consumption is indicated in brackets, which makes for a better comparison.

5 Regardless of the category, consumption is higher in the United States than in China.

6 After analyzing the data, I conclude that even if the population of the United States is four times smaller than that of China, its consumption in all of the areas addressed in this table is considerably higher than in China.

7 The table helps me fulfill my original purpose. Now, I will verify whether the data for 2009 indicates any significant changes.

Creating a Contingency Table

Method (How to go about it)

1 Define the purpose of the exercise (what you want to represent) and give the table a provisional title.

2 Select the information. Determine the headings of your columns and collect the data needed to fill in the table.

3 Construct the table.

- Draw the table. Estimate the number of columns and rows you will need. Don't forget to determine the width of the columns based on the information to be used.
- Write the headings. Don't forget to include the units, if applicable.

4 Fill in the table using the data collected. If the data are numerical, align the numbers uniformly.

5 Give the table a final title and indicate the source and year of the data.

Example

1 I want to construct a table showing the composition of municipal waste in different countries. The title could be: **The Composition of Municipal Waste (%).**

2 I need information about the composition of municipal waste in Canada, France, South Korea and Mexico. I found the information on the OECD's website.

3 I will construct the table.

	Canada	France	South Korea	Mexico
Paper and cardboard				
Organic matter				
Plastic				
Glass				
Metals				
Textiles and other				

4 and **5**

I will complete the table by adding the data, the title and the source. Since the data are numerical, I will centre-align them, thus helping to prevent errors in interpretation.

Composition of municipal waste (%)

	Canada	France	South Korea	Mexico
Paper and cardboard	47	20	24	15
Organic matter	24	32	28	51
Plastic	3	9	8	6
Glass	6	10	5	6
Metals	13	3	7	3
Textiles and other	8	26	28	18

Source: OECD, OECD *Environmental Data Compendium*, [On-line], 2008.

Components of a Graph

Title: The title provides information about the graph. It refers to the data used and often contains a time reference.

Axes and units: The axes are divided into equal intervals to make the graph easier to read. The units help define the variables and their quantities.

Sectors: A circle graph is made up of sectors, each one representing part of a whole.

Broken line: A broken-line graph is made up of points connected by a broken line.

Bars: In a bar graph or histogram, the bars are the horizontal or vertical sections. They are all the same width, as are the spaces between them.

Legend: The legend indicates the colours associated with the data. This key is essential for circle graphs and sometimes necessary for other graphs.

Source and year: The source and year indicate the origin of the data.

Explanatory note: The explanatory note provides an explanation.

Functions of Each Type of Graph

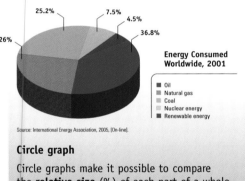

Circle graph

Circle graphs make it possible to compare the **relative size** (%) of each part of a whole.

Bar graph

Bar graphs make it possible to **compare** qualitative or quantitative aspects of different elements.

The bars can be horizontal or vertical.

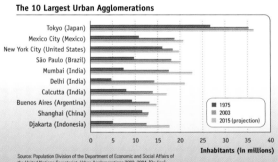

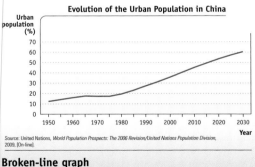

Broken-line graph

Broken-line graphs make it possible to see the evolution (increase or decrease) of a **phenomenon** over time.

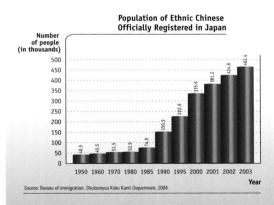

Histogram

Histograms make it possible to see the **distribution** among specific classes.

267

Interpreting a Graph

Goals (Why interpret a graph?)

- To find specific information
- To compare similar data
- To establish connections among certain data
- To get a quick overview of a situation

Method (How to go about it)

1 **Define the purpose of the exercise.** You will work more efficiently if you know what you are looking for.

2 **Read the title.** The title provides information about the theme of the graph.

3 **Determine the type of graph.** Each type of graph has specific characteristics that can guide you in reading, analyzing and interpreting data.

4 **Validate the source and year.** Verifying this information will confirm the credibility of the data.

5 **Read the legend and the axis titles.** Bar graphs and broken-line graphs are made up of a vertical axis and a horizontal axis. Circle graphs are often accompanied by a legend.

6 **Analyze the data.** Take the time to analyze the information.

7 **Interpret the graph.** Establish connections among the data.

8 **Determine whether the document helps you fulfill your original purpose.** If it does, note the information on record sheets.

Example

1 I want to assess the rural exodus within the context of the mobility of populations in China.

2 The title indicates that the broken-line graph represents the evolution of the urban population in China. Since the increase in the urban population is a result of the rural exodus, I think the graph could prove useful.

3 Since this is a broken-line graph, I know that it shows the evolution of a phenomenon over time.

4 The source is reliable. I can therefore conclude that the data are valid.

5 There is no legend. The title helps define the axes. The urban population (%) is on the vertical axis and the years, on the horizontal axis.

6 The curve begins in 1950. There is a slight increase until 1965, then there is no movement until 1975 (find out why). Then, there is a substantial increase which, according to predictions, will continue until at least 2030

7 I conclude that the rural exodus in China began around 1975 and that it will continue, since the trend appears to be ongoing.

8 This graph helps me fulfill my original purpose. The evolution of the urban population in China shows that the rural exodus is an integral part of the mobility of populations in China, since the phenomenon is increasing.

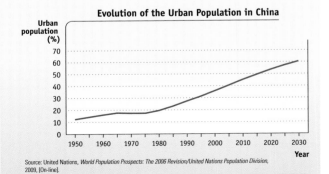

Evolution of the Urban Population in China

Source: United Nations, *World Population Prospects: The 2006 Revision/United Nations Population Division*, 2009, [On-line].

Creating a Graph

Method (How to go about it)

1 Define the purpose of the exercise (what you want to represent) and give the graph a provisional title.

2 Select the information. Organizing the data in a table is usually very helpful when creating a graph.

3 Choose and construct the graph. Think about the characteristics of each type of graph.

4 Add a legend, if applicable.

5 Give the graph a title and indicate the source and year of the data.

World population

Continent	2000	2008	2025
World (in millions)	6 124	6 750	8 011
Africa (%)	13.4	14.6	17.4
Latin America (%)	8.5	8.6	8.6
North America (%)	5.2	5.1	4.9
Asia (%)	60.5	60.4	59.7
Europe (%)	11.9	10.8	8.9
Oceania (%)	0.5	0.5	0.5

Source: L'État du monde, *Encyclopédie de l'État du monde*, [On-line], 2007.

Example

The following data is available:

Bar graph

1 I want to show the population distribution by continent in 2008.

2 I will use the data in the above table.

3 I choose a bar graph, since it is ideal for my purpose.
- I will draw the axes.
- I will graduate the axes according to my chosen interval.
- I will identify the units on each axis.

4 and **5**

I will set the height of each bar and draw bars the same width. I will write the title of the graph and the source of the data.

Broken-line graph

1 I want to show the evolution of the world's population between 2000 and 2025.

2 I will use the data in the above table.

3 I choose a broken-line graph, since it is ideal for my purpose.
- I will draw the axes.
- I will graduate the axes according to my chosen interval.
- I will identify the units on each axis.

4 and **5**

I will plot points on the graph and draw lines between them. I will write the title of the graph and the source of the data.

Circle graph

1 I want to show the portion of the world population on each continent in 2008.

2 I will use the data in the above table.

3 I choose a circle graph, since it is ideal for my purpose.
- I will draw the circle and indicate its centre.
- I will consider the data as percentages and calculate the number of degrees corresponding to each percentage.

$$\% \times 360 \div 100 = \text{number of } °$$

Africa = 14.6% ⟶ 14.6% × 360° ÷ 100% = 53°
Latin America = 8.6% ⟶ 8.6% × 360° ÷ 100% = 31°
North America = 5.1% ⟶ 5.1% × 360° ÷ 100% = 18°
Asia = 60.4% ⟶ 60.4% × 360° ÷ 100% = 217°
Europe = 10.8% ⟶ 10.8% × 360° ÷ 100% = 39°
Oceania = 0.5% ⟶ 0.5% × 360° ÷ 100% = 2°

4 and **5**

I will draw the radii using a protractor and colour each portion of the circle a different colour. I will explain the meaning of the colours in a legend. I will write the title of the graph and the source of the data.

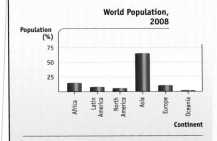

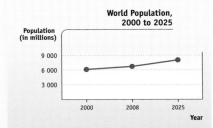

Interpreting and Creating a Graphic Organizer

Goals (Why interpret and create a graphic organizer?)

- To help understand an explanation
- To synthesize the information in one or more documents
- To recall prior knowledge and correct or enhance it using new information
- To brainstorm on a theme

Method (How to go about it)

1 **Define the purpose of the exercise (what you want to represent) and the theme, and give the organizer a provisional title.**

2 **Gather information or prepare a list of the concepts to be included.**
In the case of a demonstration or the analysis of a document, the information can make designing the organizer easier. This step is not essential to the brainstorming process.

3 **Choose the type of diagram.** This step is very important, since it will determine how you will process the information. If you are brainstorming, you will most likely use a descriptive model. However, you could use another model depending on your goal.

4 **Develop the graphic organizer.** If you are brainstorming, you should start with the central concept and develop the structure based on your reflections. In the case of a demonstration or a summary, develop the chosen structure using the available information. Use clear symbols of different colours. Don't forget that the graphic organizer must help the reader understand your message without any further explanation.

5 **Give the organizer a final title and make sure it helps you fulfill your original purpose.**

Example

1 I want to summarize the concept of sustainable development.

2 I found the following information: there are three aspects to sustainable development (Ecological, Social and Economic) and three subconcepts (Liveable, Viable and Equitable).

3 Since I am summarizing related information that explains a central concept, I choose a descriptive model. I think it will clearly show the relationships between the components of the concept.

4 and **5**
I will draw my organizer in pencil and add the information. If I am pleased with the result, I will draw it in ink and add a title.

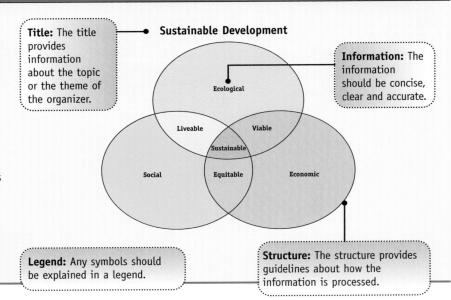

Title: The title provides information about the topic or the theme of the organizer.

Sustainable Development

Information: The information should be concise, clear and accurate.

Ecological

Liveable   Viable

Sustainable

Social   Equitable   Economic

Legend: Any symbols should be explained in a legend.

Structure: The structure provides guidelines about how the information is processed.

The Different Types of Graphic Organizers

Descriptive organizers

The central concept goes in the purple box.

Example 1

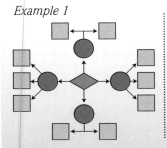

Example 2

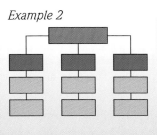

Example 3

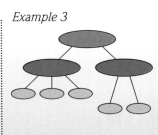

Pyramid organizer

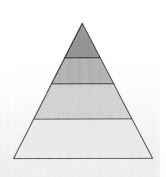

Compare and contrast organizers

Example 1

| Québec | Elsewhere |

Different | Same | Different

Example 2

| Québec | and | Elsewhere |

Similarities

Differences

Sequence organizer

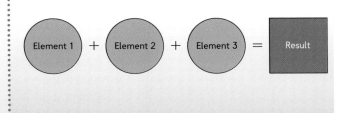

Cause and effect organizers

Example 1

Cause → Effect

Example 2

| Cause 1 |
| Cause 2 | → Effect
| Cause 3 |

Example 3

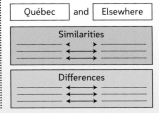

Problem-solution organizers

Example 1

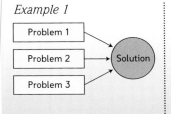

Example 2

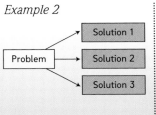

Example 3

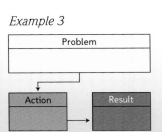

Cycle organizer

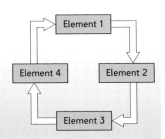

271

Preparing a Mediagraphy

Goals (Why create a mediagraphy?)

- To indicate the source of the documents used
- To identify the authors who played a role in your thinking
- To enable readers to consult the documents used

Method (How to go about it)

1 **Prepare a list of all the documents used in the research project.** Consult your bibliographical sheets or else you will have to find the documents again.

2 **Determine the order in which to present the documents and write the references.** You can classify the documents by medium and in alphabetical order. Follow the instructions below for writing the references. Use the same format (punctuation, italics).

- **Book with an author:**

  Last name of author, first name. *Title of Document.* Edition number. Place of publication: publisher, year of publication.

- **Book with no author (dictionary, encyclopaedia):**

  Title of Document. Edition number. Place of publication: publisher, year of publication.

- **Article in a periodical:**

  Last name of author, first name. "Title of Article." *Title of Periodical,* issue number (date).

- **Article on CD-ROM:**

  Last name of author, first name. "Title of Article." In *Title of CD-ROM.* [CD ROM]. Publisher, date.

- **Internet document:**

  Last name of author, first name. *Title of Home Page.* [On-line]. URL address. (Date consulted).

- **Film, documentary:**

  Title. [DVD or videocassette]. Producer, production company, date, duration.

Bibliography or mediagraphy?

The difference between the two is simple. A *bibliography* is a list of paper documents (books, magazines, research reports, etc.). A *mediagraphy* lists all the information documents used, regardless of medium (books, CD-ROMs, videos, websites, etc.). As more and more information becomes available in electronic format, mediagraphies are becoming more common.

Participating in a Debate

Method (How to go about it)

1 **Become familiar with the topic.** Start by getting an overview of the topic in question. Then, make sure you understand all of the related aspects and concepts. Focus on the key elements of the question or the statement of the problem.

2 **Take a position.** Define your point of view. Prepare a list of the arguments on which your position is based. These will be your "thesis." Your position should be rational, not emotional.

3 **Verify the debate format.** Usually, debates take place according to a well-defined process, but the process may vary from one debate to the next. Consider the type of exchange (open forum, formal debate, making a case), the topic and the amount of time allotted to each participant. You should take these elements into account in your preparation.

4 **Do a documentary search to flesh out your thesis.** This research will enable you to improve your understanding of the topic. Find arguments supporting your thesis (facts, general statements, values). Take this opportunity to examine counter-arguments (counter-thesis) that your opponents might raise.

> **Comment:** Debate is very similar to writing an argumentative text. See the methodological sheet on page 253, **3**.

5 **Organize your arguments.**

- Organize your arguments in order of importance and determine what order you will use them in. You must make choices: quantity or quality of arguments, starting or finishing with your best argument.
- Choose the argumentative strategies you will use: demonstration, refutation or argumentative explanation.

6 **Prepare for the debate.**

- Find the proper tone and make sure to respect the debate structure.
- Develop documentary support (record sheets, tables or graphs, physical evidence).

Glossary

Main Abbreviations and Acronyms

APEC • Asia-Pacific Economic Cooperation

ATTAC • Association for the Taxation of Financial Transactions to Aid Citizens

CIDA • Canadian International Development Agency

CIS • Commonwealth of Independent States

DC • Developing country

ECSC • European Coal and Steel Community

EEC • European Economic Community

EU • European Union

FAO • Food and Agriculture Organization of the United Nations

G8 • Group of 8

G20 • Group of 20

GATT • General Agreement on Tariffs and Trade

GDP • Gross domestic product

GHG • Greenhouse gas

GMO • Genetically modified organism

GNI • Gross national income

HDI • Human Development Index

IAEA • International Atomic Energy Agency

ICAO • International Civil Aviation Organization

ICC • International Criminal Court

ICJ • International Court of Justice

ICRC • International Committee of the Red Cross

ICT • International Criminal Tribunal

ILO • International Labour Organization

IMF • International Monetary Fund

IMO • International Maritime Organization

IPCC • Intergovernmental Panel on Climate Change

ISO • International Standards Organization

IUCN • International Union for the Conservation of Nature

IWC • International Whaling Commission

LDC • Least developed country

MDG • Millennium Development Goal

MSF • Doctors Without Borders

NAFTA • North American Free Trade Agreement

NATO • North Atlantic Treaty Organization

NGO • Non-Governmental Organization

OAS • Organization of American States

OECD • Organization for Economic Co-operation and Development

OIF • International Organization of the Francophonie

OPEC • Organization of Petroleum Exporting Countries

PPP • Purchasing-power parity

RSF • Reporters Without Borders

UN • United Nations

UNCTAD • United Nations Conference on Trade and Development

UNDP • United Nations Development Programme

UNEP • United Nations Environment Programme

UNESCO • United Nations Educational, Scientific and Cultural Organization

UNFCCC • United Nations Framework Convention on Climate Change

UNHCR • United Nations High Commission for Refugees

UNICEF • United Nations Children's Fund

USSR • Union of Soviet Socialist Republics

WFP • World Food Programme

WHO • World Health Organization

WMO • World Meteorological Organization

WTO • World Trade Organization

Definitions

In a definition, a term in bold indicates that this term is also defined in the glossary.

Allies • The name given to the coalition of countries, including Canada, the United Kingdom, the United States, the USSR, China and France, that fought against the **Axis Powers** during the Second World War.

American Secretary of State • The person responsible for foreign affairs in the U.S. federal government.

Anarchism • A political doctrine in which all forms of government are considered negative and unnecessary, based on the premise that a society should be built on mutual support and greater cooperation among individuals.

Anti-globalism • A movement that opposes **globalization** and raises awareness in its struggle for change to ensure that human rights and the principles of **sustainable development** are respected.

Anti-Semitism • Racism directed against Jews.

Asian Dragons and Tigers • The Asian Dragons refer to four countries (South Korea, Singapore, Taiwan and Hong Kong) that experienced extremely rapid economic expansion and modernization during the early 1960s. This growth was followed by similar economic expansion in four countries known as the Asian Tigers (Thailand, Indonesia, Malaysia and the Philippines).
▶▶▶ Wealth • *Economic Growth (pages 148-149)*

Axis Powers • The name of the alliance between Nazi Germany, fascist Italy and imperial Japan during the Second World War. By extension, the forces of the Axis Powers refers to all countries that fought against the Allies.
▶▶▶ History Headlines • *Section on the Second World War*

Big Mac Index • An index used to measure purchasing-power parity in the world by comparing the price of a Big Mac in different countries.
▶▶▶ Power • *The Homogenization of Culture (pages 134-135)*

Biodiversity • Diversity and variety of living organisms (plants and animals).

Biosphere • All living organisms (plants and animals) on the planet.

Black market • Clandestine trade with the goal of avoiding existing regulations (sale of banned products, non-payment of taxes, etc.)

Bolshevism • The doctrine held by Vladimir Lenin's political party in Russia between 1903 and 1922, based on the principles of **socialism** as a precursor to **communism**.

Capital • A sum of money used to generate income.

Capitalism • A socioeconomic system in which private entrepreneurs seek profit for their personal gain.

Ceasefire • An agreement between two adversaries to suspend hostilities in times of war.

Chancellor • The title given to the head of government in Germany and Austria.

Child soldier • An army combatant who is under the age of 18. The recruitment of children under the age of 15, in particular, is considered a war crime by the **International Criminal Court**.

Citizen • An individual who possesses **citizenship**.

Citizenship • The status of a person recognized as a member of a State and who is entitled to enjoy certain civil and political rights.

Civil war • A conflict that occurs within a State between the citizens of the same country.

Coalition • A temporary alliance between groups or individuals striving to attain a common objective.

Coastal (adjective) • That which is located on the coast.

Colonialism • The occupation and economic, political or social exploitation of a territory by a foreign State.

Common market • An economic area in which the trade of goods and services is conducted without customs tariffs or quotas and where there is free circulation and the harmonization of economic policies.
▶▶▶ Power • *Economic Associations (pages 126-127)*

Communism • A political doctrine that seeks to abolish private property in favour of collective property. This system is based on the sharing of a society's resources and means of production, so that consumer goods can be redistributed according to individual needs.

Confederal system of government • A political system in which regional governments hold most of the power, with only a small portion left to the central government. No genuine confederal State exists today, although Switzerland was one before 1848 and the United States, from 1781 to 1789.

Confederation • See **Confederal system of government**

Coup d'état • The act of illegally overthrowing a government with the objective of taking power.

Currency • A monetary unit specific to a country or a group of countries, such as the Canadian dollar, Japan's yen or the European Union's euro.

Customs clearance • The formalities related to **customs duties**.

Customs duty • A tax charged on goods when crossing a border.

Czar • Title held by the monarchs of Russia.

Debt • The obligation of a person (debtor) toward another person (creditor), particularly the payment of a sum of money.

Decolonization • An emancipation movement in which colonies free themselves from their main ties to the **mother country**.
▶▶ Wealth • *Colonization (pages 164-165)*

Demand • The quantity of a good or service that a consumer is prepared to buy at a given price.
▶▶ Introduction • *The Laws of the Market or Supply and Demand (pages 14-15)*

Developed countries • The wealthiest countries in the world, having a high **gross domestic product** per capita and a high **Human Development Index**.
▶▶ Wealth • *The Disparity of Wealth in the World (pages 152-153)*

Developing countries (DCs) • Countries that are in an intermediate position, between **developed countries** and **least advanced countries**. This expression is sometimes used to designate all States that are not developed countries.
▶▶ Wealth • *The Disparity of Wealth in the World (pages 152-153)*

Earth Summits • Major international conferences organized by the United Nations in 1972, 1992 and 2002 with the goal of finding global solutions to environmental problems.
▶▶ Environment • *The United Nations Earth Summits (pages 56-57)*

Embargo • In international politics, a coercive or punitive diplomatic measure designed to limit a country's export and import of goods.

European Union (EU) • A confederation of independent States on the European continent. Today, it is one of the most successful international political unions.
▶▶ Power • *European Union (pages 114-117)*

Executive (power) • One of three State powers, along with **legislative** and **judicial** power. Executive power seeks to ensure the implementation and application of laws set out by the legislative power.
▶▶ Power • *What Is a State? (pages 104-105)*

Expansionism • The policy of a State that is seeking to systematically increase its territory or its influence beyond its borders.

Extradition • A judicial procedure designed to return individuals to the country demanding their return, so that they can stand trial or be sentenced for their crimes.

Extreme poverty • According to the World Bank definition, a situation in which a person has less than US$1 a day on which to live.

Fascism • A political movement that promotes extreme **nationalism** and supports the ideal of a strong and absolute State to achieve its objectives.

Federal system of government • A political system in which a central government holds most of the power, only delegating a portion to the regional governments (provinces, states, cantons, etc.). *Examples:* Canada, United States, Australia, etc.

Food chain • A succession of living organisms that feed on one another.

Foreign debt • All of the debts that a State owes to foreign creditors (international institutions, other States or private creditors).
▶▶ Wealth • *The Debt Burden (pages 154-155)*

Framework agreement • A general treaty that is completed by the adoption of **protocols**.

Free trade zone • Geographic areas where industrial activities benefit from fiscal advantages, such as no controls, **customs duties**, etc.
▶▶ Power • *Protectionism Versus Free Trade (pages 122-123)*

Free trade • An economic policy based on the free circulation of goods and services. The opposite of **protectionism**.
▶▶ Power • *Protectionism Versus Free Trade (pages 122-123)*

Fundamentalism • A very strict, even extreme, attachment to an ideology, usually religious.

General Agreement on Tariffs and Trade (GATT) •
An accord establishing a framework for multilateral negotiations (involving several countries) designed to reduce tariff barriers and obstacles to international trade. Today, it is integrated into the World Trade Organization.
▶▶ Power • *International Trade (pages 124-125)*

Genetically modified organism (GMO) • A living organism (plant or animal) whose genetic material has been modified by human intervention.

Geneva Conventions • All of the treaties developed between 1864 and 1949 to define the rules for protecting people, particularly the injured, prisoners of war and civilians, in case of armed conflict.
▶▶ Tensions and Conflicts • *Humanitarian Organizations (pages 214-215)*

Genocide • The intentional extermination of an ethnic, racial or religious group. Genocide is considered a crime against humanity.
▶▶ Tensions and Conflicts • *Armed Conflicts (II) (pages 196-197)*

Geostrategy • The study of the geography, history and politics of States from a military perspective.

Globalization • A phenomenon of accelerated human exchanges at a global level, particularly with respect to the economy and the greater movement of goods, services, capital, technologies and labour.
▶▶ Wealth • *The Growth of International Trade (pages 150-151)*

Greenhouse gases (GHGs) • Gases that are present in the atmosphere and allow the sun's rays through, while trapping the heat emitted by the Earth's surface. Greenhouse gases are the main cause of global warming.
▶▶ Environment • *Global Warming (pages 40-41)*

Gross domestic product (GDP) • An economic indicator that measures the domestic production of goods and services in a given country over a period of one year.
▶▶ Wealth • *Economic Concepts and Indicators (pages 144-145)*

Gross national income (GNI) • An economic indicator that measures the total sum of income (salaries and financial income) generated by the population of a country over a period of one year. It includes investments and foreign assets.
▶▶ Wealth • *Economic Concepts and Indicators (pages 144-145)*

Gross world product • An economic indicator that measures the production of goods and services over a period of one year around the world. See also **Gross domestic product**.

Group of 8 (G8) • An annual international summit that brings together eight of the most economically powerful countries in the world.
▶▶ Power • *International Summits (pages 110-111)*

Guerrilla warfare • A combat strategy based on mobility, harassment and the element of surprise.
▶▶ Tensions and Conflicts • *Armed Conflicts (I) (pages 194-195)*

Hectare (ha) • A measurement of area equivalent to 10 000 square metres.

Holy war • A war waged in the name of a god or a religion.

Human Development Index (HDI) • A composite index used to evaluate the current situation of a State by taking into account not only the economic production of its citizens, but also their health and education.
▶▶ Wealth • *Human Development Index (HDI) (pages 146-147)*

Hydric stress • A situation in some regions of the world where the demand for water is greater than the available resources.

Hyperinflation • An extremely high level of uncontrolled **inflation**.

Industrial Revolution • The historic transition of an agrarian society to an industrial society. This phenomenon primarily took place in the 19th century.

Inflation • Economic imbalance caused by a rise in the price of goods and services and resulting in an enduring drop in purchasing power.

Insolvent • Unable to meet one's financial obligations, such as **debts**.

Interest • In finance, revenue generated by **capital** that has been loaned. The amount of this revenue is determined by a percentage (rate) established in advance.

Intergovernmental • Relations or interactions involving more than one government.

International Court of Justice (ICJ) • A judicial institution of the United Nations responsible for settling international disputes.
▶▶ Power • *Justice and International Law (pages 118-119)*

International Criminal Court (ICC) • A judicial institution of the United Nations responsible for trying war criminals under international law. Its scope of action encompasses all States that have ratified its founding statute and is therefore broader than that of international criminal tribunals.
▶▶ Tensions and Conflicts • *Bringing War Criminals to Justice (pages 216-217)*

International criminal tribunals (ICTs) • United Nations judicial institutions responsible for judging war criminals under international law. They only deal with very specific situations and are slated to be replaced by the International Criminal Court.
▶▶ Tensions and Conflicts • *Bringing War Criminals to Justice (pages 216-217)*

International law • All of the rules that govern relations between States.
▶▶ Power • *Justice and International Law (pages 118-119)*

International Monetary Fund (IMF) • A United Nations institution responsible for ensuring economic stability in the world and encouraging international monetary cooperation.
▶▶ Power • *International Finance (pages 128-129)*

Interventionism • A policy that favours State involvement in a country's economy.

Isolationism • A policy by which a State shuts itself off, limiting contact with the international community and refusing any interference from the outside world in its domestic policies.

Isthmus • A narrow strip of land separating two bodies of water and forming a bridge between two land masses.

Judicial (power) • One of three State powers, along with **legislative** and **executive** power. Judicial power is designed to settle disputes by interpreting laws set out by the legislative power and applied by the executive power.
▶▶ Power • *What Is a State? (pages 104-105)*

Laws of the market • The economic rules that establish the price of goods and services according to **supply** and **demand** in economic systems based on free enterprise or a mixed economy.
▶▶ Introduction • *The Laws of the Market or Supply and Demand (pages 14-15)*

Least Developed Countries (LDCs) • The poorest countries in the world, with a low **gross domestic product** and a low **Human Development Index**.
▶▶ Wealth • *The Disparity of Wealth in the World (pages 152-153)*

Legislative (power) • One of three State powers, along with **executive** and **judicial** power. Legislative power makes it possible to create, amend and adopt the laws that are used to manage a country.
▶▶ Power • *What Is a State? (pages 104-105)*

Liberalization • The action of freeing up international trade, based on the principles of **free trade**.

Lobby • A group or organization that practises **lobbying**.

Lobbying • Actions that seek to influence the decisions of public authorities.

Market economy • Economic system in which the principle of **supply** and **demand** is set by mechanisms said to be natural and free of any State intervention.

Market • The organization of economic trade in a given geographic area.

Martial law • A law that temporarily suspends individual rights and freedoms.

Microstate • A sovereign State that occupies a small area or has a small population, or both. *Examples:* Grenada, Cape Verde, Saint Vincent and the Grenadines, Samoa.

Military dictatorship • See **Political system (military dictatorship)**

Militia • Refers to an auxiliary force of a civilian army or of a private, non-governmental army.
▶▶ Tensions and Conflicts • *Armed Conflicts (I) (pages 194-195)*

Millennium Development Goals (MDGs) • The set of eight general goals with specific and measurable targets to be attained within the framework of global development. They were established by the United Nations in 2000.
▶▶ Wealth • *Millennium Development Goals (pages 168-169)*

Monarchism • A political doctrine that gives power to a single individual who generally holds the title of king. See also **Political system (absolute monarchy)** and **Political system (constitutional monarchy)**

Moratorium • An agreement that makes it possible to suspend certain activities.

Mother country • In the colonial system, the State that controls the colonies.

Nationalism • The awareness of belonging to a nation with a specific history, language and culture.

Nationalization • The action of transferring from the private to the public (State) sphere the ownership of certain goods or means of production. Also referred to as State control.

Naturalize • To grant someone the **citizenship** of a country.

Nazism • A word formed from the term "national socialism" (from the German *nationalsozialismus*). Refers to the ideology developed by Hitler under which the Nazi Party promoted a fascist, racist and anti-Semitic regime.

Nobel Prize • International prize awarded each year to individuals who have made remarkable contributions in various fields. For example, the Nobel Peace Prize is awarded to an individual who has contributed to bringing peoples together and to promoting peace.

Non-governmental organization (NGO) • A group of citizens that defends a cause in the public interest. NGOs act independently of their governments and are not profit-driven.

North American Free Trade Agreement (NAFTA) • An agreement between Canada, Mexico and the United States designed to eliminate trade barriers and facilitate the exchange of goods and services among the three countries.
▶▶ Power • *Economic Associations (pages 126-127)*

Organization for Economic Co-operation and Development (OECD) • An international organization that examines the economy and brings together the main **developed countries** that subscribe to the principles of democracy and the **market economy**.
▶▶ Wealth • *The Disparity of Wealth in the World (pages 152-153)*

Pandemic • An epidemic of exceptional proportions that spreads through almost an entire population.

Permanent Court of Arbitration • An international organization responsible for settling international disputes.

Permanent residency • The status accorded to an immigrant that allows that person to remain indefinitely in the host country and to work there.
▶▶ Population • *Welcoming Migrants (pages 94-95)*

Political system (absolute monarchy) • A political system in which a monarch holds all State power (**executive**, **legislative** and **judicial**).

Political system (constitutional monarchy) • A political system in which a monarch is recognized as head of State, with powers that are limited by a constitution.

Political system (military dictatorship) • A political system in which an individual or a group of individuals linked to the army holds all State power (**executive**, **legislative** and **judicial**).

Political system (parliamentary) • A representative political system (democratic) in which the **executive** power is subject to the **legislative** power. Both powers must cooperate within a parliament.

Political system (presidential) • A representative political system (democratic) in which the **executive**, **legislative** and **judicial** powers are formally separate, with the executive power (the president) having primacy.

Political system • A form of organizing of power within a State.

Pontificate • Duration of a pope's reign.

Primary elections • A preliminary election process in which a political party nominates a candidate to represent the party in a general election.

Protectionism • An economic policy adopted by a State to protect its national production and its businesses or a sector of its economy. The opposite of **free trade**.
▷▷ Power • *Protectionism Versus Free Trade (pages 122-123)*

Protocol • An accord that modifies or completes an existing treaty, which then becomes known as a **framework agreement**.

Purchasing-power parity (PPP) • A method that measures the quantity of goods and services that it is possible to purchase with a given **currency** in each of the regions or countries compared, taking into account the fact that the cost of living differs from country to country.
▷▷ Wealth • *Economic Concepts and Indicators (pages 144-145)*

Ratification • The act of officially confirming an agreement or commitment through its implementation.

Real estate bubble • A rapid and artificial rise in property values, triggered by **speculation** or an exaggerated forecast of **market** trends.

Relocation • The displacement of a company's facilities in the context of **globalization**, generally from **developed countries** to **developing countries** where labour is cheaper.
▷▷ Wealth • *The Advantages and Disadvantages of Globalization (pages 162-163)*

Right of asylum • The right of foreign persons fearing persecution in their country of origin to be protected by their host country.

Sanction • A punitive measure imposed on a group or individual for having violated a law, regulation or standard.

Schengen Accords • Accords signed in 1985 by several European countries, with the goal of gradually removing borders between member States and harmonizing their visa policies.
▷▷ Population • *Crossing Borders (pages 90-91)*

Security Council • The **executive** organ of the United Nations responsible for maintaining peace and international security, using armed force if necessary.
▷▷ Tensions and Conflicts • *The United Nations Security Council (pages 200-201)*

Shiite • A Muslim who practises Shiaism, one of the two main branches of Islam, the other being Sunniism.

Socialism • An economic doctrine that seeks to attain a more equitable distribution of wealth and to abolish social inequalities.

Speculation • A financial or commercial operation that seeks to profit from market variations, for example, by purchasing merchandise and selling it at a later date in the hopes that its price will have increased in the meantime.

Standardization • The action of imposing standards, that is, standardized requirements that seek to achieve greater uniformity.

Subcontract • The act whereby a company delegates a portion of its production to another company.

Sub-Saharan Africa • A region of the African continent south of the Sahara Desert.

Supply • The quantity of a good or service that a producer is prepared to sell at a given price.
▷▷ Introduction • *The Laws of the Market or Supply and Demand (pages 14-15)*

Supranational • Related to an institution or authority that holds power that is greater than that of a nation.

Sustainable development • A form of development designed to respond to current needs without compromising the capacity to satisfy those of future generations. It takes into account the economic, social and environmental aspects of development.
▷▷ Environment • *What Is Sustainable Development? (pages 46-47)*

System of government • A method of organizing of the government of a State.

Tidal wave • The rapid movement of a large volume of water, which usually takes the form of an enormous wave, also called a tsunami.

Totalitarianism • A political system in which only one party is permitted, meaning there is no opposition.

Unionism • A movement that seeks to unify the members of a given occupation with the goal of defending and promoting their interests.

Unitary system of government • A political system in which all of the power is concentrated in the hands of a central government. *Examples:* Japan, China, South Africa, etc.

United Nations Educational, Scientific and Cultural Organization (UNESCO) • An institution of the United Nations devoted to building universal peace by promoting collaboration among nations through education, science, culture and communication.
▶▶ Power • *UNESCO and the Preservation of Heritage (pages 138-139)*

United Nations Environment Programme (UNEP) • The main organization within the United Nations responsible for environmental issues.
▶▶ Environment • *The United Nations Earth Summits (pages 56-57)*

United Nations General Assembly • The main organ of the United Nations. Composed of all member States, the General Assembly is a forum for discussion where all members can express their point of view.

United Nations (UN) • A universal international organization that promotes international cooperation in a multitude of areas.
▶▶ Power • *The United Nations (pages 106-107)*

Universal suffrage • The right to vote extended to all adult citizens, regardless of their wealth, place of birth or social status.

Uranium • A radioactive heavy metal that is the main raw material used in the nuclear industry.

Veto power • The right bestowed on an authority to unilaterally oppose the adoption of a law or a unanimous decision. The five permanent members of the **United Nations Security Council** have veto power over the Council's decisions.
▶▶ Tensions and Conflicts • *The United Nations Security Council (pages 200-201)*

Vichy government • The name given to the government of the French State from 1940 to 1955, during the German occupation of France. Located in the city of Vichy, this government, led by Marshal Pétain, collaborated with Nazi Germany by administering the territory and denouncing members of the French Resistance.

Water table • The water that is closest to the surface of the Earth, feeding wells and springs.

Weapons of mass destruction • Nuclear, chemical or biological weapons designed to kill large numbers of people.

Welfare State • A State in which the government actively intervenes in economic and social aspects of society to redistribute collective wealth more equitably.

World Bank • In the United Nations system, a group of five financial institutions working to overcome poverty by providing advice and funding to States experiencing economic difficulties.
▶▶ Power • *International Finance (pages 128-129)*

World Trade Organization (WTO) • An international organization devoted to managing multilateral trade agreements (involving several countries), including GATT.
▶▶ Power • *International Trade (pages 124-125)*

Xenophobia • From the Greek *xenos* (foreigner) and *phobia* (fear). Hostility toward foreigners.

Index

Image References

page 100 (br): © Jon Hicks/Corbis • page 101 (t): © Bob Krist/Corbis • page 101 (c): © Toronto Star Syndicate [2003] all rights reserved • page 101 (b): © Sergio Dorantes/Corbis

Power: pages 102-103: © Justin Lane/epa/Corbis • page 108 (l): © Leif Skoogfors/Corbis • page 108 (r): © Micheline Pelletier/Corbis • page 109 (t): © Howard Davies/Corbis • page 109 (b): © Kena Betancur/epa/Corbis • page 110 (c): © Photo Itar Tass/Itar Tass/Corbis • page 110 (b): © Reuters/Corbis • page 112 (l): © Reuters/Corbis • page 112 (r): The Canadian Press/Ryan Remiorz • page 115: © Aldo Pavan/Grand Tour/Corbis • page 119: © Michael Kooren/Reuters/Corbis • page 120: © Marcel Mettelsiefen/epa/Corbis • page 121: © Sebastian Derungs/Reuters/Corbis • page 123: © Atlantide Phototravel/Corbis • page 124: © Atlantide Phototravel/Corbis • page 128: © Bettmann/Corbis • page 129 (t): © Bettmann/Corbis • page 129 (bc): © Matthew Cavanaugh/epa/Corbis • page 130: © Jean-Marc Petit/Publiphoto • page 131: The Granger Collection, New York • page 133: © Ren Junchuan/Xinhua Press/Corbis • page 135: © FCCM • page 136: © Jean Marie Leroy/Corbis • page 137: © Rudy Sulgan/Corbis • page 139 (b): © Reuters/Corbis • page 140 (t): © Gero Breloer/epa/Corbis

Wealth: pages 142-143: © Finbarr O'Reilly/Reuters/Corbis • page 145 (t): © Aaron Ufumell/epa/Corbis • page 146: © Amanda Koster/Corbis • page 147: © Sam Kiley/Sygma/Corbis • page 150: © Macduff Everton/Corbis • page 154: © Peter Turnley for Harper's/Corbis • page 155: © David Bergman/Corbis • page 157 (t): © Philippe Body/Hemis/Corbis • page 157 (b): © Reuters/Corbis • page 159 (l): © Joseph Sohm/Visions of America/Corbis • page 159 (ct): © Howard Davies/Corbis • page 160: © Hulton-Deutsch Collection/Corbis • page 162: © Phillipe Lissac/Godong/Corbis • page 163: © Michel Setboun/Corbis • page 165 (t): © Bettmann/Corbis • page 165 (r): © /Belga/epa/Corbis • page 165 (b): © Ed Kashi/Corbis • page 166: © Bill Gentile/Corbis • page 167 (t): The Canadian Press/The Intelligencer – Luke Hendry • page 167 (c): © Ronald Ssekandi/XinHua/Xinhua Press/Corbis • page 168: © Jeremy Horner/Corbis • page 169: © Yann Arthus-Bertrand/Corbis • page 170 (t): © Stephanie Maze/Corbis • page 170 (b): © Karen Kasmauski/Corbis • page 172: © Jeremy Horner/Corbis • page 174: © Howard Davies/Corbis • page 175 (t): © Pool/Pool/epa/Corbis • page 175 (cl): © Patrick Robert/Sygma/Corbis • page 175 (cr): © Bernard Bisson/Sygma/Corbis • page 175 (b): © Howard Davies/Corbis • page 176 (l): © Baci/Corbis • page 176 (r): © David Turnley/Corbis • page 177: © Morteza Nikoubazl/Reuters/Corbis

Tensions and Conflicts: pages 178-179: © Reza/Webistan/Corbis • page 181 (t): © Peter Turnley/Corbis • page 181 (b): © Ed Kashi/Corbis • page 182: © Antoine Gyori/Corbis Sygma • page 182 (t): © Peter Macdiarmid/epa/Corbis • page 182 (b): © Sean Adair/Reuters/Corbis • page 183: © Rob Howard/Corbis • page 185 (t): © Pallava Bagla/Corbis •

page 185 (b): © Manuel Litran/Corbis • page 186 (t): © Richard Dudman/Sygma/Corbis • page 186 (b): © Corbis • page 188: © Attar Maher/Corbis Sygma • page 189: © David Turnley/Corbis • page 191: © Reuters/Corbis • page 193: © Bettmann/Corbis • page 195 (t): © Corbis • page 195 (b): © Roger Hutchings/Corbis • page 196: © Lynsey Addario/Corbis • page 197 (c): © Bettmann/Corbis • page 197 (b): CP Photo/Fred Chartrand • page 198: © Bettmann/Corbis • page 199 (t): © Baci/Corbis • page 199 (b): © Leslie Neuhaus/epa/Corbis • page 200: © Reuters/Corbis • page 201 (t): © Hulton-Deutsch Collection/Corbis • page 201 (b): © Reinhard Krause/Reuters/Corbis • page 201: © Hulton-Deutsch Collection/Corbis • page 202 (t): © Patrick Robert/Corbis • page 202 (b): © Les Stone/Sygma/Corbis • page 204: © epa/Corbis • page 205: © Jacques Langevin/Corbis Sygma • page 206: © Peter Turnley/Corbis • page 207 (c): © Dominique Aubert/Sygma/Corbis • page 207 (b): © Robert Wallis/Corbis • page 208 (l): © Jose Goitia/Corbis • page 208 (r): © Reuters/Corbis • page 209: © Michael S. Yamashita/Corbis • page 210: © Kote Rodrigo/efe/Corbis • page 211: © Bettmann/Corbis • page 212: © Syed Jan Sabawoon/epa/Corbis • page 213 (t): © Luc Gnago/Reuters/Corbis • page 213 (b): © Howard Davies/Corbis • page 214: © Filippo Monteforte/epa/Corbis • page 215: © David Turnley/Corbis • page 217 (t): © Denis Balibouse/Reuters/Corbis • page 217 (b): © Michael Kooren/Reuters/Corbis

Appendixes: History Headlines: page 218 (l): © Underwood & Underwood/Corbis • page 218 (r): © Stapleton Collection/Corbis • page 219 (c): © Hulton-Deutsch Collection/Corbis • page 219 (r): © Bettmann/Corbis • page 219: © Bettmann/Corbis • page 221: © Bettmann/Corbis • page 222: ©Bettmann/Corbis • page 223: © Corbis • page 224: © Bettmann/Corbis • page 226 (l): © Bettmann/Corbis • page 226 (r): © Corbis • page 227: © Bettmann/Corbis • page 228 (l): © Bettmann/Corbis • pages 228-229 (c): © Terry Arthur/White House/Sygma/Corbis • page 229: © Regis Bossu/Sygma/Corbis • page 230: © Reuters/Corbis • page 231 (l): © Peter Turnley/Corbis • page 231 (r): © Reuters/Corbis • page 232 (l): © Reuters/Corbis • page 232 (r): © David Turnley/Corbis • page 233 (t): © Paul Souders/Corbis • page 233 (b): © Pascal Parrot/Corbis Sygma • page 234 (l): © Sean Adair/Reuters/Corbis • page 234 (r): © epa/Corbis • page 235 (c): © Imagemore Co., Ltd./Corbis • page 235 (b): © Lynsey Addario/Corbis • page 236 (t): © Jerome Sessini/Corbis • page 236 (b): © Sion Touhig/Corbis • page 237: © Gleb Garanich/Reuters/Corbis • page 238 (l): © Xinhua/Xinhua/Corbis • page 238 (r): © Bettmann/Corbis • page 239 (t): © Astaxov Dmitriy/Itar-Tass/Corbis • page 239 (b): © Reuters/Corbis • page 240 (l): © Ron Sachs/CNP/Corbis • page 240 (r): © T. Mughal/epa/Corbis • page 241: © Stephen Morrison/epa/Corbis • page 242 (l): © Gero Breloer/dpa/Corbis • page 242 (r): © Tannen Maury/epa/Corbis • page 243: © Jorge Abrego/epa/Corbis

Techniques: page 255: © Jehad Nga/Corbis • page 257: © André-Philippe Côté/Le Soleil

Atlas

North America and Central America

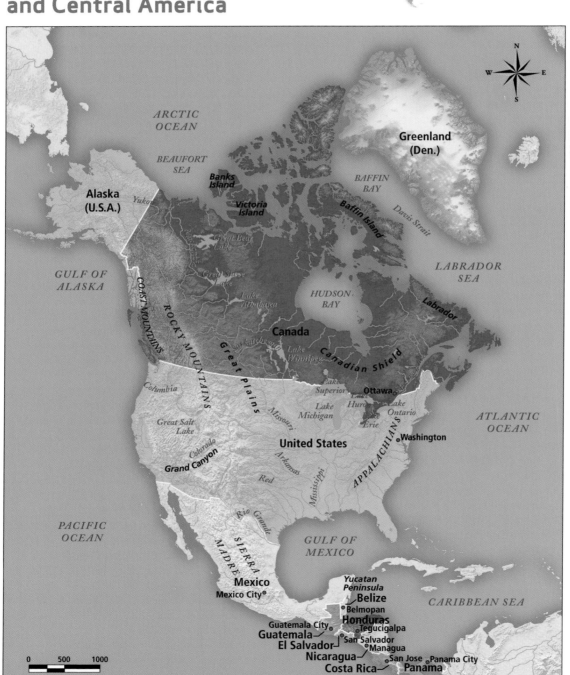

ARCTIC OCEAN

BEAUFORT SEA

Banks Island

Victoria Island

Alaska (U.S.A.)

Yukon

GULF OF ALASKA

Great Bear Lake

Great Slave Lake

Lake Athabasca

COAST MOUNTAINS

ROCKY MOUNTAINS

Great Plains

Saskatchewan

Lake Winnipeg

Canada

Canadian Shield

HUDSON BAY

BAFFIN BAY

Baffin Island

Davis Strait

Greenland (Den.)

LABRADOR SEA

Labrador

PACIFIC OCEAN

Columbia

Great Salt Lake

Colorado

Grand Canyon

United States

Missouri

Arkansas

Red

Mississippi

Lake Superior

Lake Michigan

Lake Huron

Lake Erie

Lake Ontario

Ottawa

Washington

ATLANTIC OCEAN

APPALACHIANS

Rio Grande

SIERRA MADRE

Mexico

Mexico City

GULF OF MEXICO

Yucatan Peninsula

Belize

Belmopan

Honduras

Tegucigalpa

CARIBBEAN SEA

Guatemala City

Guatemala

El Salvador

San Salvador

Nicaragua

Managua

Costa Rica

San Jose

Panama City

Panama

0   500   1000

kilometres

296

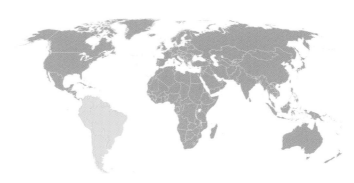

South America

Caracas
Lake Maracaibo
Venezuela
Georgetown
Guyana
Paramaribo
Cayenne
Suriname
French Guiana
Guiana Shield
Bogota
Colombia
Llanos
Galapagos Islands
Quito
Ecuador
Amazon
Peru
S e l v a s
Lima
Brazil
La Paz
Bolivia
Brasilia
Brazilian Highlands
Paraguay
Paraguay
PACIFIC OCEAN
ANDES MOUNTAINS
Gran Chaco
Asuncion
Argentina
Uruguay
Santiago
Buenos Aires
Montevideo
ATLANTIC OCEAN
Pampa
Rio de la Plata
Chile
Rio Negro
Patagonia
Strait of Magellan
Tierra del Fuego
Cape Horn

N
W   E
S

0   500   1000
kilometres

Europe

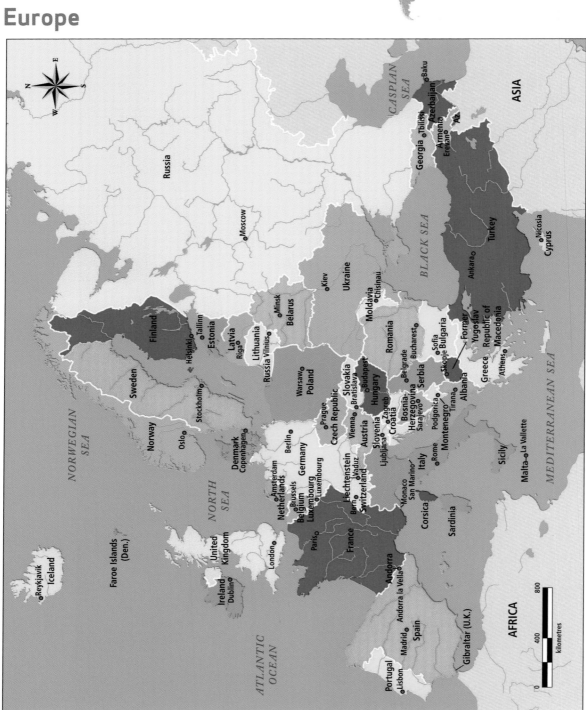

Asia

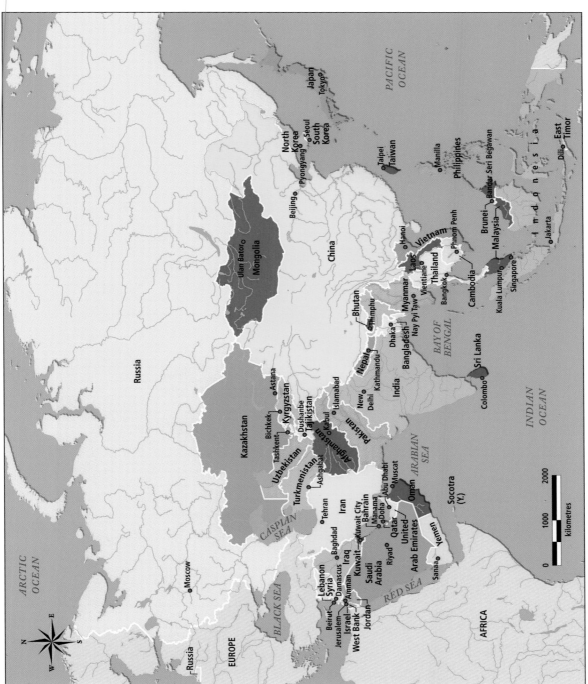

PACIFIC OCEAN

Japan
Tokyo

North Korea
Pyongyang
Seoul
South Korea

Taipei
Taiwan

Manilla
Philippines
Bandar Seri Begawan

Dili
East Timor

Beijing

China

Hanoi
Vietnam
Phnom Penh
Brunei
Malaysia
Jakarta

Bhutan
Thimphu

Laos
Myanmar
Nay Pyi Taw
Vientiane
Thailand
Bangkok
Cambodia
Kuala Lumpur
Singapore

Indonesia

Ulan Bator
Mongolia

Dhaka
Bangladesh

Nepal
Kathmandu

BAY OF BENGAL

Sri Lanka
Colombo

Russia

Astana
Kyrgyzstan
Bichkek
Dushanbe
Tajikistan
Kabul

New Delhi

India

Islamabad

Afghanistan

Pakistan

Kazakhstan

Tashkent

Uzbekistan
Turkmenistan
Ashgabat

ARABIAN SEA

Socotra (Y.)

INDIAN OCEAN

ARCTIC OCEAN

CASPIAN SEA

Tehran
Iran

Muscat
Oman
Abu Dhabi

Baghdad
Iraq
Kuwait City
Bahrain
Manama
Doha
Qatar
United Arab Emirates

Kuwait

Saudi Arabia
Riyad

Yemen
Sanaa

2000

1000

kilometres

0

Moscow

BLACK SEA

Lebanon
Syria
Damascus
Amman
Beirut
Israel
Jerusalem
West Bank
Jordan

RED SEA

EUROPE

AFRICA

Russia

N E S W

299

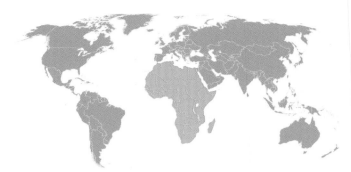

Africa

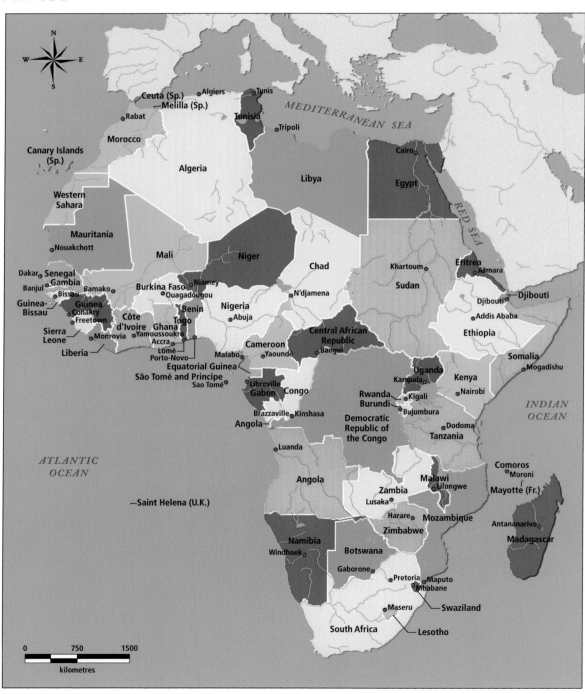

MEDITERRANEAN SEA

Ceuta (Sp.)
—Melilla (Sp.)
Algiers
Tunis
Rabat
Tunisia
Morocco
Tripoli
Canary Islands
(Sp.)
Algeria
Cairo
Egypt
Western
Sahara
RED SEA
Mauritania
Khartoum
Eritrea
Asmara
Nouakchott
Mali
Niger
Chad
Sudan
Dakar
Senegal
Djibouti
Djibouti
Gambia
Niamey
N'djamena
Banjul
Bamako
Burkina Faso
Addis Ababa
Bissau
Ouagadougou
Nigeria
Guinea-
Bissau
Guinea
Benin
Abuja
Ethiopia
Conakry
Togo
Freetown
Côte
d'Ivoire
Ghana
Central African
Republic
Somalia
Sierra
Leone
Yamoussoukro
Accra
Cameroon
Bangui
Mogadishu
Liberia
Monrovia
Lomé
Yaoundé
Uganda
Kenya
Porto-Novo
Malabo
Kampala
Equatorial Guinea
São Tomé and Principe
Sao Tomé
Nairobi
Rwanda
Kigali
Libreville
Gabon
Congo
Burundi
INDIAN
OCEAN
Brazzaville
Kinshasa
Bujumbura
Angola—
Democratic
Republic of
the Congo
Dodoma
Tanzania
Luanda
Comoros
Moroni
Malawi
Mayotte (Fr.)
ATLANTIC
OCEAN
Angola
Zambia
Lilongwe
Lusaka
—Saint Helena (U.K.)
Harare
Mozambique
Antananarivo
Zimbabwe
Madagascar
Namibia
Botswana
Windhoek
Gaborone
Pretoria
Maputo
Mbabane
Maseru
Swaziland
South Africa
Lesotho

N
W E
S

0   750   1500
kilometres

Oceania

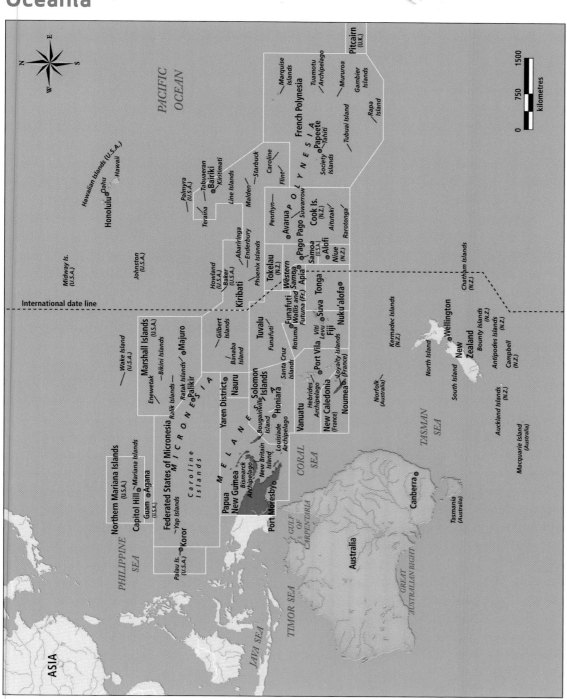

Canada

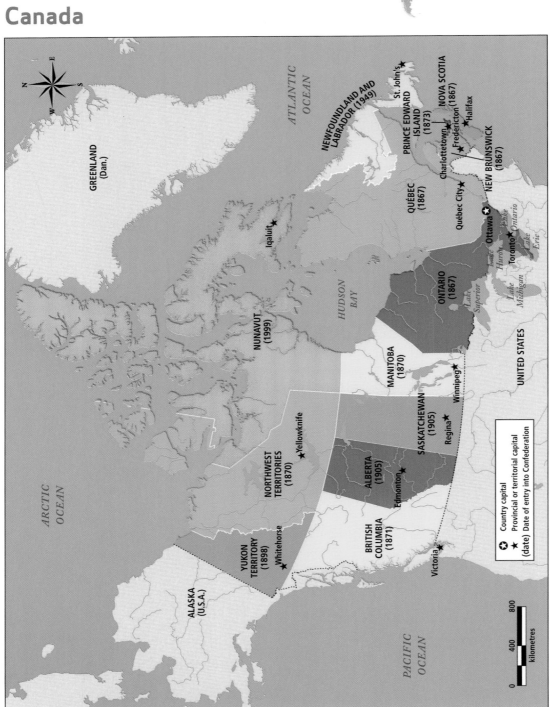

GREENLAND
(Dan.)

*ATLANTIC
OCEAN*

St. John's ★

NEWFOUNDLAND AND
LABRADOR (1949)

NOVA SCOTIA
(1867)

PRINCE EDWARD
ISLAND
(1873)

Fredericton (1867)

Charlottetown ★ ★ Halifax

NEW BRUNSWICK
(1867)

QUÉBEC
(1867)

Québec City ★

Iqaluit ★

*HUDSON
BAY*

ONTARIO
(1867)

Ottawa ✪

Toronto ★

*Lake
Superior*

*Lake
Huron*

*Lake
Ontario*

*Lake
Erie*

NUNAVUT
(1999)

MANITOBA
(1870)

*Lake
Michigan*

Winnipeg ★

UNITED STATES

Yellowknife ★

NORTHWEST
TERRITORIES
(1870)

SASKATCHEWAN
(1905)

Regina ★

ALBERTA
(1905)

Edmonton ★

*ARCTIC
OCEAN*

YUKON
TERRITORY
(1898)

Whitehorse ★

BRITISH
COLUMBIA
(1871)

Victoria ★

ALASKA
(U.S.A.)

*PACIFIC
OCEAN*

✪ Country capital
★ Provincial or territorial capital
(date) Date of entry into Confederation

800

400

kilometres

0